Is This Who We Are?

Is This Who We Are?

14 Questions about Québec

ALAIN DUBUC

Translated by Nigel Spencer

RONSDALE PRESS

RONSDALE PRESS
3350 West 21st Avenue, Vancouver, B.C. Canada V6S 1G7
www.ronsdalepress.com

Typesetting: Julie Cochrane, in Granjon 11.5 pt on 15
Cover Design: David Drummond
Copy Editors: Meagan Dyer & Susmita Dey
Paper: Ancient Forest Friendly 55lb. Enviro Book Antique Natural Cream
   FSC Recycled — 100% post-consumer waste, totally chlorine-free and acid-free.

Ronsdale Press wishes to thank the following for their support of its publishing program: the Canada Council for the Arts, the Government of Canada through the Canada Book Fund, the British Columbia Arts Council, and the Province of British Columbia through the British Columbia Book Publishing Tax Credit program. We also acknowledge the financial support of the Government of Canada through the National Translation Program for Book Publishing, an initiative of the *Roadmap for Canada's Official Languages 2013–2018: Education, Immigration, Communities*, for our translation activities.

Library and Archives Canada Cataloguing in Publication

Dubuc, Alain
[Portrait de famille. English]
   Is this who we are?: 14 questions about Quebec / Alain Dubuc; translator, Nigel Spencer.—First edition.

Translation of: Portrait de famille.
Issued in print and electronic formats.
ISBN 978-1-55380-467-3 (print)
ISBN 978-1-55380-468-0 (ebook) / ISBN 978-1-55380-469-7 (pdf)

   1. Québec (Province)—Civilization. 2. Québec (Province)—Social conditions—21st century. I. Spencer, Nigel, 1945–, translator II. Title. III. Title: Portrait de famille. English

FC2919.D813413 2016   306.09714   C2016-902121-1

At Ronsdale Press we are committed to protecting the environment. To this end we are working with Canopy and printers to phase out our use of paper produced from ancient forests. This book is one step towards that goal.

Printed in Canada by Marquis Book Printing, Quebec

Contents

SEEING CLEARLY

A few years past, we were still able to believe
in the imminent dawn of great change. Québec
seemed to both discover and accept the notion
of becoming rich. But that revolution never
came about. Lethargy took over, and resistance
to change, in my opinion, was largely the result
of our reluctance to betray our fast-held image of
ourselves. It was then I concluded that one key
to unlocking what bound us was to attack our
false self-image.

Eight years ago, I published a book called *Éloge de la richesse* (*In Praise of Riches*), which set out to make it plain that economically Québec lagged seriously behind its partners, that it was less prosperous than we thought, that our standard of living was lower, and that wealth-creation had to become a priority, not out of greed, but because prosperity is essential to reaching the objectives of a society that believes in social progress.

It garnered considerable attention, due in part to its title—almost blasphemous at the time—which caught the popular imagination, but primarily because it was part of a newly emerging pattern of thought embodied in the manifesto *Pour un Québec lucide* (*Clear Heads for Québec*)—written by an informal group of *éminences grises*, including Lucien Bouchard, André Pratte and Denise Robert. Some agreed that we were headed for an impasse and needed a serious change of direction. This too had a definite impact. Suddenly, everyone was talking about *wealth*.

One might almost have thought major change was at hand, but no, the revolution never happened, and the window slammed shut. The pendulum swung back before ever reaching the end of its arc. Québec preferred to sit tight and wait it out.

What most symbolized this resistance to change was the public debate over university fees. It may well be dubbed the "Maple Revolution," but it definitely was not about springtime: it recycled old ideas and reflexes recalling the dark and chilly days of autumn.

To consider the students' victory in convincing the new Parti Québécois government to cancel increases for the Fall 2013 semester as simply a matter of the left beating out the right was a paradigm I refused to adopt. I refused because of my profound belief that economic success is essential to the reforms needed for social progress. What won out was not the ideology of the left so much as a certain fixation on identity and historic conformism. So a virtual freeze was put on education fees, because, well, that is pretty much what we have been doing for the past forty years.

It appeared to me that the student opposition to a reasonable bump-up in fees, with the widespread support they enjoyed, was less ideological than identity-based. This sizeable activist movement was founded on a conception of Québec, a perception of its successes, needs and problems. Why, for instance, would one agree to make sacrifices dictated by budgetary constraints when one refuses to believe that the province is undergoing a financial crisis? Why agree to a fee-rise if the universities seem to be doing all right financially? Why tamper with the values of an education system which lies at the very heart of the Quiet Revolution?

Thus it becomes important to take a close look at this mental construct of Québec that we made for ourselves. We need to stack it up against the facts, so we can get an accurate read on our economic situation, our social accomplishments and our successes in general.

When I broached my intentions with those around me, many feared it would become an exercise in denigrating Québec, or that it might appear that way, in a climate where it is often hard to take a serious and critical look at ourselves without accusations of being anti-Québécois. Yet, as you will see, it is much more a matter of adjustment and deconstruction, because many aspects of the way Québécois see themselves are, in fact, relatively accurate. It so happens that we are even overly self-critical at times.

The goal is therefore not to criticize for the sake of it, but to be as lucid as possible. Collective myths often have a perverse effect. On occasion, they can indeed galvanize us and give us a sense of pride, but they can also create false reassurance from a feeling of success. America's mythology, based on its industrial superiority, can blind its citizens to the fact that their economic structure is crumbling; in France, the triumph of the French model has led our "cousins" to the edge of a precipice. In Québec, a false sense of security might lull us into not reacting when gains made in the past are actually under threat.

In our case, such false illusions leave us open to three particular dangers. When we are too self-satisfied, we see no reason to bother with improvements. If we are blinded by success, we may fail to see oncoming problems before it is too late. When we are not up-to-date, we make poor choices.

The purpose of this book is to describe Québec and the Québécois family as faithfully, clearly and subtly as we can. This we can do by chasing down our myths and deconstructing them as broadly as possible to include the economy, the environment, our culture and quality of life. We will again be asking those same questions for which we think we already have answers: Are we generous? Are we up-to-date? Do we work hard? Our answers must come from measuring our self-image against the facts as rigorously as possible . . . and having a little fun along the way. The object is not particularly academic, and although there are a number of statistics, we will also come up against glimpses of Québec that are oddly funny and captivating.

To help me in this, I have called on the Centre interuniversitaire de recherche en analyse des organizations (CIRANO—the Center for Inter-university Research and Analysis of Organizations), of which I have the honour to be a Guest Fellow. I thank its President and Director General, Claude Montmarquette, as well as its founder, Robert Lacroix, for their valuable advice. The conclusions are, of course, my own responsibility.

CHAPTER 1

REAL AND IMAGINED

This book sets out to compare and contrast our self-image with facts, statistics and verifiable data to see if we are on target or living a pipe dream. How do we see ourselves and our home? How do we compare with other societies? What do we see as our strengths or weaknesses?

For the most part, the opinions, points of view and ideas Québécois have on their own society are, in fact, quite correct, but at times coloured by their experiences and values, as well as a natural tendency to exaggerate. There are also instances of myth-making, where facts are not allowed to interfere with a good idea, leaving it to the realm of imagination.

It is by putting perceptions face-to-face with facts that we will see how clear-sighted, complacent or wrong they may be.

What exactly are these perceptions? Since I am both judge and advocate, this will be the most delicate part of the operation: defining the myths, then checking to see if they have a legitimate basis. It would be easy to drift into caricature, to concoct false ideas as straw men, the better to demolish them, or break down doors that were never locked.

In addition, there is no Facebook page, no Wikipedia article to tell us how Québécois think of themselves and their territory, so this will be done in segments, using both intuition and deduction, in order to define them as carefully as we can. Certain propositions are, of course, factual: for instance, "Québec is a paradise of natural resources," or "Québec is a society where the usual language is French." Others are more subjective: such as saying that Québec is "unique," or that Québécois are "hospitable." Still others can be classified as unspoken, like the profound conviction of many that we are less "backward" than the electorate that favoured a Harper government.

A GROUP SELFIE

Some notions we hold about Québec have been abundantly documented, such as the pivotal position held in our recent history by the Quiet Revolution, as well as the cleavage between historical fact and interpretation. It would be relatively easy to show that this fundamental undertaking gave birth to a myth which is far from fact and closer to being sacred.

One might also refer to official documents designed to describe Québec overseas, notably to investors, immigrants and tourists. These inevitably would be complacent, destined as they are to present Québec in a positive light verging on exaggeration. Still, the manner in which they do this is revealing in itself.

One can also find inspiration in the public declarations of politicians and other personalities whose characterization of Québec reflects collective images, perhaps colouring them somewhat.

While I was researching this book, the Deputy Premier, François Gendron, hailed the election of Pope Francis before the National Assembly as "giving a particular flavour to his papacy that resembles Québec values." He was referring to his reputation as "the Pope of the poor," who sought to "help the less fortunate come into a better world." This raised two questions: do we really help the poor, and if so, is it more of a priority for us than for Danes or Italians?

The matter of "Québec values" has been under intense debate recently, and is a fruitful source of ways to clarify our own self-image. Calling something a "Québec value" is certainly a way of defining Québec and underscoring its attributes, but also of emphasizing the fact that it particularly prizes certain concerns and marks itself off by respecting them.

One can consult any number of opinion polls in which Québécois define/compare themselves, or assign characteristics to Québec. There are enough of them to give us quite a good idea. In 2006, for instance, when Lucien Bouchard declared that Québécois should be harder-working, a survey showed us that his belief was far from meeting with unanimous approval: 46% agreed, and 45% disagreed, maintaining that they worked quite hard enough, thank you. Dipping into these resources, it becomes possible to establish a composite image of Québec as we Québécois see it, a sort of collective self-portrait.

FIVE MECHANISMS AT WORK

This allows us to sort out some general tendencies, mental processes— ways of seeing and reacting, which structure or colour how we look at things. Next, we can elaborate specific propositions and identify affirmations that seem to strike a common chord.

The first device to help us build our collective self-portrait is imagery from the Quiet Revolution itself. Although it is now over fifty years old, it still influences our perceptions of modern Québec. It is omnipresent and surfaces in a multitude of different domains.

The principles enunciated by Jean Lesage are part of the discussion upon which the Caisse de dépôt and placement du Québec (the Québec Deposit and Investment Fund, in which pension money is kept and used as a public source of strategic investment) is founded. We fought an increase in electricity rates by Hydro-Québec with the promises of René Lévesque in mind. The report written by Monsignor Alphonse-Marie Parent, when the parents of today's university students were still in diapers, inspired us to repudiate the unfreezing of post-secondary fees. The Quiet Revolution's secular ideal led many to support the Charter of Québec Values (on "reasonable accommodation" with immigrants and the wearing of religious or culturally exclusive garb in the public service).

The second element is the feeling that Québec is fundamentally different: "Unique! This is how Québec defines itself" is the revealing sentence that introduces the portrait of Québec on the government's official website.

That Québec is unique is, of course, true. History and sociology have laid out a very distinct path for us: a French population among the very first European arrivals in North America, who have kept their language and specificity throughout the tribulations of history, notably the conquest of New France by the British.

It is likewise obvious that Québécois make up the sole francophone community in North America, including a significant English-speaking minority, as well as native peoples and new arrivals—all of them constituting a nation with its own government, institutions and territory.

Just saying a nation is unique, however, does not clarify a great deal. All nations have specific characteristics, and even groupings which cannot claim to be nations still can be considered unique. Acadians and Texans are proud of their flags, their cuisine, their music and their lifestyles.

Fundamentally though, we all know that we stress our difference from the rest of Canada and North America. True, but hardly astonishing, and once we agree that Québec is a nation, the rest, that particular set of differences, that uniqueness, is a given.

If we emphasize that difference as much as we do, it is because there was a time when we had to protect our identity from the threats surrounding it; we had to define those distinctive qualities and underline their importance in order to protect and preserve them better. This runs parallel to the political game of deliberately emphasizing the differences in order to show that we are so distinct from Canada that we ought to leave it. The reaction of federalists was to play precisely the same game and, in turn, highlight their own nationalist fervour. The snowball effect of constantly looking for differences has led us to overlook the fact that many things we have come to think of as typically Québécois are, in fact, Canadian: shepherd's pie, hockey and our health-care system.

The third device is, in fact, an outgrowth of the second: thinking sometimes that we are not only different from but better in comparison with our North American neighbours.

This is a reflex common to all nations—a constant patriotic reflex that glorifies one's history, shows pride in one's achievements and cultural traits, often with an unavoidable hint of chauvinism. Peoples everywhere prize themselves and feel an element of superiority, be it American patriotism, French chauvinism toward the British—and vice-versa—or an equivalent reflex between Norwegians and Swedes, Spaniards and Portuguese, or Czechs and Hungarians.

It is a natural phenomenon which is probably more pronounced in a society such as Québec, adrift and smarting under the contempt of its dominant minority, feeling the legitimate need for self-esteem. Smaller societies naturally have to draw their own and other peoples' attention to their success overseas. It is apparent in the indignation that is aroused when unflattering remarks are made about us, likewise in the haste with which we seize on any sense of superiority in our achievements, or the greater morality of our values.

If the tendency toward self-glorification is present in all societies, here it takes a form of its own, derived from a certain introversion due to our linguistic insulation from the rest of the continent. We do not know the neighbours very well, and this at times provides a fourth mechanism, the tendency to appropriate "virtues" which are not exclusively ours.

In the controversy over corruption in the construction industry, the Chairman of the Treasury Board, Stéphane Bédard, commented thus on measures taken to combat the misappropriation of funds: he was "convinced we will witness the emergence of new leaders in the industry with fresh values, more in tune with Québec values." There was plenty of room for puzzlement in this. What could lead us to presume that honesty and a fundamental respect for laws—the basis of civil society everywhere—were specific to Québec? Above all, the revelations these past few years have shown the exact opposite: they are less present here than elsewhere!

This slippage in standards became evident in the debate over the Charter of Québec Values, based on a generic confusion between those principles which are considered specifically Québécois and others, which by their very nature, are universal. The French language is commonly and distinctly ours, but we cannot say as much for equality between men and women, a value widely held and vigorously defended by charter in virtually every advanced society.

Why, in its public discourse, does Québec qualify certain values as its own rather than proudly share them as an international heritage? There is a message here, but what exactly is it? Are these principles better anchored here than abroad? Are we more deeply committed to them?

A fifth mechanism, also present in other cultures, is that of "variable geometry." Here, as elsewhere, we tend to give more importance to attributes that set us apart. American patriotism relies largely on military power and attaches importance to the exploits of its troops, something not possible in Québec or in Canada, pacifism being a trait common to both. The British prize gastronomy less than the French. Québécois like to consider themselves more left-leaning than the rest of Canada, something that would not occur to an Albertan.

Such variable geometry leads us, by extension, to place less importance on areas where our superiority is not so evident. One might call this wilful blindness, and the most obvious instance is avoiding the fact that Québécois earn less than their partners and neighbours, which is amply documented, though many of us tend to forget it, deny, block out or minimize it so willingly that some actually try to prove the opposite with tenuous arguments, so as not to see what is in front of them. In this process, then, silence can be most revealing.

FOURTEEN MYTHS OPEN TO QUESTION

Decoding all this by taking account of both the mechanisms and the points of view involved, I am prepared to extract some precepts which, without much exaggeration and in reasonable truthfulness, convey the picture that Québécois retain of Québec. The following chapters will each examine one of fourteen social and economic (rather than political) myths. Preference will be given to those which can be checked with a necessary minimum of facts, data and other objective elements. Each of the fourteen will be posed in the form of a question.

Are we a unique model? The first of the fourteen addresses the conviction that, thanks to the Quiet Revolution, we have built a unique system, distinctive enough to be called a model. I can affirm in advance that this is largely a myth. Our interpretation of the Quiet Revolution has taken on mythic dimensions, sufficient to become the founding myth of modern Québécois identity, and to make us believe that to criticize the "Québec model" is to criticize Québec. This myth, our way of viewing the Quiet Revolution, engenders others as by-products, notably education, hydroelectricity, and so on.

Are we educated? As the revolution began, we undertook a vast reform to provide an entire education system (including the Ministry of Education; polyvalentes—large five-year, multidisciplinary high schools; CEGEPs—junior and vocational colleges; and the Université du Québec). Does this, however, truly mean Québec has become a society that has bet squarely on education and won?

Are we a knowledge society? This question is key at a time in history when knowledge is the main ingredient in success. Has progress in education led us to become a true learning society, one with the network of universities it needs to stand out in research and innovation?

Are we "cultural"? Québec, like others, due to the ferment of its national issue, has affirmed itself through its culture and achieved an astonishing level of cultural production by the likes of Céline Dion and Robert Lepage, known around the globe, but does this make us more cultural or cultivated than others?

Are we under threat? Québécois are a minority on the continent and fear for the survival of their culture. This is doubtless the one area where they demonstrate negativity about themselves, but are they right to do so? This a delicate theme on which to separate facts from subjective perceptions and political amplifications.

Are we egalitarian? Is Québec a haven of male-female equality? It seems important enough to us to be one of our great values. There has been undeniable progress in the past half-century, but does Québec truly stand out in the labour market, in daily life, or in the exercise of power?

Are we in solidarity with each other? This is another generally accepted description and a cause for pride: our sense of solidarity and compassion. It is applied to a number of situations such as equality of opportunity, wealth-redistribution, the gaps between rich and poor, help for the less fortunate, the generosity of our citizens, openness to others, and our leaning, in a broad sense, toward the left when compared with societies around us, but how true is all this?

Are we healthy? Québécois generally believe our health system is unique in embodying the values of the Quiet Revolution. We do not realize, however, that its uniqueness is actually a variant of the pan-Canadian system. Furthermore, how does it compare with those of the industrialized world overall? What can we affirm about the health of the population, the quality of care and the costs of our system?

Are we "green"? The conviction abounds that Québec is an ecological enclave within Canada and North America, a paradise of clean energy whose citizens are generally greener and environmentally more conscious than others. But is this borne out by our choices and our actions?

Are we hard-working? The conviction that we are a hard-working people is rooted in our folklore along with our courageous ancestors who laboured hard in the face of life's adversity. Witness our curt reaction to Lucien Bouchard's statements to the contrary in the wake of the manifesto *Clear Heads for Québec*. I shall be taking a closer look at this work ethic, as well as our productivity and attitudes in this matter.

Are we productive? Once again, the perception is that the economy of Québec, by virtue of its marginal benefits, is dynamic, capable of wealth-creation. Our economy, in fact, shows weaker growth and a lower standard of living than those of our partners, hence poorer performance. This is a subject I have already written much about, but which must ceaselessly be revisited.

Are we rich? Despite a reduced economic performance, the lot and the finances of individual Québécois are not all bad. How does their standard of living compare with those of other Canadians or of foreigners? Are we truly prosperous?

Are we happy? Happiness is a delicate but fundamental subject. Do we make up a happy society with an enviable (even exceptional) quality of life which compares favourably with that of others?

Are we viable? Here we end on a darker note. Québec society has reached a certain equilibrium, in many respects an enviable one, but not a viable one, threatened as it is by crises in public finances and deep-seated groundswells (such as demographic shock) which change the rules of the game.

These are the notions which will be addressed, one per chapter, and examined in the light of factual information, in order to help us to tell falsehood from truth with the data we possess and with the skills to permit us as much objectivity as possible in our determination.

CHAPTER 2

ARE WE A UNIQUE MODEL?

How many times have we each read or even spoken the words "Québec model"? Probably hundreds or even thousands, depending on how old we are. My second question is: have you ever actually pinned down what that is? If you have, you have most likely had some trouble doing it, especially since no two people seem to agree. This leads to my third question: how is it that something so important seems so fuzzy? How can we talk so much about something we do not understand?

My overall response, after some digging, is that there is no particular Québec model. It is a myth, surely a powerful idea that engages the imagination and imposes itself as reality, but a mental construct nevertheless. Its foundation is in the way our collective imagery has transformed, glorified and coloured the Quiet Revolution, the crowning event in contemporary Québécois history, which lies at the heart of how Québécois see themselves.

This is the moment at which we broke with our rural and religious past and entered fully into modernity—the origin of the main characteristics that distinguish today's society: rejection of the church's control over us, the creation of a state apparatus which is still very much with us, as well as the shaping of our national affirmation.

Far be it from me to slide into revisionism or deny the importance of this turning point in modern Québec. One can both emphasize the admirable qualities of the Quiet Revolution, finding it remarkable in its original context, and believe that it has passed its "best before" date, hence giving rise to a number of perverse effects. One might also say we have over-stretched the elastic and turned a rich and interesting period into a fairy tale.

In 1960's Québec, something extremely important happened. The list of innovations and accomplishments made during the Quiet Revolution is a long one: the construction of a modern state apparatus and a Ministry of Education, the nationalization of electricity and the founding of the Caisse de dépôt et placement du Québec. But the revolution itself went far beyond such institutions and programs. Most noteworthy were the spirit of the times, the winds of change, the determination to break with the past, the thirst for modernity, the energy, the thrust, the boldness, the desire to reinvent the world, and the conviction that anything was possible. Parallel with this went the affirmation of national feelings expressed in many new forms with a sense of success rather than the bitterness of defeat. The fruits of this have endured—witness, for instance, the achievements of our educational system and our very real economic catch-up, inadequate as it may be.

Still, an important gap exists between reality and the narrative that has emerged from it over the years. The fundamental action of the Quiet Revolution has also turned out to be our great national myth. Its importance has caused mistakes to be expunged from the record in a process which has taken on quasi-religious overtones. This myth rests on two instances of exaggeration: first, the Grande Noirceur ("Great Darkness" of the Duplessis period and earlier) from which we were liberated was not as dark as often believed—the epoch was less obscurantist than it was later portrayed; second, because the economic transformation had already begun, with the seeds of change planted well before the break became apparent.

Furthermore, the revolution was certainly less original and less radical than we like to believe. The winds of change in the 1960s blew not only over Québec but over the entire Western world. When we stop to think about it, the whole planet saw profound changes that started rolling early in the decade and then snowballed. Traditional values everywhere were overturned. This was the decade of the birth control pill and the rise of feminism. In the US, John F. Kennedy came to power, and civil rights came into the spotlight. Baby boomers turned to self-affirmation with the Beatles, Woodstock and the anti-war movement, along with hippy and student mobilization, leading to May 1968 in France. It was also the decade of anti-colonial wars.

In this period, our institutions did no more or less than others around them had already done: Québec simply blended into the crowd. The Quiet Revolution was essentially a vast process of catching up, as we too became a modern society. What stood out was the concentration and speed with which we did this. Reforms were made in high gear, urgently, as if it were to make up for lost time. But to what extent can this be considered a real feat?

Its principal reforms were duplicated in the rest of Canada. First came hospital insurance from Ottawa, then health insurance. The intention was to allow us all to benefit from the system invented in Saskatchewan by providing substantial funds to provinces with a system that respected the parameters defined by Ottawa. This same federal government aimed to establish the Canada Pension Plan, although Québec withdrew to manage its share through the Caisse de dépôt. Moreover, the Régie des rentes du Québec, like "the old-age pension," was Ottawa's idea. The same applied to that other segment of the social safety net, unemployment insurance, as well as welfare, inaugurated in Canada twenty years before Québec, and partly financed by Ottawa.

Québec showed guts and originality in its adaptation of Canada's reforms. It installed Canadian programs in its own way. One example is the Centre local de services communautaires (CLSCs — local community service centres). Our experience with these is certainly interesting, although not original. Thus the essence of the safety net is pan-Canadian, and the Québec welfare state is a variant on the Canadian one.

None of this detracts from the accomplishments of the period, but it does bring them down to human scale. In other words, the usual reading of the Quiet Revolution has been oversimplified, exaggerating the importance of our break with the past, and inflating our achievements.

CONSECRATION

Clearly, we have been present at the birth of a myth. This consecration is no trifling detail, nor just a cultural curiosity, but a meaningful phenomenon, important in its fallout. This consecration has had harmful side effects amounting to a betrayal of its generation of reformers. It is the myth which poisoned its source and created an interesting paradox. It has become a straitjacket not unlike what it set out to destroy. It clearly could not have grown up without being seeded, and that seedbed was the real Quiet Revolution itself, whatever its limitations and its cracks, a high point in our history, a founding gesture that would give meaning to a nation. This moment has demonstrated our creativity and energy, and affirmed itself in a way that was not traditionally our own.

It is likely that our countrymen of the day were not proud of certain features in their history that derived from defeat and were coloured by the rural resignation of those born before them to serve and be poor. The Quiet Revolution led them to erase an inglorious past and reset Québec history to 1960. This mechanism allows one to describe Québec as left-leaning and open to the world—when history says the opposite—and claim, as a pro-laic petition put it, that "this is part of Québec's heritage," though, in fact, the opposite is true. Our religious devotion has shaped our heritage.

Québécois nationalism, marked by the Conquest, was long a matter for feelings of resignation and defeat. The Quiet Revolution opened the door to a much more proactive national affirmation that would allow us to take our rightful place and confront the federal government, showing our capabilities with reforms that often outstripped those in the rest of Canada. Creating institutions proper to us, attempting to control our economic space as "maîtres chez nous" (masters in our own house)—a phrase coined by Jean Lesage that became the rallying cry of nationalists and Liberals following the death of Maurice Duplessis—carried strong autonomist overtones.

This surge in nationalism, now attuned to success, rightly became an increasingly valuable symbol and a strong reason to take pride in ourselves. We have frequently witnessed instances where understandable pride has nourished the collective ego and taken on an importance all its own. This amplification has led us to a new self-definition and the creation of a new founding myth. It may also have gained significance because the Quiet Revolution has not taken us all the way to sovereignty, which for many Québécois, would be only natural. All this is easily explained and understood, but we must remember that myths come at a cost, and the price is high indeed.

THE UNFINISHED REVOLUTION

The first effect of such a consecration, too powerful and too rapid, is to halt prematurely the ongoing revolution. Of course, the logic of the revolution continued just over a decade after the initial reforms and ended with the creation of economy-oriented state companies and health insurance. This, however, was merely a natural extension of the early 1960s. The initial impulse was gone. No doubt, this can be explained by a form of collective fatigue. A society may well need to catch its breath and digest all these reforms. This might explain the Liberal defeat and the return to power of l'Union Nationale (a modernized version of Duplessis' old nationalist and reactionary party).

There is surely another mechanism at play, one egged on by the fledgling mythology: pride, the sense of accomplishment, the feeling that Québec—now having taken great strides—had reached its peak. This was the time for us to sit back and admire our handiwork, thinking that the heavy lifting was done, when, in fact, it had barely begun. Thus the remaining efforts were carried out, but not with the same ardour. In many respects, we hit a plateau before ever reaching the summit.

There are many examples to support this. Education provides the first. The creation of a Ministry of Education and schools that offer a quality education to all young people would provide parents with a precious tool they had never owned before, and the results are indisputable: whatever criticisms and debates we have known, our system of education compares favourably with the rest of Canada and the world. This reset was a success, but it did not solve everything. Such reforms could not reach deep enough to correct one basic flaw that characterizes a backward society: the mistrust of education and the tendency not to make it one of our basic collective values. The complete indifference we have accorded to the large number of dropouts until recently, for instance, is a disaster that other cultures would not have tolerated. The prevalence of illiteracy, too, shows us to be a poor and culturally underdeveloped society. Not all traces of our traditional backwardness have yet been erased. Yet in fifty years, two generations, we have had enough time to do this. The following chapter will explore this in more detail.

A levelling-off is also noticeable in the area of economics. Québec's living standard has progressed and virtually caught up with that of Ontario, among others; yet in fifty years, a good half-century, it still has not reached the growth rate of its neighbours or outstripped the overall growth rate of Canada as a whole. We remain a poor province and one of the least prosperous jurisdictions in North America. In other words, there has been no exceptional takeoff as there has elsewhere, certainly no "Québec Miracle."

The sense of self-satisfaction mentioned earlier may be responsible for this state of affairs. Québec saw itself as prosperous before ever reaching the appropriate level of wealth. We have posed as a rich society without having the means to be such. This has certainly undermined our sense of urgency and weakened our appetite for growth.

THE MYTH OF A MODEL

This paradoxical trap finds its quintessence in the fact that we have lumped the achievements of the Quiet Revolution together under the heading "Québec Model" sufficiently for the two to become equivalent and even synonymous in our minds. It is worth taking the time to have a closer look at what this expression means.

In principle, a model is a particular way of doing things, a distinct approach that evokes admiration and emulation, as well as imitation. The Swedish model, for instance, is a unique social organization which inspired numerous other societies. As far as I know, the way we do things here, except for a handful of initiatives, has never inspired imitation by anyone. From the start, this implies that we have been self-glorifying, for who, besides us, admires the Québec model? Who has imitated us? No one as far as I am aware.

Yet the concept has another meaning as well. Using the term "model" may suggest by default that we inspire others, but it can also be used to describe the unique specificity of our practices and our mode of organization, and it is true that there are specificities about our social organization and our policies. The state, for instance, is slightly more present in our lives than elsewhere in Canada, there is a more thorough redistribution of income, there is more collaboration between economic partners, and there are more well-placed initiatives reflecting our values and our history. Still, with our social safety net and our centrist balance between the "free" market and the state, our system is a variant of that seen throughout most of Canada.

There are notable differences, of course, but to my knowledge there are no societies where governmental policy and organization are without specificities that reflect their own history, values and culture. Does that make each one a model?

If so, the phrase is pointless, but words are not without meaning and shading. Just defining what we do in Québec as a model has an impact all its own, one that fixes and traps, rendering change more difficult and favouring stasis. So, in a kind of vicious circle, the Quiet Revolution has itself produced a culture of rigidity not unlike the one it set out to overthrow. If the model concept has been developed, it is because this high point in our history has created a dimension associated with identity.

This model embodies success and self-affirmation, also describing what Québec is in the second half of the twentieth century and the first decades of the twenty-first—with its own institutions, programs and ways of doing things. Its differences, such as the Caisse de dépôt, CEGEPs and CLSCs, are often amplified as illustrations of the fact that we are indeed a distinct people, nation and society. Thus the Québec model incarnates our identity, defining us, describing what it means to be us, and so it cannot be modified or transformed without also affecting what Québec is, or risking denial of essentially who we are and therefore weakening us. Lucien Bouchard eloquently demonstrated this train of reasoning in his reply to Jean Charest (who wanted to call the model into question): "The battle undertaken against the Québec model is also a battle against the Québec identity." I do not quote this remark out of malice—it must be placed in the electoral context of the time—although it illustrates admirably a feeling still very much present in Québec.

Nothing is harder to budge than institutions or practices which relate to identity, be they bearing firearms in the United States, the health system in Canada or, in this instance, the Québec model. Thus it is that we suffer from a lack of flexibility, engendered paradoxically by the Quiet Revolution itself.

MODELS ARE SACRED

Being sacrosanct is heavy with implications. Not only does it slow the transformational process launched by the Quiet Revolution, but it also freezes time, crystallizes it, so to speak.

The accomplishments ushered in have now become untouchable, institutions are now considered standard-bearers, programs and services are seen as acquired rights. Hands off, and above all, do not question them. Hence many elements associated with the Quiet Revolution are difficult to re-examine or even modify as time passes; fine-tuning or adapting the way we do things to fit a constantly changing situation is excluded.

Even more striking is the extent to which allusion to the fathers of the revolution, or their objectives and principles are still present in public discourse half a century later, a little like quotes from Mao's "Little Red Book" in China, or references to Lenin in the USSR, or even invocations of "providence" by our own pre-war politicians.

For example, based on an implicit election mandate of the 1962 Liberal government (and carried out several years later, when SOQUIP —the government-owned Québec petroleum initiatives corporation— was established), it was argued by an odd environmental group founded by Daniel Breton, briefly Minister of the Environment in the 2012 Marois government, that the exploitation of oil should be nationalized, since private exploitation would constitute a 21st-century betrayal of the "Maîtres chez nous au 21e siècle" ("Masters in our own house in the 21st century"). Again in the energy sector, certain groups wanted wind-power production to be nationalized, as electricity had been, according to the principles invoked by René Lévesque (Energy Minister in the Lesage Cabinet, who oversaw the nationalization of Hydro-Québec).

In the matter of the Caisse de dépôt, the ghost of Jean Lesage himself, a great father of the Quiet Revolution, was called on for reinforcement. The creation of the Caisse with Young Turks such as Jacques Parizeau was a major achievement from which we still benefit. That was in 1965, though. Could one really dust off Lesage forty years later to help us work out the role and the mission of the Caisse? François Legault, Péquiste finance critic, commented on this. His reading of Lesage's speeches led him to the conclusion that the father of the Quiet Revolution had conferred a double mandate on the Caisse: returns on investment and support for Québec's economic development. At the time, Lesage felt it could be used to prevent a Québec company from falling into foreign hands. This was a sledgehammer of an argument: see, the Caisse is supposed to keep head offices from moving out . . . Jean Lesage said so!

In fifty years, the financial world has been vastly transformed, and economic development can no longer be thought of in the same terms. The definition and framework with which it was originally created cannot be imposed on the mission and strategy of a state enterprise forever.

The Castonguay-Nepveu Commission, mandated in 1966, enshrined certain principles in our health-care system which oppose any intrusion of the private sector, something that could not be foreseen at the time.

Again in that period, the commission presided over by Monsignor Parent provided the basis for our education system, and its recommendation that university be provided free is invoked to justify all opposition to a fee-hike. This is confirmed by sociologist Guy Rocher, a member of the Parent Commission. One of the rare surviving architects of the Quiet Revolution, along with Jacques Parizeau, Claude Morin and Claude Castonguay, in an interview with *Le Devoir* during the Maple Spring (the student protest movement of 2012–2013), Rocher recalled that the Commission originally supported the elimination of all tuition fees in 1965. The plan was set aside for lack of funds, "but we hoped that in the not too long term, free education would prevail. Bit-by-bit, however, the government adopted the neo-liberal *consumer-pays* principle."

The Quiet Revolution is also a reference for the debate over the Charter of Québec Values. Here, too, Guy Rocher sees an extension of the great movement:

> The projected charter cannot be understood and evaluated in and for the present alone. It has to be seen in a larger historical and future perspective. Such a charter is not conceived just for 2013, but with a view to the farthest future we can foresee. Furthermore, it is a product of our political, cultural and demographic evolution over the past fifty years, that of a particular nation—Québec.

Briefly then, the Quiet Revolution is still with us and continues to affect our debates and choices. The fundamental rigidity which turns past experience into dogma and fits our thinking into preconceived moulds has been reinforced by a plethora of other mechanisms provided directly or indirectly by the Quiet Revolution.

First, let us consider the polarization which is specific to Québec politics. Two broad camps occupy most of the terrain—the PQ (Parti Québécois) and PLQ (Québec Liberal Party)—essentially coalitions without totally unifying ideologies or social doctrines, but simply constitutional options. Neither one is fundamentally right or left, but both consider themselves heirs of the Quiet Revolution: the Liberals because they carried it out, and the Péquistes because their party was founded by René Lévesque, the most noted figure of the revolution, and because their program remains closer to the spirit of the original plan. Neither, of course, can throw this open to question and shake its own internal equilibrium or betray its declared heritage. To effect this, however awkwardly, a new party, the Action démocratique du Québec (ADQ) had to be formed outside their dogmas. After a brief time, this role was taken over by the Coalition Avenir Québec (CAQ), which absorbed the ADQ and then also lined up behind the Quiet Revolution.

Further rigidity was added by the institutionalization of the new state apparatus created by the Quiet Revolution and its absorption of a new caste which helped reinforce the myth. Our elites of knowledge and power—mandarins, thinkers, politicians and social leaders—had already long been part of the huge undertaking, rather like in France, where the criterion was whether or not one had been part of the Résistance, or China, where one had to have taken part in the Long March. Those considered Québec's great thinkers—Léon Dion, Guy Rocher, Fernand Dumont—are part of this generation, and no new recruits were ever able to achieve the same status. The same holds true for our most revered politicians, René Lévesque and Jean Lesage. Québec, basically a young society, has not granted as much power to its youth for a long time now. Attesting to this is the fact that the first baby boomer to lead the province was Jean Charest in 2003, whereas the US elected its first baby boomer president, Bill Clinton, in 1994.

The most important source of rigidity, however, came from the legions of Québécois who profited from the transformation and in turn were the first to sing the praises of a system that benefitted them. Its developing state apparatus, institutions and policies also became the guardians of its orthodoxy and protectors of their own advantages, thus creating an important pool of resistance to any change in public discourse.

The same holds true for all who, up close or at a distance, gravitate to the machinery of state, the public service, the education and health networks, plus all who benefit from state subsidies or transfers. For sociological reasons, which are obvious, all those whose well-being depends on the state and its institutions will tend to look out for themselves and fear any initiative that might change the rules of the game. As indicated earlier, this category of people carries weight in the province.

Québec, like France, is thus a society based on acquired rights, and this leads to a series of defence mechanisms which militate in numerous ways against any change in the model at hand, for fear of weakening us and our identity, or even negating who we are. This then constitutes a faithful reproduction of the type of conservative reasoning that preceded the Quiet Revolution, when defending the established order was a way of protecting what was called "the French-Canadian race."

By erecting its own dogmas and myths, the Quiet Revolution also put in place mechanisms that denied its very spirit, the power of its reforms turning into resistance against change and favouring an orthodoxy very like that against which it once fought.

BY WAY OF CONCLUSION

Does all this impel me to cast aside the Quiet Revolution as just a historical mistake? Not in the least. It was a shining moment in the history of Québec which still deserves to inspire us.

The negative fallout from it is more due to the use we have put it to than the thing itself. This revolution brought benefits, but with them, the germs of its own destruction.

Its undesirable consequences have contributed to putting Québec in a position that is disquieting in many ways. Québec is not badly off, yet it could be better, and it faces challenges that demand important and urgent changes. These reforms will, of course, be difficult, and we have delayed putting them in place.

It will require adaptation and originality to alter our habits and confront the rigidity which has become our heritage. Will this require a radical break, a ripping of the fabric we have woven, an overthrow of the sacred cows we are left with? Not necessarily. I see a search for continuity that does not require a *tabula rasa*, but rather builds on our achievements. Such much-needed efforts would be a true extension of the 1960s. We must dust off its spirit, energy and audacity in the same cause: the reach for success, excellence and a nationalism of winners.

I must conclude by admitting that this chapter has several objectives. The first is to establish that Québec does, in fact, have myths. To do this, I have begun with a theme of special clarity (supported by an example) that is easy to establish.

The second seeks to show, to any who still doubt it, that Québécois definitely possess a collective talent, as well as an aptitude for myth-building, illustrated by the exceptional divide between the Quiet Revolution as it really was and our description of it, as though each of us embodies a miniature Fred Pellerin who continually invents enchanting folk tales for us.

The third is to remind us that a myth is more than just an enchanting story. The creation of myths has tangible effects on how we discuss things and make decisions, such as school fees or energy policy.

Finally, it sets the scene for the chapters that follow, since our collectively constructed ideas of the Quiet Revolution indirectly affect other important factors such as our economic performance or educational policy, the latter being the subject of the next two chapters.

CHAPTER 3

ARE WE EDUCATED?

It matters very much that the first theme taken up is that of education. First, because some very strong symbols are attached to this initial creation of the Quiet Revolution. One of our crowning political slogans is "Learning is riches." Above all, it allows us to start on a positive note. The praiseworthy performance of our education system is no myth. We might even go so far as to say that the education system is better than most of us think.

Our governments have good reason to vaunt our accomplishments in the field of education, with our university network, our well-trained workforce and Montreal's position as a major university centre. Our education system compares favourably with others; not only is it exciting, but in many ways, it is definitely among the best in the world. Our efforts in this sphere constitute a genuine success story, although, of course, some reservations can be expressed.

The extent to which we criticize it is well known: the knowledge of our students, the competence of our teachers and school boards, the lumbering weight of the ministry, and the pedagogical overhaul of recent years. We are discontented with the way our children speak and—worse—write, and this leads to the impression that the whole system is in a state of permanent crisis.

Yet, objectively speaking, the overall diagnosis is positive . . . so much so that we need to approach the subject from an entirely different angle. Although the glass is three-quarters full, there are problems that require attention and considerable improvement. This is, however, more a matter of fine-tuning than serious existential doubt, especially since these weaknesses often have more to do with general cultural traits and attitudes than with defects in education itself. This naturally means that correctives have to be sought elsewhere.

A linear overview of the education system is called for, from top to bottom—kindergarten to university and adult education.

FROM BIRTH TO KINDERGARTEN

Schooling for a young Québécois does not begin at six when he enters the schoolyard in grade one. It begins when he is still inside his mother.

His first years are spent in an environment which determines much of what will happen in his first years at school. Success in school depends on a number of economic and psycho-social factors: the family milieu, poverty and attitudes toward education. If a child comes to school poorly equipped, it will hinder his future development and success in the system as a whole.

A study carried out by the Institut de la statistique du Québec (Québec Statistical Institute)[1] among teachers to measure the level of development in groups of kindergarten students in six areas—physical health and well-being, social competency, emotional maturity, cognitive and linguistic development, ability to communicate and general knowledge —shows that one child in four shows signs of vulnerability in one or more of these groupings. Given that the connections between level of development in kindergarten and later success have been amply demonstrated and documented, reducing the number of students with developmental difficulties could improve the school's success rate.

This means intervening at the earliest possible level before school age. Québec has made the correct choice in making kindergarten obligatory and setting up a vast daycare network which is heavily subsidized and virtually universal. This makes us the only ones in Canada to do so, which the Organization for Economic Co-operation and Development (OECD) cites as an example, thus spurring the rest of Canada to follow. Of course, the network is not perfect. It was launched without the necessary finances, with virtually uniform rates, which in turn were frozen for eternity—clearly a policy that was neither logical nor fair. There is still a shortage of available places, the main criticism being that it strayed from its original priority.

To be sure, the seven-dollar-a-day network helps parents reconcile work and family, as well as increasing women's participation in the workforce, but these centres (CPE) also have a socio-educational role to play: learning to socialize gives young children tools they may not obtain at home. This basic psycho-social element, especially important to give underprivileged children a better chance, has largely been neglected.

FIRST STEPS IN ELEMENTARY SCHOOL

First, we must take a look at how our children behave when entering the school system for the first time. There is an avalanche of statistics on our school network, and I must apologize for this, but if we are to know whether ours is an education system of quality that gives good results, we must first measure it against, and compare it with, others.

Québécois have tended to be suspicious of international contests ever since the United Nations elicited Prime Minister Jean Chrétien's affirmation that Canada was "the best country in the world." Perhaps, too, they prefer not to think of education as an Olympic discipline. Nevertheless, such studies are necessary to know whether our system of education works well, to evaluate its results and to compare them. We need to discover, for example, if the reading skills of young Ontarians or Finns are significantly superior to those of Québécois, and whether we should be asking questions.

Here again, there are those who wonder why we need to strive to be one of the best. In the case of education, we should not even be asking this: we do not wish to surpass others for the mere pleasure of it, but for our own survival and improvement. Education is the basis for all the rest: the more we have, the better our economy works, and the less poverty devastates us.

There is one such study that affords us some idea of the success or failure of Québec's primary education. The Progress in International Reading Literacy Study (PIRLS) is a vast project run by an independent organization, the International Association for the Evaluation of Educational Achievement (IEA), with over sixty member countries. The organization carried out studies of grade four children with an average age of nine and a half—not on their diction, elegance or literary aptitude, but on their reading skills, their capacity to understand a text and derive information from it.

This study is repeated every five years, the last dating from 2011 (the 2016 study has taken place but the data are yet to be released). In the 2011 study, Hong Kong led with 571 points, well over the average of 500. Next came Russia, Finland, Singapore, Northern Ireland and the USA. Canada, with 548 points, came in 12th. Québec had average results of 538, in 21st place, but ahead of supposedly exemplary countries like France, Australia and Norway.

It is worth noting that most of the other provinces did better than Québec when it came to preparing their children to read. Québec placed

PERFORMANCE IN READING IN 4TH YEAR OF ELEMENTARY SCHOOL
RESULTS OF PIRLS, AVERAGE GRADES, 2011

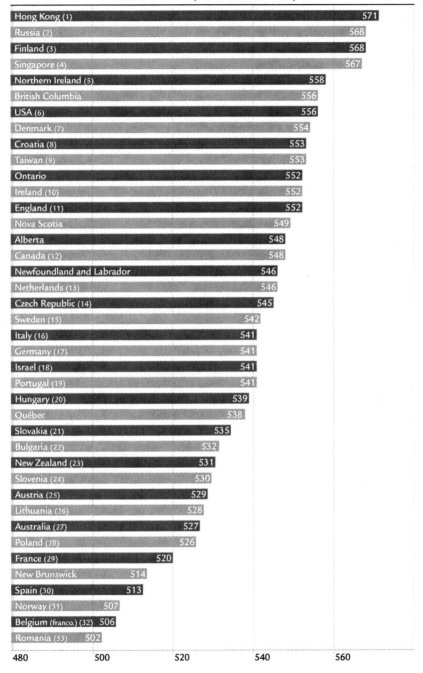

Hong Kong (1)	571
Russia (2)	568
Finland (3)	568
Singapore (4)	567
Northern Ireland (5)	558
British Columbia	556
USA (6)	556
Denmark (7)	554
Croatia (8)	553
Taiwan (9)	553
Ontario	552
Ireland (10)	552
England (11)	552
Nova Scotia	549
Alberta	548
Canada (12)	548
Newfoundland and Labrador	546
Netherlands (13)	546
Czech Republic (14)	545
Sweden (15)	542
Italy (16)	541
Germany (17)	541
Israel (18)	541
Portugal (19)	541
Hungary (20)	539
Québec	538
Slovakia (21)	535
Bulgaria (22)	532
New Zealand (23)	531
Slovenia (24)	530
Austria (25)	529
Lithuania (26)	528
Australia (27)	527
Poland (28)	526
France (29)	520
New Brunswick	514
Spain (30)	513
Norway (31)	507
Belgium (franco.) (32)	506
Romania (33)	502

480   500   520   540   560

Source: PIRLS (Progress in International Reading Literacy Study), "PIRLS 2011, Canada in Context."

8th out of nine provinces, ahead of New Brunswick—with Prince Edward Island absent. British Columbia is near the top internationally with 556 points (7th in the world), followed closely by Ontario in 11th place with a score of 552. The results for 2011 are comparable to those of 2001 and 2006.

Generally speaking, francophones, wherever they may be, do not perform very well. Young francophones from Québec, with 537 points, do less well than Anglo-Québécois at 545. New Brunswick francophones, with 514, are in 31st place, but this province is just behind France in 30th place, and ahead of Belgium at 33rd. Does this mean that the complexity of French language and texts takes more time for children to master? Perhaps when compared with English, but this does not explain the success of young Russians or Chinese.

When we dig a little deeper, we discover that this delay cannot be explained by economic inequality or educational deficiencies, but rather by cultural factors well documented by PIRLS: the links between society and reading. The study in effect shows that Québécois children live as comfortably as others, with parents as educated and professional as elsewhere, with equal or superior living conditions: individual rooms, Internet access, etc.

The difference is in the home. Because parents are the first to educate their children, they were asked to specify the frequency with which they took part in reading-associated activities with their children before school age—reading books with them, etc. Those children with early exposure to reading obtained 35 more points on the test. These questions have permitted the establishment of a scale to measure these advanced activities. Canada, with a score of 10.7, was above the international average of 10, but there was an important spread within the country. Québec, at 10.2, came last in Canada, very far behind certain provinces (Newfoundland obtained 11.9). Québécois results seem to be explained by the fact that less reading is done with children at home.

TEENAGERS

Now for some good news: if, at the primary level, a certain delay in reading is observable among Québécois children, they do catch up in adolescence. This appears in another important study by the OECD titled *Programme international pour le suivi des acquis des élèves* (PISA—Program for International Student Assessment) carried out for over 15 years on our "secondary 4" students with a series of exams. A total of 65 countries or economies (e.g. Chinese cities such as Shanghai) took part, including over 200 schools and 4,000 students in Québec. This study measured the aptitudes of young people in three areas, triennially: reading, mathematics and sciences. The latest results are for 2012. PISA is a highly respected piece of research and serves as a reference. The results are stupefying. Québec's educational system is excellent, even exceptional, in fact one of the world's 10 best, second in the West to Finland.

In mathematics, Québec, with 536 points, ranks 7th worldwide behind Shanghai, Singapore, Hong Kong, South Korea and Taipei, and is equal with Japan. In mathematics, Québec has obtained the best results in the West. It is considerably ahead of Canada in 13th place (518 points).

In reading, Canada overall is 9th with 523 points, behind those same Asian tigers and Finland. If Québec were considered a country, it would be just behind the whole of Canada, in 10th place with 520 points.

In science, things are not as bright. Canada is 10th with 525 points, but Québec, which has lost ground since the 2009 survey, saw its score drop from 524 to 516, leaving it ranking 18th in world.

There are several ways to establish world standings. I have chosen to do it by using the final scores of the participating jurisdictions in these three disciplines. At 1572, Québec thus comes 10th behind Shanghai, Singapore, Hong Kong, South Korea, Japan, Taipei, Finland, Estonia and Liechtenstein, but ahead of Macao, Canada, Poland, the Netherlands, Germany, UK, France, Denmark and the US, respectively. Québec's placement in the world's top ten is no small thing, but some nuance is required.

First, the entities included are not all equivalent, notably Chinese cities whose system of education is undoubtedly out of sync with the rest of the country, or others, such as Liechtenstein (with 40,000 inhabitants, the fourth smallest independent state in Europe). Such anomalies are bound to affect ranking.

The second nuance consists of Québec not being the best in Canada.

HIGH SCHOOL PERFORMANCE

PISA RESULTS, 2012

RANK	COUNTRY	RESULTS IN MATHS	RESULTS IN READING	RESULTS IN SCIENCES	TOTAL
1	Shanghai	613	570	580	1763
2	Singapore	573	542	551	1666
3	Hong Kong	561	545	555	1661
4	South Korea	554	536	538	1628
5	Japan	536	538	547	1621
	British Columbia	522	542	544	1608
6	Taipei	560	523	523	1606
7	Finland	519	524	545	1588
	Alberta	517	529	539	1585
8	Estonia	521	516	541	1578
9	Liechtenstein	535	516	525	1576
	Ontario	514	534	527	1573
	Québec	536	520	516	1572
10	Canada	518	523	525	1566
11	Netherlands	523	511	522	1556
12	Switzerland	531	509	515	1555
13	Germany	514	508	524	1546
14	Ireland	501	523	522	1546
15	Australia	514	512	521	1537
16	Belgium	515	509	505	1529
17	New Zealand	500	512	516	1528
18	UK	494	499	514	1507
19	Austria	506	490	506	1502
20	France	495	505	499	1499
21	Denmark	500	496	498	1494
22	Norway	489	504	495	1488
23	USA	481	498	497	1476
24	Italy	485	490	494	1469
25	Sweden	478	483	485	1446

Source: OECD, *Measuring Up: Canadian Results of the OECD PISA Study.*

In fact, three provinces place ahead of it: British Columbia with 1,608 points, Alberta with 1,585 and Ontario with 1,573.

Our chauvinist ardour is chilled when we are forced to contemplate the fact that success is not only Québécois, but also Canadian. Four Canadian provinces show very good results, and are right at the top. It is hardly accidental that four essentially distinct systems just happen to be at the same level. Evidently there must be a common denominator to these four provinces; it is their adherence to the same federation with common determinants of success in school.

The third nuance would be that Québec's relative standing is in large part thanks to our results in math. Here, Québec, with 536, leads British Columbia (522), Alberta (517) and Ontario (514). In this discipline, the other provinces have less to brag about, and it has prompted serious reflection in English Canada and some attention to the "Québec model"! Still, in sciences and in reading, Québec places 4th in Canada. Honourable as this may be, one thing still stands out: how is it that in Québec, the part of Canada where linguistic questions are most important and defence of the language is crucial, mastery of this language by our children is not better? There is surely a link to the delay in grade-school reading aptitudes mentioned earlier.

A fourth nuance has to do with the structure of our secondary system and the weight carried by private institutions. Twenty-one percent of students (one in five) go to private schools and help to raise Québec's overall average in PISA, although the public schools—while not quite as high—are most satisfactory. These private schools are nevertheless an integral part of the Québécois school system and follow a common program.

Thus there is no impediment to exceptional reading performance on our part . . . better than France, Belgium and the USA, 10th, 12th and 13th respectively. These data have stirred up considerable controversy in France, and it certainly did not hurt our ego to know we far surpassed our trans-Atlantic "cousins"—supposedly the guardians and reference —in reading.

Here is what PISA measures that, in part, explains this success. It evaluates literacy, i.e. the ability to use reading in various contexts, to understand what is read, to use the information, and to think on the basis of quoted sources, be they literature, articles or diagrams. It is, therefore, a functional definition in the logic of transversal competence, which measures more than just the accumulation of knowledge or literary culture.

FORGOTTEN DROPOUTS

The encouraging results of Québécois students in this international study should not, however, neglect some darker corners of the picture. If our high schools perform well, they do leave some students out of the process, especially those whom the education system cannot support from start to finish: the dark side of success, dropouts or those who cannot hold on to the end, or maintain "persévérance scolaire," as our bureaucrats like to say. It has even occurred to me that possibly our PISA results might be partly attributable to the fact that some young people have dropped out and thus managed not to bring down our average overall.

That numerous Québécois have no diploma is nothing new. The problem is an old one that carries the weight of the past. The proportion of those with no diploma has historically been high: over 40% for those born in the 1930s, 25% for those born in the 1940s, 20% in the 1950s, and 15% in the 1960s. The rate of non-graduates in Québec (as well as the Maritimes) has traditionally been among the highest in Canada.[2]

Québec still ranks 9th in dropout rates, and this can no longer be blamed on Maurice Duplessis. Rather, it is a collective responsibility, for if we were all convinced of the importance of education, we would never have tolerated this state of affairs. It is true that in recent years we have finally begun to acknowledge the problem and have reduced its impact impressively. All well and good, but this is not enough. We remain at the rear of the pack, and this shows we can do better. Each dropout represents a personal drama that contributes to the overall national drama.

There are many varying statistics, each defining the phenomenon a little differently. Still, altogether, whichever figure one chooses, things are improving, albeit not enough. The prime and fundamental measure is the number of young people leaving high school with their diplomas after five years, and this is the norm. For young people entering high school in 1998, and therefore graduating in 2003, the success rate was

57.7%, or, put another way, 43.3% did not graduate high school in the requisite time. For those entering in 2007, however, the rate was 63.3% graduating with a diploma in 2012, a considerable step forward. Still, this should not allow us to forget that more than one-third of young people—36.7%—do not complete their secondary education in five years.

It is worth noting that Québec has been making important efforts to gather in its strays. Even if only a little over 6 out of every 10 students graduate in 5 years, more than 7 out of 10 (73.4%) manage it in 7 years, a statistic that is, however, unchanged since 1999.

The Ministry of Education defines "dropping out" as leaving school with no diploma or qualifications—in other words, young people leaving school without paper in pocket. This rate was 21.9% in 1999–2000, and it long remained the norm, then suddenly began a spectacular decline to 18.4% in 2008–2009, 17.4% in 2009 and 16.2% in 2010, an impressive six-point drop, even stronger among boys (often much likelier to drop out than girls). In 2008–2009, for example, the overall rate of dropouts was 18.4%: it was 22.6% among boys and 14.3% among girls.

This success can be explained by the campaigns carried out, but also—according to the Ministry—by a new training stream in the second cycle of high school, one which offers new opportunities that bring more young people back onto a desirable path.

Québec has further managed to improve things with a variety of measures such as adult education and reinsertion activities. This has caused Statistics Canada to base its figures on another concept, that is, the percentage of young people from age 20 to 24 who have no diplomas and are not attending school. Known as "federal dropouts" and measured from its data on the Canada Census, this particular population is found to be constantly dropping. This can be seen in the following comparisons from Statistics Canada with sliding triennial averages which render the fluctuations less abrupt.

For 1991–1993, Québec showed a dropout rate of 17.4%, which continued falling to its 2010–2012 level of 10.6%. This is substantial and sustained progress, but the same thing can be observed in the other provinces, as indicated in the graph on page 41. Dropout rates were very high elsewhere too, but underwent even more spectacular reductions than in

Québec. The Canadian average of 15.7% in 1993 was almost halved to 8.1% by 2012. In 1993, Québec, at 17.4%, was in 7th place, ahead of three Atlantic provinces: 19.9% in Newfoundland, 18.9% in Prince Edward Island and 17.8% in Nova Scotia. Yet everyone has apparently tackled the problem with more ardour than we have, for in 20 years we have slipped from 9th place to 10th. The sliding averages again placed us dead last in 2009–2012, with a dropout rate, as was indicated, of 10.6%.

Fortunately, there has been a turnaround, which began in 2009 with an atypical intervention by Jacques Ménard, head of the Bank of Montreal in Québec. He published a report that proposed concrete, manageable and convincing solutions to reduce the catastrophic dropout rate in Québec. Entitled *Savoir pour pouvoir* (*To Know and Be Able*),[3] it was not the response to any governmental request. It was simply the initiative of one citizen, a member of a group of business people around the globe, along with members of community associations and officials in regional development as well as the public sector—an unusual assemblage which accounts for the convergence of economic development goals with those of social justice.

It worked. The Ménard Report galvanized the Liberal government at the time, and results were achieved because of the variety of approaches. They had observed this type of functioning elsewhere and absorbed all its best practices. Objectives were set and benchmarks established. Experiments which worked most effectively were derived largely from regional dynamics, mobilization of the milieus and definitions of solutions adapted to each case. The state, with its broad policies and its logic adapted to grand systems, was not capable of such things.

Above all, they began to understand the gravity of a problem that had persisted for decades and had elicited only the weakest of responses. School dropouts, after all, are less a school problem than a social one, and must be resolved in and by society. The fact that the number of young people leaving school too soon is particularly high in Québec—more so than elsewhere—is first a question of poverty and an expression of social values that lend too little weight to education. Thus it is more important to bring energy and a state of mind to it rather than money, new-wave teaching methods, project calendars, or on student-teacher ratios.

DROPOUT RATE IN CANADA
1990–1993 AND 2009–2012, IN %

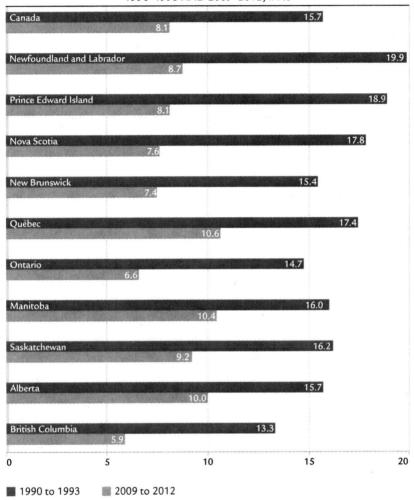

	1990 to 1993	2009 to 2012
Canada	15.7	8.1
Newfoundland and Labrador	19.9	8.7
Prince Edward Island	18.9	8.1
Nova Scotia	17.8	7.6
New Brunswick	15.4	7.4
Québec	17.4	10.6
Ontario	14.7	6.6
Manitoba	16.0	10.4
Saskatchewan	16.2	9.2
Alberta	15.7	10.0
British Columbia	13.3	5.9

■ 1990 to 1993   ■ 2009 to 2012

Source: Statistics Canada, Census.

The stakes, though, still remain high. Dropping out incurs huge losses in salaries, productivity and fiscal revenues. Furthermore, a society with a labour shortage and in need of increasingly qualified manpower cannot afford the luxury of sending young people onto the job market with inadequate training.

This drama is both individual and societal. Dropouts will earn less, be more vulnerable and more frequently unemployed. In Québec the job rate for 2010 of those with no secondary diploma was 53.7%, but 72.2% for those having completed their secondary education, and 81.3% for those having gone beyond secondary.[4]

We know there is a strong correlation between results and social origin. Children from underprivileged backgrounds have less schooling, which limits their capacity to escape the cycle of poverty. The struggle against dropping out is a potent tool that gives students from a vulnerable milieu what they need to succeed in school.

THE CEGEP INTERVAL

The word "interval" is used here, because this is in some ways the role played by colleges (CEGEP—Colleges of Professional and General Education) in our system. This network, inserted between secondary school and university, does not exist elsewhere. At the outset, it was a noble idea to extend universal free education and, at the same time, combine two major streams under a single roof: one leading to a university degree and the other to vocational studies.

Can we call it a success? It is too soon to tell. Creating the CEGEPs was one of the recommendations of the Parent Report, a pillar of the Quiet Revolution, truly a noble beginning. Furthermore, the consolidation of an institution at this level has allowed Québec to distinguish itself with a level of teaching that is unique on this continent. Its dual nature has helped to reaffirm the network's existence, hence defending it from undue interference.

Although creating the CEGEPs might not have been the idea of the century, it would be nearly impossible to go back on it, the task being far too costly and complicated. Quality institutions with their established traditions would have to be destroyed, their personnel and their programs abolished. In the outlying regions they have become poles of development. This would also inflict undue pressure on the secondary schools and universities to take up the slack. It would be far wiser to adjust to them as fully as possible, provided the colleges play their role well.

Yet, in almost any discussion of education, CEGEPs have slipped under the radar because attention has been riveted on the secondary schools and universities. It would be no crime of *lèse-majesté* to accord similar attention to the college network and insist that it fulfill its mission fully, particularly as it represents an investment of $1.5 billion a year. Is it doing so?

Québec, with its unique system, has a higher graduation rate than anywhere else in Canada, but it also has a lower rate of university registration, as will be seen below. Thus we have two problems: upstream and downstream—just before and after CEGEP. We are forced to wonder if the colleges themselves are part of the problem, impeding the transition from high school to university rather than helping it. Since high school lasts one year less here than elsewhere, perhaps it is not enough to help young people to weather a crucial stage in their career—especially boys—because there is another leap to come between college and university. The need to adapt to three different types of school at ages 16 to 19 might prove a hindrance to keeping them in school: more so, since CEGEP results are by no means overwhelming.

In the pre-university stream, students obtain their diplomas in an average of 2.4 years (2005 to 2010), which seems acceptable, but the flip side of this figure means that barely 43.3% of students finish in the "normal" time of two years, less than half, which is not much.

It would be even worse if the private colleges did not raise the average. In 2007–08, the rate of success in the CEGEPs over two years was 66.3% in private establishments. In the public ones, hardly 39.9% succeeded in finishing their studies in the allotted time.

Over a five-year period (the usual barometer used by government) the rate of graduation in the pre-university stream was still 71.7% (2009–2010), meaning that nearly 30% in the general program end up dropping out.

The average time taken for completion of studies in the technical stream is 3.3 years (for a three-year program), and barely 33% of students do so on time—or 52.2% in five years.

Can we consider this normal? Is the pass rate high enough? Is this the best way to prepare them for adult life? Frankly, I am at a loss to say.

THE UNIVERSITY MALAISE

This much I can state with certainty: the data we now have confirms what we suspected. CEGEPs are definitely not a good springboard to university.

We have a long way to go. In the summer of 2013, Statistics Canada published the education portion of its census. In it, we are told that among those 25 to 64 years of age, 23.3% of Québécois have university degrees, well behind the Canadian average (25.9%) and Ontario (28.9%). In fact, we rank 5th behind British Columbia, Alberta and Nova Scotia. This is not edifying for a region that loves to refer to itself as a "knowledge society."

Nor can this lag be attributed simply to the leftover effects of a formerly archaic system of education. The data exclude those Québécois over 65 who may have been subject to those defects, and they concern only baby boomers and those who followed them, thus removing much of the effect of these inherited deficiencies.

Nevertheless, there has been progress, especially among the younger population (ages 25 to 29) who are much more likely to attend university than their elders. The percentage of those with a university diploma is 29.6%, although the same rise can be noted across Canada and worldwide.

Canada's graduation rate is 32.1%, rising to 35.3% in Ontario. The gap between Québec on one hand and Canada or Ontario on the other is smaller than before, but just barely. Québec remains in 4th place, again behind Nova Scotia (33.5%) and British Columbia (31.8%), but slightly ahead of Alberta (28.2%).

In summary, Québec has fewer university diplomas than other urbanized provinces without the additional need for an accelerated catch-up. It is as though, after rushing ahead during the Quiet Revolution, we have taken a break . . . for too long.

BY WAY OF CONCLUSION

What can we draw from this? First, the education our children are receiving is of good quality and compares favourably with other systems.

The challenge is not saving our schools from disaster, but obtaining still better results, and to make education an available and fairly distributed asset. We have, for example, much criticized the pedagogical reform, yet the young Québécois taking part in the PISA research, and who were 15 years old in the spring of 2012, are the children of the latest reform, and their results are as good as those in 2009.

This changes our perspective completely. It is not a matter of pulling our system out of a nosedive, but of improving an already good network. We are not talking about rescuing our children, but of helping them go farther in greater numbers.

These data especially tell us that we are in a position to define extremely ambitious objectives. Québec, for example, could very well have an education system among the best in the world now that we know it is possible.

Obstacles to improving it come less from the system itself, whatever rigidity might afflict it—unionization, ministerial bureaucracy, duplication, the need to redefine the role of school boards—than from attitudes prevalent in society over all.

For example, behind the failures in attaining graduation lies a larger problem, and I reiterate it: Québécois have never been impassioned about education. Politicians who examine the polls know the theme is not a very saleable one, and they have never tried to impose it as a top priority. The problems of graduation and even the lack of attachment to our universities are, I believe, based on our relationship with education and knowledge. I see this as an unfinished task of the Quiet Revolution.

It is no accident if, in various interprovincial comparisons shown in this chapter, Québec is often in the same grouping as the Atlantic provinces. In several respects, when it comes to education and knowledge, we find ourselves closer to New Brunswick than Ontario. There still remains much work before all will value learning and knowledge. That is where we must concentrate our energies.

The Québec of the 1950s with which the Quiet Revolution attempted to break was in several regards a backward society, a poor one both materially and culturally, and this poverty contributed to a mistrust of education. The traditional suspicion has not yet dissipated completely. Our society still bears traces of the old Québec, relics of cultural poverty.

CHAPTER 4

ARE WE A KNOWLEDGE SOCIETY?

In the preceding chapter, we have seen how Québec society is, in fact, an educated one. We may even say that our secondary education is one of the world's best. Our university network is excellent, and our diplomas and universities themselves are recognized and excellent on many levels. But when attendance and graduation rates leave something to be desired, is this enough to consider Québec a knowledge society?

It is a matter of more than just statistics. It is a state of mind. Our graduation results reveal something else which is disturbing: a malaise that alienates the population from its universities, a lack of attachment and pride, a lack of knowledge about the important role they play. This state of mind seems also to prevail for several other requisites of a knowledge society, such as the place accorded to our large cities or our aptitude for innovation.

I am also disturbed by the level of university enrollment; it may be adequate, but we must do better if we are to say that universities fully play their role in the development of society. At a time in history when knowledge holds the keys to success, and constitutes one of the principal levers that would allow us to make up for some of the obstacles to modernizing our economy, it is an essential tool for a small nation to possess and use to affirm itself.

AN UNHAPPY MAPLE SPRING

Québécois appear to consider higher education important, enough so to devote considerable collective energy to a debate which, by and large, concerns the universities. I am speaking, of course, about the battle of the "red squares" ("carrés rouges," so called for the bits of red cloth worn by those supporting the student strike) against fee increases and hence the barriers to universal university access.

I say "by and large" because the university network emerged from this campaign quite battered. The reason for this seems evident: the "Maple Spring" was not so much a mobilization for universities as a broad movement for the preservation of acquired rights and a certain social status quo, in which universities were sacrificed to other objectives.

The student movement, which obtained a degree of victory, opposed the idea that the universities could be under-financed, and successfully discredited administrations accused of waste. A collection of student groups, under the name of CLASSE (Coalition large de l'Association pour une solidarité syndicale étudiante), accused the universities of being too research-oriented.

This hostility to the university as an institution is present not only in the street and during demonstrations, but was implicitly endorsed by the Québec government under Pauline Marois, whose policies sought to bring an end to the strike by simply giving in to student demands.

The result was utterly surrealistic: a summit on higher education to cap several months of public consultations, complete with background documents and regional assemblies. Through all this, the Marois government had created a precedent by opting to remain neutral, while student associations and university administrators debated. Notable among the themes was financing, itself an anomaly in that university governance is in many respects mandated by the state itself.

What was bound to happen did happen. The two-day summit of February 2013 looked more like a prescribed ritual than anything else. The government rubber-stamped the students' vision and version of the university "problem," not a good idea, because the student associations were essentially corporatist, and their agenda was more to impose their demands than propose the disinterested view that society needed.

Thus the Péquiste government abolished the increased fees of the preceding Liberal government and replaced them with a much more modest 3% "indexation." Not only was this a victory for the students, but also a decision rendering university finances even more fragile, and closing the door, for years and years to come, on any and all new financing formulas, as well as any possibility of asking more from students.

The latter's way of thinking also triumphed over university administrations, which became whipping-boys in the whole process. One can, of course, understand students taking their example from union struggles and opposing the presidents as though they were bosses, but this attitude, reprised by the state, effectively transformed the summit into an inquisition with the heads of universities in the box—something like Mafia contractors before the Charbonneau Commission (Québec's much publicized inquiry into corrupt construction and public contracting practices) while denying them any real right of reply, for it was difficult for them to oppose the government that held their purse strings.

Thus the summit resulted in two "worksites" focused on controlling and managing university administrations and increasing their account-ability while sacrificing part of their freedom. These controls were all the more surprising for leading one to believe that universities are somehow less well run than any other part of the public sector. The result was to discredit university leaders, now weakened, along with their institutions.

The other great student victory made inroads into the belief that uni-versities are not under-funded. If certain polls are to be believed, this is now a widely held credo among a majority of Québécois. This opinion was shared by the former premier, who said at the time, "I would not say that the university network is under-funded, but funding could certainly be better managed." How could a government now ever convince the public to make sacrifices elsewhere—say, in health—to provide further collective investment in universities?

MORE FIGURES

All this occurred during a post-crisis period in which several economies, including ours, were still very fragile from the shock of 2008–2009, also a context in which higher education was on the trail of some very promis-ing solutions. According to an OECD study during the crisis, education might prove to be the way out of unemployment.[5]

Canadian young people of ages 25 to 34 with a higher education saw only 5.4% unemployment, as opposed to those with only a secondary di-ploma (8.1%). This is reinforced by a salary gap, and very significantly, those with a higher education earn 40% more than those with only high school. A Québécois slogan of the 1960s—"Learning means earning"—is still true today!

This surely is excellent motivation to do better, to which must be added the imperative of social justice, the impact of education on creativ-ity and innovation, as well as their effects on culture and democracy. Obviously the arguments of economics apply as well, by virtue of the fact that the principal sectors in the future are going to be knowledge-based.

Much still remains to be done, and without falling prey to an avalanche of statistics, I would like to add some more data in the form of a Statistics Canada summary[6] rather different from that of the preceding chapter. This one is more precise and uses the same method as the OECD, comparing Québec to the rest of the industrialized world.

Among those aged 25 to 64, Québec's, graduation rate of 24% is below the Canadian average of 26% and ranks 4th, tied with Manitoba and Nova Scotia behind the three richest provinces. Among 25–29-year-olds, it is once again 4th with 29%.

When these results are twinned with data from the OECD, we see that Canada, with a university graduation rate of 27% for 25–64-year-olds, ranks 10th among the 34 countries polled, behind the English-speaking and Scandinavian countries. With 24%, Québec ranks 17th, barely above the 23% average for 25–34-year-olds.

This is because many countries have progressed to higher and higher university attendance among the very young. With a graduation rate of 29%, Québec is slightly short of the 30% average of OECD countries, and ranks 19th. In other words, we are not even in the running, but are outclassed by the best!

There are, of course, other well-performing countries with low university graduation rates—France, for instance, with 18% and Germany with 16%, although the latter makes up for it with a highly organized professional training program. We must also take our surroundings into account, and being in North America, our main partners and competitors are both Canada and the US, with very high attendance rates. Thirty-two percent of citizens hold a university diploma, far more than our 24%.

ODDLY PARADOXICAL

Strangely, we find ourselves facing a contradictory situation: on the one hand, our universities are less well attended, and on the other, they are highly rated. Québec universities draw more than their share of federal research funding, and not because they make the most of cost-sharing mechanisms. Montreal is renowned as a university city with four large institutions and seven other university establishments, for a total of

UNIVERSITY GRADUATION RATE
AGES 25–64 AND 25–29, 2011

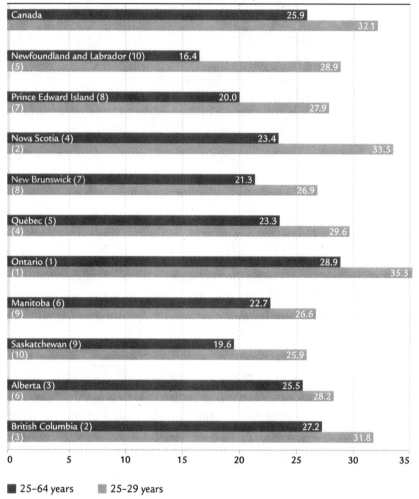

Canada — 25.9 / 32.1

Newfoundland and Labrador (10) — 16.4 / (5) 28.9

Prince Edward Island (8) — 20.0 / (7) 27.9

Nova Scotia (4) — 23.4 / (2) 33.5

New Brunswick (7) — 21.3 / (8) 26.9

Québec (5) — 23.3 / (4) 29.6

Ontario (1) — 28.9 / (1) 35.3

Manitoba (6) — 22.7 / (9) 26.6

Saskatchewan (9) — 19.6 / (10) 25.9

Alberta (3) — 25.5 / (6) 28.2

British Columbia (2) — 27.2 / (3) 31.8

■ 25–64 years   ▨ 25–29 years

Source: Statistics Canada, 2011 Census.

170,000 students. "Greater Montreal" is the metropolitan region with the highest ratio of university students in North America, ahead of even Boston, the intellectual capital of the US. On paper at least, this is enough to speak of it as a knowledge city.

According to the *QS Best Student Cities*[7] produced by a British corporation specializing in education, Montreal places first in Canada's top university cities, 2nd in North America and 9th in the world. This is explained not only by the intrinsic quality of its teaching, but also by other factors that are likely to attract students, such as the cost of living, intake structures for visitors and other less university-related considerations like the legal drinking age or the tolerance of certain substances!

With figures such as these, one might expect Québécois to be further encouraged by our low tuition fees compared to the rest of Canada, as well as our relatively generous loan and bursary programs, and beat down the doors. Well, no!

This prompts us to note that the modest fee-scale intended to boost university access doesn't seem to be working. The other large provinces draw more students, despite much higher fees, and no amount of catch-up seems to be in the offing. This, in turn, leads one to believe that the main obstacles are not economic; hence the "red squares" may have missed the point. Elements farther upstream must be playing a more important part here, notably high school graduation rates and psychosocial factors, such as the value attached to education both in the society and in the family.

THE FUNDING DRAMA

I believe this attitude explains yet another problem haunting our universities: under-financing. This is less a result of the impasse in public finances than a social and political choice, once again reflecting the fact that the future of our universities is not seen as a priority by governments or citizens. Under-financing is both a problem and a symptom.

The Conference of Québec University Rectors and Principals—rebaptized the Office of University Co-operation in January 2014—updated its study on the under-financing of universities in early 2013, and showed a widening of the gap between Québec and the rest of Canada to $850 million in 2009–2010. Over a period of seven years, this gap has risen to $4.5 billion, based on a comparison of revenues.

Economist Pierre Fortin challenges this calculation and prefers to compare expenditures instead. He estimates under-financing at $300 million. He maintains that outlays need not be so considerable in Québec, since our cadres and teachers are paid less. However, this argument tends to lead us in circles, because these lower salaries form an obstacle to recruitment and to retention of personnel. Be that as it may, all agree on one thing: under-financing very likely exists and can be situated between these two points.

If there is a deficit to make up—say, $500 million—this is not because the Québec government is stingy. Our universities receive proportionately $72 million more from the state than those of other provinces. Nevertheless, we do know that lower tuition fees deprive them of around $700 million, and their meagre endowments prevent them from receiving another $200 million. This has consequences for the resources available, for the quality of teaching, for their capacity to attract top-quality professors and students, as well as for research.

And while Québec is unconvinced that it needs to catch up to the level of financing in Canada as a whole, other provinces are also worried by their under-financing relative to universities in the US.

NOT FEELING THE LOVE

Any important reorientation, then, would be less economic than political. Generally speaking, as our attendance rate shows, we have difficulty "selling" education, even more so higher education. Families are saving up less for their children's studies than elsewhere in Canada—this is evident from the amounts invested in Registered Education Savings Plans —and provide less support to their children's school work, which in turn is reflected in the political choices they make.

Betting on education is probably not a winning proposition in Québec. Hence few politicians have ridden that particular war horse with the exception of François Legault, former Education Minister under the PQ government, and now head of the CAQ. Why is this? No doubt because public opinion considers help to the universities as elitist and a gift to the more privileged members of society.

This probably explained the very strong support the Charest government enjoyed in the controversy over student-fee hikes. Some of those supporting the government were preoccupied with university funding, and I am convinced that a great many Québécois rejoiced, especially at the refusal to give in to "spoiled children."

Despite the divergence in approach, a similar train of thought prevailed when the Marois government took up the argument presented by student associations that showed the pointlessness of a hike by resorting to a caricature of universities as either poorly managed or too spendthrift when it came to research. The Marois government certainly went populist on this and considered university-bashing a viable tactic. The consequences of this will be most important.

The duty of a responsible government would have been to counter this line rapidly and clearly. Universities, as institutions of teaching and research, play a strategic part in training manpower for advanced societies, in seeking out talent and in stoking motivation. This is the key to economic development, and it is essential that Québécois, like other nations, support their universities unreservedly, are fully aware of their role, agree to deploy individual and collective efforts to ensure their success and view them with pride.

THE ROLE OF RESEARCH

Still, one cannot live on love alone. The link between universities and society must also be measured in dollars. It is that much more important to support our universities as they play a key role in research and development, a vital activity in which we truly distinguish ourselves.

Our expenditures on research and development reached $7.9 billion in 2011; this is equivalent to 2.28% of GDP, which is considerable. It is the highest in Canada and slightly superior to the only other outstanding province, Ontario, whose research accounts for 2.23% of GDP. Québec is well above the Canadian average of 1.74%. It should be mentioned that Québec's advance has decreased in recent years due to the financial crisis, as well as difficulties in the pharmaceutical industry. In 2008, with a research and development rate of 2.59%, Québec was well ahead of Ontario at 2.35%. It is still true, however, that Québec is doing well enough to nourish grand ambitions. It has as its objective to increase research and development to 3% of GDP.

This new direction is necessary because Québec, above the OECD average until 2010, was slightly below in 2011. Québec nevertheless ranks 8th among the wealthier countries for research and development, led only by Finland, Japan, Switzerland, Denmark, Germany, Austria and the US.

This success rests largely on university research. In 2011, university expenditures on research reached $2.8 billion, or 35.5% of Canada's total ($7.9 billion). This corresponds to 0.81% of GDP, versus 0.75% in Ontario and 0.66% in Canada. It is the dynamism of our universities and their lion's share of federal research funding that accounts for this, supported by the efforts of our government. We can be proud of taking this route. Canada is proud to be first in the G7 for university research, ahead of Germany (0.52%), France (0.47%), the UK (0.46%) and the US (0.39%). Québec is also 3rd in the world, behind Denmark (0.94%) and Sweden (0.90%).

However, we must be aware that this success has its limits. There is an important difference between research and innovation, interconnected as they are, and if research is essential—regardless of where it is conducted (laboratories, businesses or universities), and whatever its nature (fundamental or applied research), or its goals (health, engineering, mathematics or social sciences)—research cannot be said to directly affect economic activity.

The ferment of growth is due to innovation, and this need not be a particular discovery or invention. It is the idea that turns innovation or discovery into action, be it a product, a service, a process, a form of commercialization, or a way of organizing. Innovation occurs when an idea leads to economic activity, to sales, to jobs or to viable commercial exploitation. This is the nerve of war.

Even though our governments recognize the importance of innovation, their margin for manoeuvre remains limited, especially by political restraints, such as the fact that innovation is difficult to explain to the general population. There are also economic restraints, especially insofar as it is hard for governments to get a toe-hold on something related to attitudes or state of mind. The state cannot simply decree innovation in a company any more than it can force managers to embody the entrepreneurial spirit.

This is why governments fall back on what they can control or act upon, such as university research—largely grant-supported—or governmental research This does not always culminate in economic activity, because victory is not won in laboratories, but often on the cold, hard ground.

The indirect way to observe real success in Québec in research and development is not simply by measuring innovation but the expenditures devoted to them—26.7% of the Canadian total for 2010—whereas inventions counted for only 18.1% of all Canada's patents. This figure is, of course, approximate, but it does illustrate the fact that research alone is not the whole story. Québec has one advantage, the overlap of efforts by two governments. This, along with culture, is another example of the benefits of having two of them to provide financing, provided, of course, that the philosophies of federal and provincial agencies evolve in such a way as to favour innovation, though not at the expense of research.

Encouraging innovation is a long-term job which depends not just on programs and subsidies. As with entrepreneurship, it is in large part a matter of awakening then nurturing a state of mind, of developing attitudes, on a collective culture both in the training of young people and in public discussion, as well as economic policy. This is the challenge of not just a government, but a generation.

THE BENEFITS OF DUALITY

Innovation is by no mean the sole instance where values, state of mind or attitude play an important role in a society's ability to take knowledge in hand. Let us take a specific example of the need to develop knowledge by acting on several fronts at the same time: linguistic duality.

The fact that Montreal is a city where francophone and anglophone communities coexist, has been, and continues to be, a source of tension to the point that we find it difficult to admit that it shows Montreal is a bilingual city. These tensions, however, can also be creative. This duality helps to define Montreal's hybrid identity, with its British-constructed heritage and its French face. It is this that makes Montreal more than "Québec writ large," which gives it an enormous competitive advantage and contributes to its numerous economic successes.

A very concrete demonstration of this duality is the duplication of its institutions (universities, hospitals, cultural venues, neighbourhoods).

This enriches intellectual life by dipping into two traditions, and it goes a long way to explaining our university vocation. If we did not have two networks, there would not be four institutions in Montreal, two francophone and two anglophone, nor would we attract so many foreign students and be ranked one of the QS's best universities in the world, or compare ourselves to Boston. Yet we regularly hear complaints about the privileged position held by McGill with its endowment funds and suggestions that this imbalance be corrected . . . without taking account of the fact that it is also thanks to McGill that Montreal holds such a high rank internationally with its 21st position according to QS, or 35th for the *Times of London*. The Université de Montréal places 92nd and 106th, respectively.

This duality also allows Montreal to be several things at the same time: at ease in both La Francophonie and the Commonwealth, with roots in two cultures, able to be the interface between two worlds—both very North American, yet more European than any other city on the continent. It certainly helps explain the success of certain industries, such as information technology and the development of video games, an area in which Montreal draws businesses from both France and the US.

It also allows Montreal to be more creative by favouring diversity and tolerance. Tensions can contribute to the ferment of cultural life. This is evident for francophones who affirm their identity largely through theatre, music, literature and film. In the past several years, there has been a surge in Anglo-Montreal creativity which has nourished both the city and the province. Without this meeting of cultures, Montreal would not enjoy its trademark image as an "in" city. This should be remembered when we decry certain things which are merely the legitimate manifestations of the English-speaking community. If we think in terms of a knowledge society, Montreal's duality is a precious advantage that needs to be preserved and even encouraged, although we cannot be certain that Québec society is quite ready for that.

THINKING IN BIG-CITY TERMS

The other major tool in the economic development of a knowledge society is urban policy. It is generally in big cities that new ideas, new industries and new products are born. In all logic, a society seeking the "knowledge" label must focus on its cities. Breakthroughs are much less likely to emerge in the countryside, and this also requires an enormous change in the way Québec sees and sets its priorities; it is essential to accept the fact that Québec has become a truly urban society.

This has been addressed with much vigour in my columns, conferences and other initiatives to support the development of our metropolis as well as our provincial capital. I have also submitted a report on the matter for the cities of Montreal and Québec, *A New Pact for Québec's Large Cities*, which provides the basis for many of the pages which follow.

Cities have a drawing power all their own. In contemporary society, bombarded by television and the Internet, cities derive even more appeal from studies, employment possibilities and the quality of life that characterizes an urban milieu—commerce, entertainment, culture, freedom, lifestyle. These qualities also attract more young people and those who are better educated and more productive, which also helps to reinforce the impact of cities.

The other factor contributing to modify and reinforce the role of cities radically is globalization, which has transformed their very nature. Not only do cities carry serious economic weight, but they also exhibit greater dynamism, which allows them to play their locomotive role. Big cities generally have a disproportionately higher level of productivity than the territory they occupy, and their contribution to GDP surpasses their true weight.

These cities become nerve centres for the worldwide circulation of information, exchanges, mobility of capital and people. This new reality is well described by the concept of the city-state or city-region—the most current term is that of world cities—which defines great cities as true poles of development within their respective countries, capable of developing their own strategies within a global network.

The acceleration of all forms of exchanges has, in fact, drawn the great world cities closer together. They interact while still competing. They battle for investments, talent, markets and recognition. They become increasingly the conveyors of economic strategies. Their dynamism and energy, which make the difference between mediocrity and success, will also depend on the synergies and climate that an urban milieu can create. This new reality has brought about an evolution in economic thought: in other words, the awareness that cities, in the present context of globalization, play an even more strategic role than before, and that their development and success are absolutely essential to the success of their respective countries.

A society whose success and growth capacity are increasingly based on knowledge, higher education, innovation and the presence of cutting-edge industries will unavoidably depend on the vitality of its cities, and especially its large ones. That is where the concentration of universities, research centres and high-performing industries occurs. This concentration of advantages provides necessary critical mass and allows the growth of competition.

Numerous specialists and economic organizations are now placing cities at the heart of development strategy. The rate of urbanization in a society has become a criterion of its potential success. Specialists such as Richard Florida, geographer and professor of urban development at Columbia University, are now crusaders in this cause. Canada will not reach the desired level of prosperity if it fails to energize its large cities or does not take heed of the others. The same holds true for Québec. If we do not invest in them, we will not create as much wealth as we should, nor make up for its historic lateness, a preoccupation that seems to be lacking at both levels of government. A city is not a country. It is a unique entity with economic needs and challenges of its own. Wealth-creation depends very much on the vitality that cities exude, as well as their image and their capacities of attraction, for they are both crucibles and magnets at the same time. The former bring about a certain alchemy, and the latter draw in talent, business and capital.

The question of talent is crucial, because traditional hiring patterns have become inverted. It used to be manpower that migrated toward employment, but in a knowledge economy, businesses frequently gravitate to labour pools. Clearly, on the world stage, Montreal remains a city of modest size and importance, unable to rival the globe's great urban centres, and even more so Québec City, which, with a population of under a million, simply does not rank at all, although both cities can depend on several attributes of large urban centres. Despite their size, the approaches adopted elsewhere can and must apply. Reinforcing these attributes can help them develop.

The most influential measure of a city's success over the past decade has certainly been that developed by Richard Florida in his book *The Rise of the Creative Class*. It constitutes a revolution in our thinking about cities. The determining factor in the success of cities, he says, is the presence of a creative class composed of those whose job requires thought— professionals and managers in occupations linked to science and technology, culture, education and training, plus communications. Florida's approach is not universally accepted, but it should be noted that several elements of his analysis can be found in most studies of cities and their assets. The Conference Board of Canada has published two reports on the role played by cities in this country, and they lead toward the same conclusions.

The second document is *City Magnets II*, from the Conference Board of Canada, which classes 50 Canadian cities according to their capacity for attracting skilled labour and a mobile population "because cities incapable of acting as magnets and attracting new people will have difficulty remaining prosperous in decades to come...." Is this what allows a world-class city to stand out? This term, "magnetism," could, in fact, serve as a common denominator for most indicators associated with success. These include the ability to attract business, capital, activity and people, especially those who, by their specialization and their talent, can support a knowledge economy and the ingredients that make for such attraction and economic dynamism—measured by growth, social level and the attributes of knowledge. Also included is the ability to attract a pool of specialized labour—measured by graduation rates, creative class and quality of life. Massive investment in universities is one of the main tools for reinforcing cities and helping them play the role that is theirs in a knowledge society.

In Québec, however, we can take none of this for granted. Most governments have great difficulty in focusing their energies on cities, especially the two largest—Montreal and Québec City—even though these two urban areas account for nearly 60% of the population. This hesitation can be explained in large part by political factors. Our electoral structures give the outlying regions far greater political weight proportionately, and the political gains which turn into victories occur more often in the countryside. Montreal's electorate is fixed, along basic linguistic lines among others, and the chances that a riding will swing from one party to another is limited, which makes attempts to win the metropolis barely worthwhile. This political context is not confined to electoral behaviour. The reticence of governments to give the impression that they favour, or are even concerned with, larger cities is palpable. The mistrust of cities by the rural communities is party to this, as are the very real problems these regions face.

Liberal, Péquiste and Caquiste political discourse is based on the principle that the cities are prosperous and not the locus of our real problems. A glimmer of hope resides in the possibility of conferring special status on Montreal and Québec City, which would be a veritable and far-reaching revolution for the regionalistic concept of Québec. Governments rarely pay attention to the specificity of the large centres, hence the quasi-freeze on tuition fees, which penalizes large research universities competing with those in the rest of the world, and which are, of course, in the larger urban centres. Further, the egalitarian philosophy by which tuition fees and government grants are uniform throughout our territory, regardless of the size, importance or vocation of each university, once again penalizes the large cities.

A NEW DIRECTION IS NEEDED

The moral of the story? Apart from a few obvious successes, we have quite a long way to go if we are to transform Québec into a veritable knowledge society. We definitely have university success stories, and we have cutting-edge industries. Of course, we are not alone on the planet, and the rest of the world is using roughly the same strategies. To go farther, we will need to follow paths that require a change of mentality: for instance, accepting Montreal's cultural duality—a true ferment of creativity—committing to our large cities (though our reflexes remain regional), and investing, especially in our universities . . . and attending them.

CHAPTER 5

ARE WE "CULTURAL"?

If there is one area where we are proud of
ourselves, it is certainly arts and culture. Québec
is proud of its stars and the overseas success of
its artists and its creators, and with good reason,
since their cultural production is remarkable
in its quality, quantity and exposure abroad.
This is all the more astonishing for a small
nation of eight million.

The pride in our culture is not a myth. Rather it exists in the conviction that these successes belong to us all by association, and thus we must be an exceptionally cultivated people, when, in fact, there is a wide gap between the importance we say it deserves and the concrete effort we give it, collectively or individually. There is a large rift between creators and the people they come from. There is above all a world separating the cultural production of our artists and the consumption of cultural products by the average citizen at home.

Robert Lepage may be known round the world, but it is Mike Ward (a stand-up comedian known for his vulgarity) that the public goes to see. Michel Tremblay is a monument in theatre and literature, yet most of us have never seen his plays or read his novels, for the simple reason that we do not read much. In fact, all too often, we do not really know how to read.

I am not the specialist to analyze Québec's cultural activity definitively, and I am aware of the limits of my approach (which is to favour whatever can be measured) when it is applied to an area for which statistics have little relevance, but these tools, however limited, are quite sufficient to answer the question we are asking here: "Are We Culturally Oriented?" The difference between reality and the image we have of ourselves is striking enough to answer "NO."

THE IMPORTANCE OF CULTURE

Let me be frank about how culture fits into my framework. I am one of those who believe in its importance, and in the necessity of much more investment in culture than we currently accord to it.

My daily life would not be the same without the books, newspapers and magazines I read, or the films, shows, concerts, and plays I go to, or the radio I listen to and the TV that I watch. I also believe in it from a professional angle, because my craft depends on reading habits. On a collective level, I believe in it because it is an essential tool for social progress and for the affirmation of Québec. As an economist I believe in it because culture is a major element in civilized economic development.

To begin with, it is an industry which generates activities and expenditures, while putting people to work. It has an indirect but enriching impact when we stimulate it.

Precise evaluations of its power in the economy are rare and dated. In 2007, according to the Conference Board of Canada, culture accounted for 3.8% of GDP.[8] The Observatoire de la culture et des communications du Québec (OCCQ) evaluated cultural activity at $9.8 billion in 2003, or 4.1% of GDP. Roughly then, culture represents 4% of GDP, more than double that of agriculture. According to the 2006 census, Québec provided 118,765 jobs in this sector—taken in the broadest sense, around 3.3% of manpower, notably professionals in publications, graphic artists, architects, designers, library staff—much more than just artists in the strictest sense, and lots of money as well.

According to the OCCQ, cultural expenditures in Québec reached $8.5 billion in 2009, and in 2012, we spent $267 million on tickets to shows, $170 million in movie theatres and $678 million on books.

It is much more than a matter of mere round figures though. It is not just an industry with a market and economic spinoffs all its own. It also plays an indirect, less visible but probably more important role in the ferment of economic development.

It nourishes and stimulates creativity, not only of artists themselves, but also of those with whom they connect. It contributes to society's general state of mind. It is this which gives rise to theses, such as that of urban development specialist Richard Florida, to the effect that the presence of a creative class, in which artists and the world of culture hold a defining place, rubs off on society as a whole and assumes major importance in economic success.[9]

It is one of the elements which help a city become a pole of attraction for students, artists, researchers and professionals, and convince businesses to establish themselves there. The quality of life is certainly a factor contributing, for example, to the resurgence of Montreal.

Such indirect effects are surely as important as any measurable impact.

To this we must add social outcomes, even more diffuse and difficult to measure, beginning with social cohesion and the enrichment of civic life that art and peaceful assemblies provide. The Festival International de Jazz de Montréal is a particularly interesting illustration of this, for it unites English-speakers and French-speakers. Likewise the Festival d'été de Québec (Québec Summer Festival) draws a major segment of the population. Another social effect is cultural enrichment, which facilitates access to free or low-cost shows that not only entertain people but get them out of the house to discover new horizons and a more open mind. It goes without saying that such events give meaning to a city, allow us to live in a different manner (be it the Plains of Abraham, the Quartier des spectacles or Saint Helen's Island, with Osheaga, for instance), and render the downtown attractive and relevant in an era overwhelmed with urban sprawl.

As should be clear, the importance of culture is not first and foremost economic. It breathes soul into a society. It contributes to reinforcing and enriching the area's identity. This is all the more essential for a small society, in a definite minority on the continent. In the struggle to affirm and defend its right to exist, culture is both a rampart and a springboard.

For all these reasons, I have believed over these many years that culture must be one of the great priorities of the state and the collectivity: for their socio-economic benefits in the very broadest sense, but also because Québec collectively needs culture as a tool to build its identity. It is an excellent one that propels us forward, fills us with pride and a sense of ownership, but without keeping us in defence mode as the reinforcement of language laws do, or worse, the ethnocentric retrenchment that has characterized the debate on the Charter of Québec Values.

I may not be an enthusiastic supporter of state omnipresence and lavish public spending, but I deeply believe that culture—an area where the market does not supply answers—should be a major axis in which we have to invest more.

EXCEPTIONAL IMPACT

One thing that the figures cannot measure is the remarkable transportability of our culture in all its forms. There is an obvious imbalance between the size of Québec society and the vigour of its cultural production, its renown and its ability to penetrate international markets.

The examples of our international success are so many (cinema, literature, classic and popular music, visual arts, song, theatre, circuses, humour, television, etc.) that to try and draw up a list would be very risky. It would be a long one, from Robert Lepage to Xavier Dolan, Céline Dion to Yannick Nézet-Séguin or Leonard Cohen to Arcade Fire among English-speakers. Is it exceptional though?

It is difficult to show that our international success is, in fact, exceptional, that Québec does better and spreads its culture farther and wider than other societies of similar size—all the more so when one realizes that there are subjective elements to the way we view such things. We have a legitimate tendency to highlight them and trumpet Oscar nominations, for instance, just as other countries with modest populations achieve international successes which they publicize highly, though they may gain less attention abroad. We have no valid basis for comparison, for example, with Denmark and Norway, each with a population of five million; they have a world-renowned film industry. We may well be proud of Dany Laferrière's entry into the Académie française, though we may not be aware that the "Immortals" already include writers from Algeria, Belgium, Luxembourg and Lebanon.

The impression that our success is somehow exceptional comes also from our habit of comparing ourselves with the rest of Canada, which is less visible on the international cultural scene. This too may partly be accounted for by the fact that Québécois media are less aware of what is going on in Canada. Much was made of the May 2014 opening of Xavier Dolan's latest film as an official competition entry at the Festival de Cannes, but not much of two other Canadian films. Who here had heard of Alice Munro before her Nobel Prize for literature? In our linguistic bubble, we do not always distinguish between what is Canadian and what is American, though there may be real differences.

Why spoil the party? We are indeed successful, but we must wonder where it comes from. Why do Québécois stand out when it comes to culture? Mere luck? Our history? Well thought-out public policies? A propensity for culture in our soul or our DNA?

Clearly these successes emerge mostly from a nationalistic impulse that gathered power in the 1960s, a huge developing awareness of a people desiring to affirm their nationhood, to be recognized for it and to be treated as equals. This nationalistic sentiment gave life to cultural expression, which in turn added energy to the initial impulse. The words of the song "Le grand six pieds" by Claude Gauthier, in which he says "Je suis de nationalité canadienne-française" (I am of French-Canadian nationality) were changed to "Québécoise française." Michel Tremblay also dared to write in our own popular language for one of the great popular spectacles *L'Osstidcho* (*One Helluva Show*) at our mythic June 24th holiday.

It also had a "bubble" effect. Francophones, isolated in an English-speaking ocean, were still cut off from the language for lack of bilingualism, yet too North American to identify with European French productions. The response was to develop local production—especially in television—with Québec's own soap operas and drama series, often shows of very high quality, with their very own star system, which in turn lent strength to other forms of expression, such as cinema and the theatre. This is why television is at the living heart of our culture and nourishes it, challenging our familiar and common references, unlike the US, where movies play this central role.

Québec has also benefitted from institutions that provide structure as well as a base for creation and broadcasting. Perhaps most notable is Radio-Canada/CBC, which was once a long-standing monopoly and implicitly founded on the two-nation model, with an English service (based in Toronto) and a French service (based in Montreal). There is also the important federal institutions such as the National Film Board and the National Theatre School of Canada. Also important is the duplication of funding organizations—the Société de développement de l'entreprise québécoise (the Québec Business Development Corporation), Telefilm Canada, the Canada Council for the Arts and the Conseil des arts et des lettres du Québec (the Québec Arts and Letters Council). In the political arena, of course, overlapping and duplication are denounced, but they are beneficial to the arts, having allowed for an increase in the funds available, while instilling a healthy spirit of emulation.

Regulation and laws have also played their part: for example, the requirements for francophone Canadian content imposed on radio stations by the Canadian Radio-television and Telecommunications Commission. This artificial protection might well have encouraged mediocrity, but that did not happen; on the contrary, these rules provided a springboard for a music industry of considerable quality.

We must be aware that behind these creators and artists were visionaries and risk-takers who have played an important part in Québec's culture boom. Suffice it to mention, among others, the genius of René Angélil behind the talent of Céline Dion, the vision of Guy Laliberté behind Cirque du Soleil (crucial for Montreal), Alain Simard (Festival International de Jazz de Montreal, etc.), Spectra (a major production company), or Gilbert Rozon (Just for Laughs Festival), and many more.

WHAT HAPPENED TO THE PUBLIC FUNDS?

Behind all this is money. There is, of course, considerable investment in culture, but not as much as we might suppose. One would think successive Québec governments would plunk huge amounts into "identity issues," especially when they accord so much importance to culture, but on the contrary, we are not the province that invests the most.

The statistics here are truly astonishing. Québec comes second for such expenditures—both governments combined—with $3.044 billion in 2009–2010, behind Ontario with $3.517 billion overall (though in proportion to its population, it is ahead with 30.1% of the $10.1 billion for all of Canada).

For the sake of comparison, it would be wise to confine ourselves to the proportion of expenditures per inhabitant. Québec, with $388.20 per person, is still the province where public investment is the highest, well above the Canadian average of $303.30. Two other provinces dedicate large amounts to culture: Prince Edward Island ($354.50) and Saskatchewan ($312.80).

What is surprising is the origin of this Québec advance, for it does not come from the provincial government, as we might expect, with $125 per capita, which is behind Newfoundland at $154, and Saskatchewan with $148. Similarly, if we combine expenditures by municipalities—

PUBLIC EXPENDITURES ON CULTURE PER CAPITA
IN 2009–2010 $

	FEDERAL	PROVINCIAL & MUNICIPAL	TOTAL
Newfoundland and Labrador	119.40	183.80	303.30
Prince Edward Island	192.60	90.60	354.70
Nova Scotia	136.70	159.60	296.30
New Brunswick	118.80	144.30	263.30
Québec	187.30	200.90	388.20
Ontario	109.80	160.70	270.60
Manitoba	90.10	171.90	262.00
Saskatchewan	62.00	250.80	312.80
Alberta	71.30	200.10	271.50
British Columbia	53.30	154.90	208.20
Canada	123.80	177.60	301.40

Source: Statistics Canada.

themselves creatures of the provinces—Québec's total comes to $200.90 per person, behind Saskatchewan, which is well ahead at $250, and barely leading Alberta at $200.40.

The exceptional support for culture in Québec actually comes from the federal government, and it is here that the most money from Ottawa is spent ($1.468 billion of a total $4.1 billion for the rest of Canada—35% of the total) much of this is no doubt due to the presence of federal institutions such as Radio-Canada.

The Canadian government spends $187.30 per capita in Québec, well above the national average of $119.40, although tiny Prince Edward Island receives more. Without such substantial support, Québec's cultural assistance would be far less exemplary. If Québec received what other provinces receive on average, $104.52, then the total public expenditures on culture in Québec would be $305.42 per inhabitant, ranking third behind Saskatchewan and Prince Edward Island, just ahead of Newfoundland.

These figures give us something serious to reflect on: firstly, concerning Canadian federalism, not always a bad thing for Québec; secondly, a certain incoherence in public discourse that likes to crow about the importance of culture, yet curiously does not bestow the funding to match its verbal enthusiasm. Is this "all talk and no (or little) action" as the adage would have it?

A MORE CULTURAL PROVINCE?

The fact that Québec is not the cultural paradise that the government claims—at least not in terms of concrete support—is also reflected in the place that culture occupies in the economy. Contrary to what is generally believed, the importance of culture to the economy is no higher in Québec than elsewhere in Canada.

Statistics Canada data on the share of each industry in GDP—a very imperfect measure—indicates that culture in the broadest sense represents 4.19% of Québec's GDP, which places it 3rd behind Ontario (4.65%) and British Columbia (4.53%), with Nova Scotia close behind (4.04%). This essentially reflects the concentration of cultural activity in the large urban centres.

It leads us to similar conclusions when one considers the area of employment in cultural enterprises—again in the largest sense, including radio and television, cinema and recording, books and newspapers, performing arts, bookstores, newsstands, heritage sites, etc. Québec accounts for 45,907 jobs in these sectors, again according to Statistics Canada and the Institut de la statistique du Québec. This amounts to a total of 1.32% of all jobs, placing Québec in first position, well above the Canadian average of 1.1%, slightly more than Ontario (1.2%) and British Columbia (1.01%) and far ahead of Alberta (0.08%).

Québec, with 22.6% of all jobs in Canada, holds 25.84% in cultural employment, though one can observe a similar overemphasis comparable in Ontario, with 37.95% of total employment and 39.35% cultural employment. Further statistics provided by Hill Strategies,[10] based on the 2006 census—more precise in asking people's occupations and concerning itself with "real artists" (actors, artisans, authors, composers, dancers, musicians, painters, producers, etc.)—showed an average of 0.77% working in all of Canada. Two provinces showed larger-than-average proportions: Ontario with 0.81% and British Columbia with

1.08%. Nova Scotia placed 3rd with 0.73%, and Québec 4th with 0.71%.

What do all these figures add up to? Pretty much the same thing: at a quantitative level at least, Québec is an important cultural centre, but not much more so than other large cities or cultural loci in Canada.

THEORY AND ACTIONS

There appears to be a split not only between our perceptions of Québec as the principal centre for culture in Canada and reality, but also between the quality and quantity in our cultural production on one hand and the cultural habits of Québec's citizens on the other.

Let us begin with quality. If the state fails to support the arts as it should, are ordinary citizens taking up the slack? Not if we take a close look at how Québécois consume culture. Two phenomena are worth noting.

The first is that the consumption of cultural products is declining. This is not obvious at first glance. The OCCQ says cultural consumption of our households remained stable enough from 1997 to 2009, when it amounted to $2,520 in 2009, which represents 5.8% of total family expenditures.[11] In all, then, Québécois spend about $8.6 billion a year on culture. Enormous as this may seem, it relies on a very broad definition of culture that contains a multitude of things.

Of the $2,520 spent by the average household, $1,376 is set aside for goods such as TV sets, video material, computers and the Internet, etc. Then we have $162 spent on the materials required (art and photographic supplies, etc). Next come $448 in distribution (cable and satellite). Of the $2,520 per family, we are left with only $534 for "true" culture: newspapers, videos, movie tickets, books, magazines, shows and museums— around 21% of the total.

Furthermore, this dips when we realize the overall amount spent remains stable (5.6% to 5.8% of total family expenditures), but more and more is being spent on "hardware"—cable and satellite subscriptions— which exploded in 1997 to reach $769 by 2009, if one allows for inflation. The real proportion of expenditures thus went from 39.9% to 21.2%.

This is a heavy downward trend away from culture per se and toward technology. This must surely be happening elsewhere too.

The second phenomenon, however, is distinctly Québécois. Expenditures here are clearly weaker than outside Québec, according to a troubling study by Hill Strategies, which shows that, on average, 2008 expenditures—per person, not by household—in Canada amounted to $841[12] as opposed to Québec's $716, placing us 10th among the provinces, well behind Ontario ($880) and still further behind Alberta ($963). This includes cultural expenditures by the very broadest definition. This may be skewed by, for example, the size of flat screens purchased.

This study shows expenditures reaching $5.4 billion in 2008 in Québec, or 2.7% of total consumption, "the weakest of all Canadian provinces." Québec's citizens spent twice as much as both levels of government—$2.8 billion for the year in question. This again is the weakest in Canada: Ontarians spent 3.5 times as much as all three levels of government.

With regard to "purely cultural" products, the picture of expenditures on shows and museums is hardly inspiring. Québec came 6th at $38 per inhabitant, well below Canada's $44. It was 10th in the purchase of art works: $12 versus $29; 4th for books ($41), close to the Canadian average of $43, which to me is explained more by the price of books in French rather than our voracious readership. This will appear below.

However incomplete, this data allows a preliminary but obvious conclusion: we spend less than our neighbours in the rest of Canada on culture. Hence, we do not stand out for the importance we accord to it in everyday life, or for the support we show our artists.

QUANTITY AND QUALITY

If not stellar in quantitative terms, do Québécois at least make up for it qualitatively, in the tastes, habits or finesse of the choices we make? Unfortunately not, for there is a third negative tendency. It is not my intention to deliver a value judgement on us Québécois, but we can say without fear of contradiction that there is no connection between what we celebrate and what we are ready to enjoy. With the one notable exception of Céline Dion, the stars known around the world are not generally our household favourites. The films, plays and artists which achieve international success are not those we hold most dear.

Let us begin with the stage: shows, classical concerts, theatre, dance,

SHOWS PRESENTED IN QUÉBEC

TYPE OF SHOW	SALES IN MILLIONS	QUÉBEC'S SHARE
Theatre	33.4	88.2
Dance	9.4	64.1
Music	29.5	47.0
Song: in French	29.2	79.3
Song: in English	69.9	13.7
Humour	42.6	100.0
Circus	35.3	100.0
Total	**267.6**	

Source: Observatoire de la culture et des communications du Québec.

popular music and variety shows. The activity is enormous: in 2012, there were 7,250,625 spectators for 17,411 shows and receipts of $267 million.

Of this total of $267 million, two huge sectors accounted for two-thirds (61%) of all box-office receipts: English-speaking songs with $69 million (25.8%)—essentially major world tours for popular music groups —and variety shows with $94 million (35.2%). This can be broken down into three types of presentation: humour ($42.5 million), circus ($35.3 million) and music-hall ($16.3 million).

What is most striking is the strength of humour with $42 million in ticket sales, equal to theatre and dance combined. Similarly, English-speaking songs earn double the receipts of francophone music. Theatre, however, takes in $33 million (12.5%).

Still more interesting is the small number of shows that account for a considerable part of overall attendance and box-office receipts. The most attended 20 drew 33.1% of all receipts and 20.8% of all audience members. The top 50 attracted 46.5% of all ticket sales and 32.8% of attendees. There is plainly a high concentration of successful shows, and an analysis of them should tell us much about public thinking and tastes.

Humour dominates the top 50: sixteen of these shows drew 35% of all audiences in 2012—in order, Lise Dion, Patrick Huard, Claudine Mercier, Jean-Marc Parent, Philippe Bond and Sugar Sammy. Next is the circus with 17% attendance, Cirque du Soleil coming first with *Amaluna, Michael Jackson* and *Saltimbanco*. Surprising as it may seem, theatre comes third with 14%, but this is thanks to *Broue* (a star-studded laugh-out-loud farce which has been frequently reprised for at least two decades). Behind that is English-speaking music, with 13.1% for Madonna, *The Wall* and Coldplay (U2 had preceded these in 2011). Francophone music pulls through with 11.4%, thanks to *Star Académie* 2012, Chantal Pary, *Mixmania 3* and those of our stars making a comeback.

WHAT CONCLUSIONS CAN WE DRAW?

Firstly, when they go out, Québécois show a clear preference for entertainment over cultural exertion. They love to laugh, whether at stand-up comics or *Broue*, and they love the magic of a circus.

Secondly, they massively prefer Québécois shows. It might not be an absolute objective for a society to prefer its own cultural products systematically. One may mobilize for self-reliance in food and strive to eat locally. In culture, however, we must be open to the world, to see and hear what is unfamiliar. We need to look for a reasonable balance between such openness and support for our own artists.

Of course, it is good news for Québec's cultural industry that 21 of the 25 most popular shows were ours, and that they captured 50.86% of all audiences, but on the other hand, we cannot help finding something a bit circular and incestuous in it too. Fundamentally, when it come to performing arts, Québécois go to see who and what they know from television: humourists and singers from "reality" shows.

Thirdly, one can suppose—although this would be hard to verify statistically—that we are expressing our specificity in so choosing. The phenomenon of humourists is unique to Québec. They are everywhere, to be sure, but the degree of their popularity and show-business dominance is distinctly our own. Our enthusiasm for circuses is also specific to us, which explains the origin of Cirque du Soleil and the overall quality of what is available in this area.

MOST SUCCESSFUL TICKET SALES FOR SHOWS
IN QUÉBEC, 2012

RANK	TITLE	ARTIST	TYPE
1	Amaluna	Cirque du Soleil	Circus and Magic
2	Tournée Star Académie 2012	Various artists	Song: In French
3	Le temps qui court	Lise Dion	Humour
4	MDNA World Tour 2012	Madonna	Song: In English
5	The Wall Tour 2012	Roger Waters	Song: In English
6	Le bonheur	Patrick Huard	Humour
7	Dans le champ	Claudine Mercier	Humour
8	Torture	Jean-Marc Parent	Humour
9	Michael Jackson: The Immortal World Tour	Cirque du Soleil	Circus and Magic
10	Chantons sous la pluie	Various artists	Musical Comedy and Music-hall
11	Sagesse reportée	Peter MacLeod	Humour
12	First One Man Show	Philippe Bond	Humour
13	Saltimbanco	Cirque du Soleil	Circus and Magic
14	You're Gonna Rire	Sugar Sammy	Humour (bilingual)
15	Le retour de nos idoles	Chantal Pary & Claude Barzotti	Song: In French
16	Wicked	Various artists	Musical Comedy and Music-hall
17	Tel quel	Jean-Michel Anctil	Humour
18	Les Belles-soeurs	Théâtre d'Aujourd'hui	Musical Comedy and Music-hall
19	Mike Ward s'eXpose	Mike Ward	Humour
20	Broue	Various artists	Repertory Theatre
21	Alexandre Barrette... and others	Alexandre Barrette	Humour
22	Casse-Noisette (Nutcracker)	Les Grands Ballets Canadiens de Montréal	Classical Ballet
23	Messmer le fascinateur	Messmer	Circus and Magic
24	Les confessions de Rousseau	Stéphane Rousseau	Humour
25	Mylo Xyloto Tour	Coldplay	Song: In English

Sources: Institut de la statistique du Québec, Observatoire de la culture et des communications du Québec.

Fourthly, except for shows by the Cirque du Soleil, the most successful performances have no connection to the international acclaim of our culture. Most of them are quite simply not exportable. Such is the case with most of our humourists, barring a few lucky incursions into the French-speaking markets of Europe. The same holds true for French-language singers and composers: the greatest of these are not our most popular, but rather the stars produced by reality shows like *Star Académie* or *La Voix* (*The Voice*).

FILM COMEDY

The rift between reality and public declaration is most striking in the movies. Québécois don't go to the cinema that often. On average, they see 2.6 films a year as opposed to 4.1 in Canada and the US, or 3.1 in France. And when they do, it is not to see Québécois films, much less those celebrated beyond our borders. When a local film does well in Québec, it is one of the many features that do not make it elsewhere . . . the *Les Boys* cycle (a comic series about very amateur hockey players), for instance.

The balance sheet for these past few years is catastrophic: since 2003, Québec cinema has garnered 9% to 13% of box office sales, with the notable exception of 2005, when three films—*C. R. A. Z. Y.*, *Aurore* and *Les Boys IV*—raised the figure to 18.2%, only to fall as low as 5.3% in 2012 and 5.6% in 2013.

Our cinema has to deal with enormous pressure from the Americans, who pull in over 80%, although we can perhaps console ourselves with the fact that receipts are not the sole measure of success. In all, 1.2 million Québécois watched one of their own films in 2012 and a million in 2013.

Especially striking is the disconnect between critical and overall success. Québécois films are celebrated the world over—creating a definite sense of pride—but these are rarely the films we go to see. The only true success in 2013 was *Louis Cyr* with 473,370 tickets sold, followed at a considerable distance by *Gabrielle* at 154,528 tickets, well received overseas and winner of an award in the People's Choice category in Locarno. *Sarah préfère la course*, entered in the "Un certain regard" (alternative film) category at Cannes and quite an accomplishment, drew only 19,167 cinephiles, i.e. almost no one. At the time of writing, it is too soon to gauge the success of *Mommy*, applauded at Cannes in 2014.

In 2012, there was no runaway hit. *Omerta*, in first position, pulled in 295,386, followed by *Les Pee-Wee 3D* at 231,884. *Laurence Anyways*, winner of a Best Actress award at Cannes and in the "Un certain regard" category, and winner of Best Canadian Film in Toronto, sold only 50,574 tickets. *Rebelle (War Witch)*, despite a nomination for Best Foreign Film at the Oscars, was snubbed with a mere 16,813. The preceding year, *Monsieur Lazhar*, also nominated for an Oscar, did somewhat better (358,000), likewise, *Incendies* also a nominee at the Oscars in 2010 (430,816 filmgoers), but even these prestigious honours were no guarantee of triumph here in Québec. Of 27 Québec films screened here in 2013, barely 9 attracted more than 20,000 filmgoers. Again in 2012, 9 out of 27 films and in 2011, 14 out of 31 reached that level.

In part, this is because Québec cinema tends to be in a niche known as "cinéma d'auteur" (art film), seen mainly in festivals and in the sole Oscar category to stray from Hollywood dogma, Best Foreign Film. Out of this, Vincent Guzzo, owner of several theatres, created a tempest by stating flatly that the Québec industry did not produce enough popular films. Well, let us admit we have not found the magic formula for perfect balance between accessibility and quality.

I am not making a judgement call, but this much is clear: our cinema does not fill us with pride, and so we fail to support it by buying tickets. In fact, our main link with the cinema that represents us so well abroad is involuntary: we support it through taxes channelled into subsidies, without which our film industry could not survive.

BOOKS

These cannot be approached in the same way as the cinema. Here, we do answer the call . . . those of us who read. The problem is not how we split the pie, nor particular choices, but rather the size of the pie—the size of the book market, the number we buy and read overall. We read too little, so little, in fact, that it is tragic.

The number of books we produce is impressive. In 2011, we published 6,564 works: equivalent to one book per 1,000 inhabitants! Press runs, however, are ridiculous—2,273 copies on average. These figures suggest that we publish far too many books, although I say this with no thought of muzzling those wishing to express themselves in print, even more so since I myself have written books with this kind of sales figure, usually kept confidential.

In 2009, Québec's share of the market was 42%. That is a lot, and we should be happy about it, even if sticking solely to our own books is not a social objective.

Furthermore, book sales as a whole are not increasing. They reached $678 million in 2012, 12% less than the $763 million in 2009; this can be explained by the end of the schoolbook boom that followed the pedagogical reform. Sales, in fact, have stagnated for over a decade.

Is $678 million really that much? Is it too little? To find out, we need to compare provinces, and data here is rather fragmentary. In a study on book purchasing conducted by Hill Strategies in 2008, 44% of Québec respondents claimed to have bought books,[13] not many, for we rank 7th ahead of Newfoundland and Prince Edward Island. Québec fares a little better in expenditures per family, with $212—below the Canadian average of $226—still in fourth place behind Ontario, British Columbia and Alberta. Yet this placement is due not to the love of books, but rather to the higher price of them in French than in English.

Another study by Hill Strategies, based on census data from 2006 shows our expenditures per inhabitant at $37.10, placing 4th behind Ontario at $50.16, British Columbia at $48.62 and Alberta at $42.54. Nova Scotians spend $36.12, New Brunswickers $31.51, Prince Edward Islanders $30.92, Saskatchewanites $27.88, and Newfoundlanders $25.72. These numbers do not tell everything by any means, for they conceal something much deeper: reading habits, of which I shall say more in the following chapter.

A CONSIDERABLE CHALLENGE

Behind these figures lies the problem of a society that does not value reading, and which, 50 years after the Quiet Revolution, has still not fully thrown off the weight of the past.

Québec laboured under a cultural time lag and a relationship of the majority with reading, culture and learning that was similar to those of the poorer Atlantic provinces. The Quiet Revolution allowed us to break with this past and believe, no doubt, that mere institutional reform would do the rest. While the baby boomers were educated in a deconfessionalized school environment (non-denominational schools) and in brand new polyvalentes and CEGEPs, family culture did not keep pace.

The statistics quoted earlier show that, in passing on their values to these boomers, their parents had not left them with fertile ground for reading or inculcating the reading habits of an advanced society. Thus, despite society's generalized efforts, the Quiet Revolution was not completed, and it still is incomplete 50 years later.

This is heavy with consequence, because this connection to reading had an impact on our attitudes toward education, and thus excluded a part of the population from fully participating in social life. It also, therefore, obviously affects our purchases of, and relationship with, books and the book world in general, as well as our film and TV habits and our choice of shows. Even in the digital age, writing still remains a pillar of the cultural world, the foundation of all cultivated life.

This constitutes a major societal problem; our lag in reading reveals a social fracture and a problem of identity, since the development of a minority language relies on the capacity of citizens to wield it, to read and write it. The encouragement of reading and the exercise of great prudence with regard to anything that might compromise this effort has to become our central common objective.

Until we have eradicated our very real delays and regained lost ground in this regard, we cannot claim openness to, or a penchant for, culture as a mark of Québec society. We produce great artists distinguished the world over; this alone does not make us particularly cultured citizens.

CHAPTER 6

ARE WE UNDER THREAT?

The Québécois nation is challenged largely by its language and the fear for its future. We are ready to fight for it, but we do fundamentally nothing to reinforce it. There is a flagrant contradiction between the love we proclaim for our language and our weak propensity to protect, read and write it.

Were you aware that on a pan-Canadian scale, Québécois are those that read the least? Furthermore, the number of illiterates is higher than those of other provinces and the majority of advanced economies.

It may seem strange to begin a chapter on a subject this important and having so much to do with our future as a people, as well as our ability to survive as a linguistic minority on this continent with remarks on reading, but I feel it is the correct way to present the problem.

By insisting more than usual on questions such as reading within the framework of a linguistic discussion, I have four messages to convey. The first concerns the intrinsic importance of language. The quality of French and the mastery of writing constitute the foundations of success for our language, more so than concerns about the presence of English business terms like Second Cup or the inability of a Korean convenience store owner to serve his customers in French. The vigour and quality of a language depend largely on writing, and this is what structures it, anchors it in time, and protects it from becoming mere folklore. The oral tradition has its limits. The written language cannot play its fundamental role if people read less and less. Not exactly a matter for headlines. A notice on literacy from the Conseil supérieur de l'éducation in 2013 went largely unnoticed, unlike indignant revelations in *Le Journal de Montréal* on the presence of English in downtown Montreal.

The second message is that the main enemy, in several respects, is not others but ourselves: a people who claim to love their language but do not read, a people who must endure minority status but do not replenish their population—then complain of their declining demographic strength, especially begrudging the importance accorded to immigrants. An enemy we do not speak sufficiently about, when it comes to language, is the enemy within.

The third message is a plea to cast a fresh eye on the language issue. We indeed must "think outside the box." The discussion so far has been frozen in time with the same tools and laws, fears and reflexes as those of two generations ago. Fifty years ago, we battled department stores for refusing to serve clients in French, and big business for refusing to promote francophones. Now we wonder how technology giants will manage their multinational activities. The problems—and threats, if they exist—are of another kind and must be approached differently if we are to stop spinning our wheels.

The fourth and most important message is yet another paradox. Québécois are proud by nature, ready to take up a challenge and sometimes given to exaggerating their accomplishments. Yet, when it comes to language, we display a pessimism not evident in other facets of our collective life, a pessimism which leads to a "loser" complex and reflexes which are out of sync with the economic and cultural dynamism we show otherwise. While some may accuse me of being too sombre or critical, I am an optimist about our language. Yes, of course there are problems to solve and challenges to take up, but let us stop being so afraid.

I do not claim to have dealt completely with the linguistic question, particularly since my method consists of testing opinions and perceptions with facts, and in this it has its limits. It is curious that this discussion is awash in statistics, as if the question of language could be solved with accountancy. Yet, if such data are useful, they cannot help us definitively, because our reading of them is highly subjective and coloured by political opinion, personal experiences and anecdotal observations. The reading I offer is my own and, I believe, lucid, but will not achieve consensus. Nevertheless, I hope to be able to show what a huge difference there is between perception and reality.

THE THEME OF DECLINE

The linguistic debate comes in waves which never seem to cool us off. The question of language disappears from public discussion for long periods of time and generally regenerates itself with the publication of statistics, court judgements, or headlines. In sum, it comes up, one minor crisis at a time.

The word "decline" is among the most frequently used terms to describe the situation of French in Québec, recurring whenever imposing studies by l'Office Québécois de la langue française (OQLF—the guardian of the French language) come out, as in the fall of 2011, or linguistic data from the 2011 census, or the 2012 figures from Statistics Canada.[14]

The census revealed that, in the nine English-speaking provinces, the percentage of those who spoke mostly English at home went from 84.2% in 2006 to 83.7% in 2011, a drop of 0.5%. Yet, as far as I know, no one in the Toronto or Vancouver media has remarked on the decline of English! The reason for this is simple: immigration is important, and it is normal for the proportion of foreign-speakers to increase while the ratio of the majority, in this case, English-speakers, decreases.

The phenomenon is identical in Québec as a result of immigration; hence the proportion of French-speakers in Québec has dipped from 81.8% to 81.2%. The same causes have given rise to similar results; greater reactions in Québec are predictable, however, because English dominates the planet, while French is in the minority on this continent.

Does this justify talk of a decline in one case and not the other? Words matter, regardless of where they are uttered. The description provided by Statistics Canada of a very minor slide in the ratio of francophones is correct, but it hardly provides for striking headlines or ominous speeches in the National Assembly.

"Decline" is a much-used term in the media, and it carries a lot of weight. In any dictionary, we see decline of an empire, decline of an offer, decline in one's health: it is anything but neutral. It signifies the beginning of the end, certainly not a launching or takeoff. It is not how one would describe a language, but rather a conclusion, and it should not be used for a modest dip unless it constitutes the start of an inexorable process in the extinction of French.

Clearly, this is the view of those who feel very serious concern for the language. Mouvement Québec français talks about a "considerable decline." The former Péquiste member of the National Assembly, Pierre Curzi, considers that "anglicization is ongoing." Jean-François Lisée, the then minister responsible for the metropolis, affirms that "the proportion of francophones is becoming marginalized" without defining what he means by "marginal." Former Minister Pierre Duchesne, not wanting to be left out, has said, "The continued existence of our nation is far from certain."

All this fallout comes from an infinitesimal dip in the proportion of francophones whose number has, after all, *increased in absolute figures* by 259,000 in five years, while the migration toward French over English has improved. Although the relative strength of francophone numbers may be reduced, it is not due to the rise of English, which is traditionally seen as the threat, but to an increase in the immigrant population.

The abuse of "decline" reminds one that this discussion is heavily politicized. The arrival of greater and greater numbers of immigrants creates challenges to integration in all of our large cities. Here, the challenges are even more considerable but could be more easily taken up with a little less theatre, verbal inflation and political manoeuvring.

A MINORITY ON THE ISLAND OF MONTREAL?

Whether real or feigned, the principal source of worry about our language does not spring from Québec City but Montreal, especially on the island. Reactions were vivid when, in 2011, the OQLF published demographic and linguistic data.[15] Concern and indignation rose to the surface in response to one particular figure among the massive 682-page, 60-part document and its mass of data and graphs: 47%. This was the number of francophones projected to live on the island in 2031. "French Retreats in Montreal," "French Downswing Continues," "French Headed for Perpetual Decline in Montreal" said the headlines.

These data foresaw, in fact, a continuation of phenomena we were already aware of, revealed by an arithmetic we already knew. People of Québécois stock, for lack of offspring, were counting on immigration to assure their demographic growth. It was then inevitable that the proportion of immigrants among the population would increase, above all in Montreal where they were most concentrated. By 2031, it will have risen from 20.6% to 29.5%, whereas the proportion of francophones will drop from 54.2% to 47.4%. To this must be added yet another process, the displacement of francophone families to the suburbs.

These figures do not lead us to talk of anglicization. On the contrary, the proportion of English-speakers is also falling—from 25.2% to 23%, sufficient to put them in 3rd place. The projected figure of 47.4% for francophones in 2031 carries definite symbolic weight, because a drop in number to below 50% opens the door to their becoming a minority. This conclusion, however, has three strong failings.

The first consists in the fact that, in order to describe francophones as a minority, one has to isolate the island from the rest of the greater Montreal region. Yes, they are a minority *on* the island, but a majority *all around* it, due to urban sprawl. Their number has not diminished; they have simply moved a few dozen kilometres away. Geographically isolating the island like this, without seeing the metropolitan region as a whole, cannot give us a reliable linguistic picture. Can the St. Lawrence and Rivière-des-Prairies be considered some sort of wall around language? This type of reasoning cannot help but mislead us. The number of francophones in Montreal drops if a family leaves Ahuntsic for Saint-Lambert, but not if the same family moves to nearby Pointe-Claire!

The second flaw shows francophones as a minority only if the numbers of English-speakers and allophones are fused to make a single group, which is obviously nonsense. They do not impinge on linguistic balance in the same way at all. Add to this that many French-speakers, or those who are nearly so (Haitians and North Africans, for instance), are described as allophones because they use their first language at home, but function as francophones in their daily lives. Most others will also become francophones. This is a perilous adventure, too, because it unavoidably leads to presenting immigrants as a threat.

The third weakness arises from the fact that those who fear that francophones are a minority on the island are concerned that they are not numerically strong enough to absorb newcomers. They are not looking at the correct set of figures, however. They are focused on the question of one's mother tongue, the language used at home, since many on the island, after moving to the suburbs, revert to it from French in the evening with family. Thus, when night falls, there are fewer French-speakers on the island. The next day, they are back in force, studying, working and shopping in French, and this is when they will rub against francophones and draw them closer to the language.

THE CHOICE OF IMMIGRANTS

Allusions to a decline brought on by immigration arise from the fear that newcomers will massively abandon their languages in favour of English. Looking at the census figures without analyzing them too closely can lead us to this conclusion. The 2006 census could lead us to conclude that only 51% of immigrants have chosen French as the target of their linguistic transfer. This too is a magic number which has elicited inflammatory reactions because it suggests that half of all immigrants opted for English. It does not really describe the choice of language for new arrivals though, but of those who abandoned their mother tongue over decades, sometimes two generations after they arrived, a process begun long before, like Greeks going to English schools. Figures from 2006 do not reflect the attraction of English today, but often of choices made before Bill 101.

In fact, much data shows that, as time goes by, more and more immigrants opt for French. The proportion of allophones having transferred completely or partially to French is in constant progression: 34.7% in 2001, 38.6% in 2006, 40% in 2011. Inversely, the proportion of those choosing English is in constant decline: 34% in 2001, 31.6% in 2006 and 29.9% in 2011. The high number of allophones who stick to their maternal language explains why these figures do not add up to 100. Such a significant turnaround is the result of Bill 101, schooling in French, and the increasingly francophone (or quasi-francophone) make-up of immigration, including Haitians, North Africans or "francotropes"[16] whose languages lead more naturally to French, such as Latin-Americans. What is important to remember is that things are moving in the right direction.

THE LANGUAGE OF EVERYDAY

The liveliest discussions emerge, however, from an abundance of less formal or systematic documents which often attest to the irritation of ordinary citizens, such as the investigations of *Le Journal de Montréal* into language used by salespeople in downtown Montreal or complaints for violation of the rules on signage. In each instance, it is difficult to draw a definitive conclusion, because nothing is harder than measuring preferred language usage in conversations and economic dealings. How can we define progress or slippage? To what must we compare our observations? We scarcely know.

We are in the domain of anecdotes and poorly validated observations which can easily be turned into a major issue whose range and degree of subjectivity cannot be measured, but which depend on the political party we support, or where we come from or where we presently live. We may see progress if we can order in French in Chinatown, but deplore the halting French of a Tamil convenience-store owner. We may rejoice in the multi-ethnic nature of Montreal, yet feel that downtown has become a Tower of Babel dominated by English.

These perceptions betray two sources of confusion. First, in Québec we tend to view the immigration agenda through a linguistic lens. Accordingly, the rise of English in the downtown is largely in reaction to the increase in immigration and to the presence of large visible minorities. Doubtless, those not regularly accustomed to being downtown will feel out of place. They hold this in common with people in large cities the world over. Here, however, it is seen as an English-French problem.

Second, we forget that the goal of linguistic battles in the '60s and '70s was never to get rid of English altogether, but rather to restore French to its rightful place, showing a French face and making certain that francophones can work in their own language . . . not making Montreal into a giant Catholic and unilingual version of Chicoutimi. The reactions of many, especially the most exalted, suggest denunciation not merely of the abusive use of English, but of the very presence of anglophones themselves.

Montreal's challenge is not its multiculturalism, banal enough in any metropolis and not particularly remarkable compared with Toronto or Vancouver. What is unique is the duality in being composed of a large francophone majority and an anglophone minority. Montreal is one of the world's rare bilingual cities where we live with two of the greatest universal languages. Naturally, the word "bilingualism" becomes a snag, because legally and institutionally Montreal is a French city. This leads everyone to verbal acrobatics to describe what is evident—without uttering the taboo word of "bilingualism."

There are consequences to this: English-speaking Montrealers often congregate in specific neighbourhoods, just as francophones do, and use their native language not only at home, but at school, at work, and in shops. As long as this presents no barrier to French, it is just part of life. It is normal to hear English spoken in the streets, in movie theatres and in restaurants, all the more so because downtown is still, in several respects, an English-speaking district. This is primarily true because francophones frequent it less, and because the pull of English is reinforced by the presence of two universities and multinational offices, with tourists and business travellers naturally gravitating toward the downtown area.

Yet, even though much has changed, a great deal of energy in the linguistic debate is still directed against English. Examples are manifold: a part of Bill 14—with which the Marois government sought to reinforce Bill 101 by removing bilingual status from municipalities whose English-speaking population dipped below 50%—was an irritant not needed for the reinforcement of French; or the intense campaign against nefarious "bridging schools," which sought to get around the French Language Charter directing students to French schools, but which affected only a few hundred; or the idea of forbidding francophones and allophones from going to English CEGEPs, which would weaken these institutions; or repeated attacks on McGill; or reconsidering the construction of an English-language super-hospital. There is a whiff of anglophobia to all these issues.

THE *LINGUA FRANCA*

All this energy has been misdirected. A battle from 50 years ago has been plastered over today's realities. The linguistic struggle in Québec was to correct an imbalance favouring English domination at work, in signage and in the public arena, plus its inordinate power of attraction, particularly to immigrants. The language laws sought to correct an injustice and ensure the survival and development of French. It was in part a fight against the English minority, especially those who refused to give up their privileges, and it did contain some coercive aspects which brought about the exodus of a number of those who refused any change to the status quo.

This battle has been won and is now over; the injustices are a thing of the past. English speakers are in decline and those who have chosen Québec have largely accepted the new rules of the game, especially by being bilingual. Today's problems have to do with company names and insignia, as well as the increased use of English in the workplace—these are not holdovers of the old injustices, but the results of another phenomenon: English as the new *lingua franca* imposed on the whole world, the Latin of our millennium, the language of commerce, culture, technology and universities.

The new battles are not against English speakers themselves, but something else entirely: the dominance of English is creating problems globally. Here, they are more serious because this universal language happens to be that of Québec's minority and the majority in Canada as well as in the majority of our gigantic neighbour to the south, which only increases the pressure. It is ever-present, from show business to universities, but also in the daily lives of our children under bombardment from Facebook and YouTube, where they "like" photos and "follow" tweeters.

English is the indispensable tool for those who study, travel or want to know what is happening on our planet and aspire to professional success. Yet there is an evident malaise when it comes to finding a way for young people to learn English properly in school: the proposal to give intensive English courses in grade 6, for instance. These challenges differ greatly from those taken up by Bill 101, and there is a disconnect in applying 35-year-old solutions to the present day: same language, same fears, same solutions? No, this is a very different type of problem from those which mobilized Québec a few decades ago, and cannot be resolved by the same old methods.

The use of English in Montreal head offices is one example, even when these are the Caisse de dépôt et de placement du Québec, Bombardier, or the Banque Nationale headed by unilingual English-speakers favouring English Montrealers. It is annoying and reveals a reversal of the traditional dilemma. Paradoxically, this is in a way the price of success. We are not talking about "foreign" businesses imposing English on their employees, but French-Canadian companies that have become multinationals and expanded beyond our borders. English is necessary to them because it is needed to communicate with clients, foreign markets, suppliers and partners.

Knowing this can only continue, what do we do? Our large businesses cannot develop worldwide if they hire only francophones or create linguistic barriers. This will not be solved with threats, witch hunts or rigorous application of the Charte de la langue française, nor will bureaucratic norms adapt to a perpetually changing reality.

This also applies to another great challenge of years past, and one we do not really know how to solve: the exemption of small businesses with fewer than 50 employees from Bill 101, a considerable gap in our regulatory arsenal. We all agree on the basics. Work is where immigrants become integrated, and it constitutes a public space where francophones have a right to function in their own language. But how do we accomplish this without crushing small and middle businesses under a mountain of bureaucracy and paperwork? There must be another way, without resorting to Bill 101.

The other important linguistic matter which needs rethinking is immigration, which is not really linguistic, after all. Our society, like all industrialized societies, must come to grips with an increasingly significant migratory flux from countries whose cultures are far removed from ours, and this demands increased efforts to integrate them.

A NATION OF NON-READERS

The time has come for all Québécois who truly believe in this issue to concern themselves more with language itself and less with politics, a little less with English-speakers and more attentively with francophones, forgetting about symbolism—often hollow, though emotionally charged. They must involve themselves in "the real thing," concrete problems which may lend themselves less to headlines but are still of capital importance. Among these is our rapport with reading, essential for citizens to master their language, to keep it alive and give it the solidity it needs.

A study of several hundred pages by Heritage Canada and based on an in-depth poll by the Québec firm Créatec in 2005, highlights "Québec reading rates as the lowest in Canada."[17] Québécois placed last. Fewer than 46% read regularly, as opposed to between 53% and 60% in the other provinces: truly an enormous gap. Likewise, far fewer of us read literature (37% against 45% elsewhere).

Furthermore, fewer books are read by francophones (13.9 books a year) than by English-speakers (17.6), and less time is devoted to leisure-time reading (3.9 hours vs. 4.8 among Anglo-Canadians).

A little digging leads us to the root of the problem. The Créatec poll asked respondents if their parents read books. Here the gap widens: 64% of English-speakers in the other provinces said "yes," but only 49% of Québec francophones. When asked if their parents talked to them about books they had read, 47% of English-speakers in the rest of Canada replied in the affirmative, as opposed to 37% of Québec francophones.

If we read less, it is partly due to a relative lack of contact with books in the past, and it is truly terrifying that this tradition seems bound to continue. These days, 55% of Québec francophones say they read to their children daily, far below the 75% of Anglo-Canadians, and when asked if they start reading to their children by the age of one, only 25% of Franco-Québécois said "yes," but it was 59% among Anglo-Canadians!

These are alarming statistics borne out by a yet another study—the PIRLS mentioned in the chapter on education. This broad international investigation tested not only the reading aptitude of nine-year-olds, but also inquired into their cultural environment. When parents encouraged literary activities with their pre-school children—reading books, story-telling, singing, playing alphabet or word games, discussing what one has done or read, or letter-writing or reading posters out loud—their reading test results climbed. And this is where Québec society is sorely lacking.

The proportion of families with more than 25 children's books is much weaker in Québec (78%) than anywhere else in Canada: British Columbia (84%), Alberta (88%), Ontario (84%), New Brunswick (85%), Nova Scotia (93%), and Newfoundland (94%). Likewise, Québec trails in the number of households with more than 100 books per household with 28%, barely above the international average of 27%—this includes Third World countries—and well behind Nova Scotia (41%), British Columbia and Newfoundland (38% each), Alberta and Ontario (37% each) and even French-speaking New Brunswick (29%).

Let us top this off with the killer-question: do you like reading? Québec comes in last (29%) against a Canadian average of 41%. We also hold the record for those who dislike reading—16%, twice as much as anywhere else.

LITERACY: A CATASTROPHE OF OUR OWN

This tragically difficult relationship with books and reading contains the explanation for yet another problem: around 1.2 million Québécois have such poor reading skills that they are not functionally literate. One notes also that 2.2 million Québécois cannot read well enough to develop themselves fully.

This is a true catastrophe in the personal life and work of each, and for society as a whole, which is in need of skilled workers as well as citizens well adapted to an increasingly complicated environment.

A "Notice" from the Conseil supérieur de l'education sur la littératie[18] in September 2013 went largely unnoticed, like the results of a vast study by the OECD in October of the same year. This study, the Program for the International Assessment of Adult Competencies, carried out by the OECD in 22 countries, measures the reading aptitudes (literacy) of persons 16 to 65 years old, as well as their ability with figures (numeracy) and their mastery of new technologies.

Canada places slightly above the OECD average with a score of 273.5 out of 500 on reading, in 10th place among the 22 countries measured, but Québec (with 268.6) is 8th out of 10 in Canada, ahead only of New Brunswick and Newfoundland. Internationally, we place 17th, while Alberta is 7th. Such results on a series of tests to evaluate "comprehension, evaluation, assimilation and the use of written texts needed to take part in society, achieve objectives and develop one's knowledge and potential" are most troubling.

Those attaining level 1 or less in terms of the study are too weak to be functionally literate, and Québec outnumbers every province but Newfoundland. Nineteen percent of us are at the bottom of the scale, in other words, 1.2 million adults who, though not wholly illiterate, cannot decode above the simplest of texts. That is a lot of people. In Ontario there are only 15% of them, 12.8% in Australia and 11.9% in the Netherlands, which leaves Québec 20th out of 22, ahead of Italy and Spain.

Québec also has a high proportion of citizens at level 2, functional, but not sufficiently enough to cultivate themselves in a modern society. Combining these two groups gives us the figure of 3.4 million—53% of Québec adults—who do not have what they really need to be functional. These are the worst results in Canada and in the industrialized world, ahead of only Spain, Poland, Austria and Ireland.

How could it be otherwise? One cannot have good literacy skills if one does not read, and without reading, one progressively loses the benefits of education already acquired. Such troubling behaviour would indicate that, 50 years after the start of the Quiet Revolution, we still have not completely caught up culturally from the "Grande Noirceur" (the Great Darkness of the Duplessis and pre-Duplessis eras). Yet there is something deeper, a kind of fatalism which, in many respects, betrays an attitude of "losers." Otherwise, we would do all in our power, collectively and individually, to support and develop our language.

A CULTURE UNDER THREAT

Concentrating one's attention on external threats with origins beyond our control seems to be a natural reflex, and it is this which nourishes, decade after decade, a dynamic fear of sensing one's future threatened, of feeling in decline, even though this impression may not be based in fact.

Despite improvement in the status of French these past few years, this culture of fear has gone on to new heights. The political context has much to do with it.

The linguistic debate, emotional as it is in Québec, often follows the contours of the national question. Federalists tend toward optimism regarding the future of French. Sovereigntists are more likely to express concern. This is in part due to the latter banking on fear and indignation as powerful tools for mobilization. This is not merely calculated. Many sovereigntists are genuinely worried, which is why they favour independence. However, the impasse that their project finds itself in has added new intensity to the linguistic debate.

The unionist Gérald Larose, President of the Conseil de la souveraineté (Sovereignty Council) in 2011, could not rule out the disappearance of French within 20 years. Gilles Duceppe, after leaving the Bloc Québécois, also in 2011, brandished the horror of assimilation: "If Québécois do nothing in the next 15 years, inevitably we will find ourselves on the same slippery slope as Franco-Canadians and Acadians: plunged into assimilation. We cannot allow ourselves to hide from this reality," he said, even alluding to Cajun gumbo. Pauline Marois, for her part, asserted: "Where there is a national minority . . . I think there is always a risk of assimilation." Waving the scarecrow of assimilation is idiotic. It is also a worrisome aberration.

Words have meaning, and assimilation would mean that francophones in Québec would cease massively to speak French in order to become English speakers. This is simply beyond the pale, for despite Québec's tormented history, it has always resisted assimilation very well. The history of Canada shows us that this process occurs when a population is in a distinct minority, deprived of tools and institutions for its own protection—the absence of French schools, for instance—or subject to unjust laws like those forbidding the speaking of French in schools or in the workplace. None of this applies to Québec, where francophones are, and will remain, in a very large majority, have their own government, laws and institutions, as well as an economic base. The comparison simply does not work.

Gilles Duceppe's nightmare scenarios are a copy of the eighteenth-century Acadian model, or the twentieth- and problematic twenty-first-century models of the western provinces. It injects a certain confusion between older fears (traditionally of the English, and more recently of immigrants). This confusion is evident in the planned Charte des valeurs québécoises (Charter of Québec Values) with which the Marois government systematically drew a parallel with Bill 101, the first continuing the combat initiated in the second.

There have been moments in history when francophones feared for their survival—their defeat and domination at the hands of England, the doomed plans for assimilation in the Durham Report, massive English-speaking immigration, the exodus of French-Canadians to the USA, and, of course, the fate of French-Canadians outside Québec. This fear of extinction and the feeling of being victims are also part of our DNA; even though the initial causes may have disappeared, they seek expression in terms of other threats, real or imagined. Clearly, immigration has unconsciously become the new threat. Immigration, for example, makes francophones a minority on the Island of Montreal. In the 2015 election campaign, François Legault, leader of the CAQ, made the most explicit link between these two fears when he said that the Charter aimed to protect our identity.

We can agree that the Charter took aim at highly conservative Islamism for conflicting with our values, at its position against women which was unacceptable to us, and at certain behaviours which are fundamentally incompatible with our society. One may be indignant or irritated by such fundamentalism, but are we under threat? Does it so threaten our sense of identity that we need to be protected, despite the small number of hard-and-fast Muslims? Why would Québécois be especially threatened more, say, than other societies? Québécois, on this subject, have held onto their reflexes as a minority, even if they are now the majority in a landscape where they do control things.

This unfortunate situation reveals that the fear of a threat, of disappearing, is a vector of our identity. The menace which justifies fear comes in altered forms, but nevertheless endures. I have been looking through our history for those moments when our francophone nation was truly under threat, weakened to the point where one might have feared for its survival. It has always been protected by demography, territory, and control of its political institutions (often including those of the federal government). What we have endured is not threats to our survival but being held in inferiority, treated as second-class citizens, kept away from economic power. The fight has not been for survival but for justice, equality and dignity.

The fear of disappearance was in part one of our myths, a collective cement, an unattractive common value, because fear feeds intolerance. It amazes me that speeches which contribute to this fear come from political currents which ought, on the contrary, to nourish our pride. The sense of being threatened simply prolongs reflexes born of impotence, which in turn encourage "loser" behaviour.

CHAPTER 7

ARE WE EGALITARIAN?

We know the official story: Québec was for too long a hidebound society which denied women their rightful place. Since then, however, these unflattering lapses have been eradicated in the remarkably rapid progress toward equality of the sexes and a better integration of women into the labour market. The activity rate of women has thus made a gigantic leap, particularly when it comes to the vast program of subsidized daycare, to the point that Québec has become an egalitarian society. The election in 2012 of a female premier reflects this. The importance of women in Québécois society is such that the government of Pauline Marois decided to enshrine this principle of equality in the Charte des valeurs québécoises, and was, in fact, a pillar of the document. Now let me relate a piece of history which is more realistic than heroic, though still impressive.

As in so much else, the portrait is neither black nor white. The high point of feminine literature is better viewed in shades of grey . . . perhaps fifty of them. It is entirely true that Québec has made immense progress. But this is neither unique nor exceptional when compared with what has been done elsewhere, particularly in the rest of Canada. Today, after considerable delay, Québec has certainly joined the ranks of open and egalitarian societies, but it is often far from setting the pace, and there is still much to be done.

Equality between men and women is one of the all-important markers of modernity and an indisputable condition for the economic and social success of a society. Without doubt, this is non-negotiable. By virtue of its importance, equality between men and women is a matter which must be faced squarely and clearly, for, great as our successes may be, we must not allow our tendency toward self-congratulation to obscure the progress still to be made.

How do we measure what is yet to be accomplished? The classic indicators can measure the status of women: those used by the Conseil du statut de la femme (CSF—Council on the Status of Women), ISQ (Institut de la statistique du Québec—the Québec Institute for Statistics) or international organizations such as the OECD. Some concrete elements are easily measured: the place of women at work, for instance. There are many intangibles, however, such as prejudices, attitudes and behaviour, whether in daily life or in love, which must be taken into account, but which fall outside the task I have set myself.

A LOT OF CATCHING UP TO DO

Without going back to the days of colonization, we must recall that Québec has been a rural society heavily marked by Roman Catholicism, and that is quite a ball-and-chain to be dragging. The vote for women in Québec—possibly the greatest symbol of the fight for equality—was accorded as late as 1940, after a long battle going back to the 1920s. To put ourselves in the context of those times, this was a right acquired in ostensibly less enlightened countries such as Thailand, Burma, or El Salvador sooner than it was here. On the other hand, Catholic European countries such as France, Spain and Italy had to wait for the end of Second World War.

This revolution, was practically a matter of chance, because the Liberal Adélard Godbout beat Maurice Duplessis in 1939 and used his five years as premier to bring about this reform before Mr. Duplessis could regain power and embed himself for another 15 years. This short Liberal reign allowed Québec to shorten the duration of its shameful situation, but still it was troubling, since in fact, Québec had stood out in a Canada where the federal government had already adopted the vote for women in 1918. Even then, Ottawa was outstripped by Manitoba, Alberta and Saskatchewan, who had done so in 1916, followed by British Columbia and Ontario in 1917, then Nova Scotia in 1918, New Brunswick in 1919, Prince Edward Island in 1922 and Newfoundland, not yet part of Canada, in 1925. Québec, then, had been the sole holdout.

In other areas, we were less tardy. Québec women were less evident in the workplace, but hardly less than other Canadian women. The data of economist Pierre Fortin show that the proportion of women at paid work was for a long time similar in Québec and Ontario: the ratio was 24 women for 100 men in 1931, 28 in 1941 and 30 in 1951.

A DELAYED TAKEOFF

However, when the winds of modernity did begin to blow during the decade that followed the war, they seemed to pass Québec by. In Ontario, women stormed the workplace, and their numbers reached 42% of the active population, as opposed to 33% in Québec—stagnation in fact. The Quiet Revolution at first appeared not to engage this issue: education was deconfessionalized and rethought; then a state apparatus was raised up; yet still a certain number of traditional values held fast.

The weight of this past was still being felt in 1976, nearly 15 years after

GAP BETWEEN MEN & WOMEN IN THE LABOUR MARKET
FEMALE RATE OF PARTICIPATION AS A % OF THE MALE RATE, 1976 AND 2013

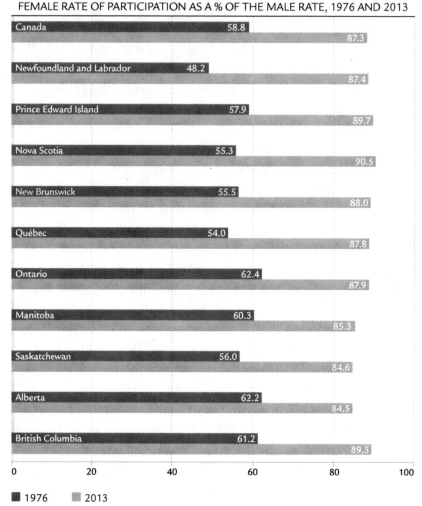

■ 1976   ▨ 2013

Source: Statistics Canada.

the Quiet Revolution. I mention 1976 not because it marked the rise to power of René Lévesque and the Parti Québécois, but because it was the first year we gained access to complete statistics. The gap separating Québec and the rest of Canada was still considerable. The rate of employed women in Canada was 45.7%, and Québec came 7th in the country with 41.4%, slightly better than Nova Scotia and New Brunswick, and barely ahead of Newfoundland. Even more remarkable was the gap between urbanized and rural provinces.

The participation of women in the workforce not only reflects the relation between men and women in society. It also depends on economics. This rate would be higher in a developed province and weaker in a province with low employment.

We get a better idea of women's place on the labour market by comparing their rate of activity with men's. Thus the presence of women at work in Québec, was 54% that of men in 1976, much, much less, for example, than Ontario's 62.4%, again Canada's worst performance apart from Newfoundland.

THE BIG CATCH-UP

In 1976 then, there still remained a lot to be done, and it was. Women's activity rate exploded from 41.4% (1976) to 61.0% (2013). The gap between men and woman thinned appreciably. Feminine participation now accounts for 87.8% of that of men, up from 54% in 1976. This is progress we can justly be proud of.

Official history does not tell us that this type of progress—also occurring elsewhere—was specific to Québec, nor that it stands out for its vigour. The participation of women may have increased as much as 47.3% from 1976 to 2013 here, but the same progression hit over the 50% mark in the Atlantic provinces, who were coming from even farther behind: thus they did better.

Today, contrary to what we might think, Québec is still 6th in Canada, both for women's activity rate and for their participation compared with men. A rate of 61% is good, but less so when we consider Manitoba's 63.3%, Saskatchewan's 64.1% or Alberta's 66.8%. Likewise, 87.8% of the figure for men looks good, but not so good next to that of Prince Edward Island, Nova Scotia, New Brunswick, Ontario or British Columbia, and this leads us to three remarks worth making.

First, the weight of the past always counterbalances these statistics, for they include older female workers from generations in which changes were less profound. If we confine ourselves to women from 25 to 44 years of age—people young enough to have grown up free of the Duplessis influence—then their performance is exemplary. Their rate then climbs to 84.5%, higher than the Canadian average of 82.7%, also the highest in Canada with the exception of the home province of Anne of Green Gables. In Québec, these younger women work out to 94.3% of men's rate, the best in Canada.

Second, the economic situation of each province can have impressive effects on the presence of women. Generally speaking, it is in the poorer provinces that women's participation is closest to men's. In the Prairies, it seems that inversely there is a levelling off for women.

Why? Is it because the type of development defined by resources leads to traditionally masculine jobs and, further, attracts male employees from other provinces? Is it because prosperity discourages female employment, thus inversely explaining that women in the Atlantic provinces work more in order to make ends meet?

Thirdly, the progress in Québec's network of subsidized daycare has also been spectacular and has been credited with some of this progress, but certain provinces such as Nova Scotia, New Brunswick and Saskatchewan, without such encouragement, have done better. This weakens the argument that daycare makes a big difference. Still, although its role in getting women into the labour market is not as great as might be thought, daycare is of prime importance in itself and for the general quality of life in the work-family equation.

WOMEN PAID LESS . . .

The other great measure of equality between men and women is salary. The gap in hourly wages has decreased dramatically between 1997 and 2013, particularly over the past decade. In 1997, the typical Québécoise earned 84.47% of a man's salary. In 2012, women averaged $22.52 an hour for full-time work, whereas men averaged $25.09. That is 89.76%. Canada saw the same rate go from 82.95% to 87.93%. Not only is the salary gap weaker in Québec, but we seem to be increasing our lead over Canada year by year.

However, comparing data this way can be misleading, because average figures tend to conceal important disparities within Canada. The salary gap is increased by the three richest western provinces where men

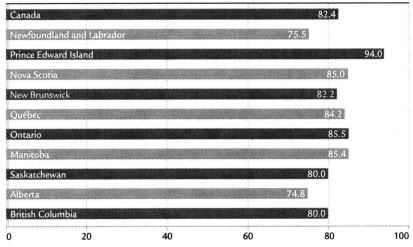

WOMEN'S PAY IN PROPORTION TO MEN'S
WEEKLY, FULL-TIME PAY, 2013

Canada	82.4
Newfoundland and Labrador	75.5
Prince Edward Island	94.0
Nova Scotia	85.0
New Brunswick	82.2
Québec	84.2
Ontario	85.5
Manitoba	85.4
Saskatchewan	80.0
Alberta	74.8
British Columbia	80.0

Source: Statistics Canada.

do much better: in Alberta, women earn only 80.2% of men's salary, in British Columbia 85%, and in Saskatchewan 87.2%. Yet these are weaker than in Québec, the Atlantic provinces, Ontario and Manitoba, which once again puts us in 6th place. It is worth noting that hourly pay in Prince Edward Island is higher for women than for men, a reflection, I believe, not so much of social progress as the special nature of the labour market.

The measure of equality is perhaps more realistic if we compare weekly salaries for full-time work. In 2013, men on average earned $980.63 a week, compared with $825.47 for women, or 84.2% of a male salary. By this yardstick, Québec once again places 5th and above the Canadian average. Progress has occurred, but other provinces are doing better, and there is still a large margin to recover.

. . . BUT BETTER EDUCATED

This is in no way the case when it comes to education, where women have caught up and clearly surpassed men. School grades are clear on this. In the latest PISA results for the OECD for 15-year-olds, girls in

Québec obtained better scores in reading than boys: 537 to 502. The 35-point gap applies to the rest of Canada as well. Like everywhere else, however, girls trail boys in mathematics (a 10-point difference) and are nearly head-to-head in sciences (one point behind boys), but do better in Ministry high school exams, with an average of 76.7% in 2011, ahead of boys at 73.9%. Their pass rate (94.7%) also surpasses boys' (91.5%).

It is likewise known that girls drop out much less than boys. In 2012, according to the federal definition of student retention, the dropout rate was 9.4% for Québec, 7.4% for the whole of Canada and 6.2% for Ontario. The dropout rate for girls was largely constant throughout Canada: 5.8% in Québec, 4.6% in Ontario, and 5.6% overall. Thus, Québec stands out only when it comes to the graduation rate for young Québécois males (12.8%), which is much higher than the rate for Canadians (9.2%) or Ontarians (7.8%).

Likewise, and for similar reasons, the number of women with at least a high school diploma outstrips men: 87% as opposed to 84% in 2010 for 25–64-year-olds. Québec girls outdo Québec boys, but remain 8th in Canada.

Women's advantage is still more notable among later generations, younger women doing better than men. Among 25–34-year-olds, women's graduation rate (92%) is five points ahead of men. Comparison with Canada shows two differences: Canadian graduation rates are higher for both men and women, but the gap between genders is less, because the number achieving high school graduation is also lower.

Women maintain their lead when it comes to post-secondary education (university graduation). Of Québécoises aged 25 to 64, 25% hold university diplomas, and this figure climbs to 34% among 25–34-year-olds and 35–44-year-olds. Women largely outstrip men, with 27% for the two age groups respectively. Nine and seven percentage points are enormous. In other words, one woman in three holds a university diploma in Québec, but only one man in four does! This phenomenon is the same for the rest of Canada, as are the disparities.

There is a new tendency to be observed: this domination by women in university is fairly recent. It was only at the turn of the millennium that the proportion of women university graduates outdid male graduates, and the gap has continued to widen for graduate degrees (masters and doctorates), with men leading before 2012, but losing ground.

UNEQUAL PAY

Women's successes within the education network shed new light on the wage gap. Here injustice and paradox hold sway: women earn less than men, even though they do better in school and are consequently better educated.

There are several factors to explain this: discrimination, pure and simple; poorer remuneration in predominantly feminine jobs—whence the under-estimation of the associated abilities; the relative scarcity of women in the more lucrative areas such as data processing; pregnancy and childcare, which interrupt careers and cause women to spend less time at work.

These inequalities in the labour market have a rebound effect on living standards and the poverty rate. Injustices occur, then, at the bottom of the scale. According to CSF (Conseil du statut de la femme—Council on the Status of Women), 76% of single-parent family heads in 2011 were women.[19] In 2012, 57.4% of those earning the minimum wage were feminine. Women without a high school diploma were possibly less numerous because they received less, but they were the most penalized: 41.2% of them earned less than $20,000. Men with no diploma did much better, with only 24.9% earning less than $20,000.

Injustices also exist at the top of the scale. A study by the ISQ published in March 2014[20] compared the average hourly wage of five typically masculine professions and five typically feminine professions. The "men's jobs" are better remunerated than the "women's jobs." There are tendencies: engineering, architecture, surveying and data processing pay around $40 an hour, while feminine jobs (teaching, psychology, etc.) offer around $35 an hour.

Other data lead one to note that remuneration can vary within a single profession. In 2012, a masculine upper cadre received $51.81 an hour, compared with $33.91 for a female equivalent: in other words a proportion of 65.5%. This case is extreme, for in general, a health-care professional is situated at 93.9% of a masculine salary, while teaching is at the same rate, and social science is at 87.5%. These gaps seem comparable with the other provinces. "Analyses," stresses the ISQ study,

> reveal that a wage-gap generally exists between men and women within a single profession. This gap gives cause for reflection. Even when women gravitate toward a typically masculine field, such as engineering, their remuneration is not as high.

According to CSF data, only 26.6% of women with a bachelor's degree earn more than $80,000 a year. This figure doubles when we examine men's salaries (54.3%).

WEAKER FEMINISM

My numerous comparisons between Québec and the rest of Canada should not be taken as a profession of faith in federalism. They are justified because we still live in a single country with common institutions, laws and practices which make such comparisons possible.

But there is another reason. Canada provides a useful standard, being an advanced country with regard to the equality between men and women, and thus we must dispel a Manichaean myth, the idea that Québec is a unique model alone in a sea of backwardness. The data presented thus far shows that Québec compares adequately with Canada, though without standing out in particular. In some cases, it is ahead; in others it is behind, and the same might be said for the US.

This is because Québec has not been a leader, but a follower busy catching up, partly because it is unable to erase all traces of the past, and partly because of its historic backwardness, and the particular forms its awakening has taken. All the energy of our rapid modernization has been devoted to questions of identity and the national question. Our vital forces are very much taken up with constitutional matters. Many women, moreover, who would be committed to the battle for equality, have diverted their energies to the national struggle. The same dynamic has played itself out on the question of the environment.

If there have been pioneers of feminism in Québec and demands made, we cannot claim to have been in the foreground as much as English Canada and the US, a country which, whatever its prejudices, is in many respects a leader in this matter, as well as on the question of wage discrimination. Québec, as elsewhere, has caught up institutionally and acquired the political tools to make considerable gains with its daycare system and parental leaves—which are unique in Canada—and its law on wage equality, as well as the CSF, which have definitely had an impact.

In the following pages, I shall attempt to situate Canada and Québec on the world stage, which is not easy, given the difficulties in comparing them.

AN ODD WAY OF RANKING

At its annual meeting in Davos, the World Economic Forum published a study, the Global Gender Gap Report, which proposed a true ranking of countries. In the February 2014 version of this highly researched 397-page document, Canada ranks 20th of 136 countries, rich and poor.

Detailed as it may be, its unusual methodology limits what we can learn from it, for it fails to measure the level women have attained in several respects, considering only the gap that separates them from men. Hence the results are surprising. For instance, Malawi is furthest ahead in female participation in the workplace, because women there work more than men. Lesotho leads in secondary school attendance, despite serious handicaps, because girls go to school more than boys: 37% versus 23%. Sweden comes in 75th, because boys do as well as girls, with 93%.

While it is useful to note the progress of developing countries, this clearly does not help us in defining Canada's position among similar nations. If we limit our comparison to the industrialized countries, Canada takes 14th place. Iceland is far ahead, followed by Finland, Norway, Sweden, Ireland, New Zealand, Denmark, Switzerland, Belgium, the Netherlands, Germany, Great Britain and Austria. Canada, however, leads the US, France, Australia and Spain. Why? Canada places 5th among the advanced countries in the first category measured: economic participation (rate of employment, wage gap, women's presence in technical professions). In health (mortality rate, female births), we come 5th among rich countries, although I fail to see reason for elation in this. Along with others, we are 1st for education, but we lose all our points for the participation of women in politics, where we drop to 14th among wealthy countries. We will return to this shortly.

OECD INDICATORS

More useful measures are likely those of the OECD, which gives neither ranking nor awards, but keeps an up-to-date set of key data on the progress of women. This also serves to remind us that economic organizations accord greater importance to women's success in society, definitely a measure of progress, but also a *sine qua non* for development and prosperity. We shall examine these indicators one by one to see, as far as possible, where Canada and Québec come in.

First, let us look at *the rate of employment* for working women from 15 to 64 years of age in comparison with men. Canada comes 7th of 40 countries measured by the OECD, with 69.6%. The gap between men and women (5.8%) is about average. Canada as a whole ranks just below the Scandinavian countries—Iceland, Norway, Sweden, Denmark—as well as Switzerland and the Netherlands. Québec fares a little better, with a higher employment rate (70.1%) and a smaller male-female gap (4.2%).

When it comes to *wage gaps*, Canada registers 19% according to the OECD data, one of the largest, far in the rear at 23rd position in a field of 28! We will not be astonished to learn that the situation is worse in Japan and South Korea, with gaps of 37% and 27% respectively, or Germany and Austria (around 20%). The OECD average is 15%. The US (17%) is less inegalitarian than Canada and most countries of northern Europe (between 10% and 15%), with the exception of Norway, outstanding at 7%.

Knowing that the wage gap in Québec is two points lower than Canada, we can place the province at about 20th, near the USA and Great Britain, which does not merit high praise.

Part-time work is a ludicrous response. There is little part-time work available for women in poorer countries such as Greece and Portugal. Firmly implanted, however, in prosperous countries, it is seen as a progressive situation that helps to reconcile work and the family, as in the Netherlands, where 60% of women are involved, or 40% in Germany and the UK. Other prosperous countries, however, tend to link progress to a limited prevalence of part-time feminine work, a symbol of equality between women and men on the labour market. It is below 20% in Sweden, USA and Finland. Canada, for its part, places 15th, near the OECD average, with prevalence at 25.6%, slightly more than double that of men. Results are similar for Québec (25.4%), where two phenomena are apparent: the proportion of women working part-time went from 17.4% in 1976 to 26.0% in 2013, but also increased greatly for men, from 4.4% to 12.8%. In other words, forty years ago, part-time work was four times more frequent among women than men; now it is twice as much.

In *unpaid work*—hours spent at domestic tasks—Canada places well enough (one of the 10 best, along with Scandinavia) among those countries where women spend 250 minutes or less per day at unpaid tasks, and the number of minutes for men is not too far off. In Canada, women spend 255 minutes a day performing domestic work, compared with 150 minutes for men. This ratio is close to Sweden (250–170), the US (250–150) and Denmark (240–180).

Concerning *education*, the OECD pays close attention to the PISA exams (see Chapter 3), and especially to the different results between boys and girls. Canada and Québec are within the norm: i.e. girls do better in reading, slightly less well in sciences, and less well in mathematics.

With regard to *pre-schooling* and the proportion of three- to five-year-olds served by the school system—crucial to the quality of life—Canada is simply out of the running. In nearly all developed countries, 80% to 100% of children are in daycare or pre-kindergarten. In Canada, scarcely 50% are because the provinces have no universal daycare plan for pre-schoolers. Québec's CPE (Centres de la petite enfance—child-care centres) are compulsory, as is kindergarten, and put us out in front: around 75% of three- to five-year-olds are registered. Nevertheless, we lag behind the European social safety nets.

The OECD studies *the power of women* through their membership on boards of governors. Canada shares last place with the Netherlands, Japan and Germany. Canadian boards include only 7% women versus 38% in Norway, 19% in Sweden, and 18% in France. These gaps are mainly due to institutional decisions. Norwegian law prescribes a minimum 40% female membership on boards. Québec has a committee set up under the Charest government—the Table des partenaires influents

(TPI—Influential Partners' Table)—which proposed that business be encouraged, rather than forced, to have women on boards.

In this, Québec fares a little better than Canada. Catalyst,[21] a not-for-profit organization, promotes the involvement of women in business. Québec boards included 19.8% women in 2014, 3rd in Canada, behind Nova Scotia (25.7%) and Saskatchewan (23.2%). These data, however, account only for state-owned companies for which a threshold of feminine representation is set. The proportion for Canada is 15.9%.

According to the TPI, around 15% of administrative posts in 100 large Canadian companies listed on the stock exchange in 2011 were occupied by women, while 26% of businesses had not one woman on their boards. In the US, according to Catalyst, the proportion is similar, with some 16% of women in *Fortune 500* corporations.

The same holds true for key management positions. In 2011, 17.7% of top cadres listed in the *Financial Post 500* were women. Companies headquartered in Québec showed 17.8% women in equivalent positions.

We are behind the times, and the reasons are both obvious and numerous. They may spring from the fact that men are more desirous of rising in the hierarchies. Women also suffer discrimination, which is often unconscious, and they are excluded from the old boys' networks. This problem is serious enough to wonder if it would not be better to resort to coercive laws, as in Norway.

The political power of women in Canada is such that we have women occupying 76 of 305 seats in Parliament (24.9%), which puts us in 17th place, just below the UK, but still far behind northern Europe.

Québec, with 41 female members out of 125 (39%) in the National Assembly after the 2012 elections, seemed to fare better. We were ahead of other provinces like Ontario, which had 25.3% women in the Legislative Assembly, British Columbia with 35.3%, and Alberta, 26.4%. In the fall of 2012, when Pauline Marois headed the government of Québec—the first woman to become premier of the province—one had the impression that Québec, like the rest of Canada, was at the dawn of revolution.

She was not alone, however. Of 12 provincial first ministers in the provinces and territories of Canada in 2013, six were women, sufficient for the traditional meetings to begin to look like a ladies' club. This did not last long, which only served to underscore the fragility of gains made by women in the corridors of power.

Of the original six, only two remained in June 2014: Kathleen Wynne in Ontario and Christy Clark in British Columbia. Pauline Marois was defeated on April 7, 2014; Alison Redford, Conservative premier of Alberta left after a power struggle within her party (though she was replaced in 2015 by Rachel Notley of the New Democratic Party); Kathy Dunderdale, resigned as premier of Newfoundland and Labrador; and Eva Aariak of Nunavut chose not to run again.

Québec also slid backwards in overall feminine representation. In the 2014 elections, the number of women elected dipped from 41 to 34, bringing their proportional representation to 27%. Québec thus rejoined the Canadian average.

CONCLUSION

What can we conclude from this overview? First, it should be noted that we do not have all the pieces of the puzzle, especially since—I must reiterate—all these comparisons and evaluations rely on what can be calculated and measured, which leaves out many basic elements, all unspoken: conversations behind closed doors, day-to-day sexism, male attitudes toward women, poverty, the apportioning of tasks, violence, the biases in institutions, laws and the justice system, social behaviour, etc.

Second, if we compare Québec to the rest of Canada, we are no exception. Overall, we equal the Canadian average, perhaps a little behind in some cases, a little ahead in others.

Some gains have been won, as we have seen with the recent improvement of women's place in the political arena, but these are still so very fragile.

On a worldwide scale, Canada and Québec both behave very much according to the English-speaking model of the US and the UK, with women occupying a more enviable place than in many other countries, including France, with whom we often like to compare ourselves. Neither Canada nor Québec figures among the resolutely egalitarian societies of northern Europe, and much remains to be done.

CHAPTER 8

ARE WE IN SOLIDARITY WITH EACH OTHER?

"In solidarity"—these are certainly words by which Québec defines itself. The speeches of our leaders are full of them, whatever their colour, and they pepper the vast debate between the "clear-eyed" and those "in solidarity," including a small political party (Québec solidaire, a left-wing sovereigntist party). Across the province people have these words on their lips, but the transition from words to action is another story. Québec may be "in solidarity," but it is not evident that its inhabitants are.

So much is the term "in solidarity" part of our self-definition that it oc-curs in the second paragraph of "Portrait du Québec" on the Québec government's website, where Québec is described as a "société moderne et solidaire." What, in fact, does "in solidarity" mean? This is not such an easy question, and surely means different things for different people. The party which chose to call itself that really means "socialist." Others use it to describe a generous, open and altruistic approach that refuses to abandon people to their fate.

Even the Liberals include it in their vocabulary. Finance Minister Raymond Bachand tabled a budget for 2012–2013, with a section on re-ducing inequality titled "Québec et la lutte à la pauvreté: pour un Québec solidaire," in which we read that "a better apportionment of wealth and the reduction of poverty correspond to a vision of society that constitutes a consensus within Québec: we must make sure that economic growth benefits all and especially helps improve the well-being of the under-privileged in our midst."

His Péquiste successor, Nicolas Marceau, in turn delivered a budget in 2014–2015, which said, "Solidarity is a fundamental value for Québécois. It is a pillar of government action in the 2014–2015 budget; we must re-inforce solidarity."

Obviously, it is a consensual word, but does it correspond to reality? In several respects it does. In its mores, Québec is indeed one of the most egalitarian societies in North America. Its policies are more redistribu-tive than most. Yet solidarity does not consist merely in fiscal policy and transfer payments; it is also a spirit of justice, generosity, openness and tolerance.

Generally speaking, I would say that society in Québec is character-ized by a passive form of solidarity working through the fiscal system, and less by an active solidarity requiring effort, commitment and genuine sacrifice.

A MORE EGALITARIAN SOCIETY

I confess to being somewhat astonished by some results of my research, having truly believed from all I had read and heard for so long, that Québec really was the Mecca of income equality in North America. This was not quite the case. Most provinces do better than Québec on this.

The Gini coefficient is the principal measure of income equality, arrived at by averaging a number of complex calculations. The number 1 denotes a society which is wholly non-egalitarian and where one person alone acquires the total income, whereas as we move down toward zero we come closer to a society which is completely egalitarian and where everyone earns the same amount. This indicator is universally recognized and followed for international comparisons. Note: the lower the figure, the better it is for those (myself included) who wish Québec to be egalitarian.

When we compare ourselves with the Canadian average, Québec looks good. The Gini coefficient for families was 0.378 in Québec in 2011, versus 0.395 in the rest of Canada. Yet, when we take a closer look, Québec's performance is less positive. Contrary to what one may think, it is not 1st among the provinces, but 6th for income equality! Three Atlantic provinces and two Prairie provinces (Manitoba and Saskatchewan) lead the list. This might not be what we expected, and why would the Atlantic and the Prairies be ahead of us?

It is surprising that Québec, with heavier taxes and social programs, plus its "cult" of solidarity, cannot build a more just society than Manitoba or New Brunswick. There is at least a partial explanation.

Inequality is due to the initial distribution of disposable income throughout society, then come mechanisms of redistribution to reduce the gaps. In Canada, there are quite simply fewer high-income taxpayers in the poorer provinces than in the rich ones. Thus income distribution is less unequally distributed from the start. Next, the redistributive mechanisms are more powerful in poor provinces, notably because of the amount of federal transfers—guaranteed income supplement,

INEQUALITIES IN CANADA
GINI COEFFICIENTS, 2011

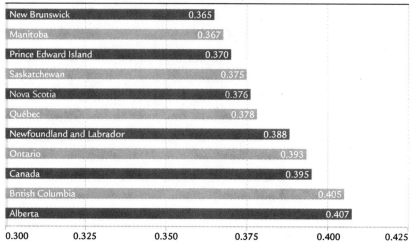

New Brunswick	0.365
Manitoba	0.367
Prince Edward Island	0.370
Saskatchewan	0.375
Nova Scotia	0.376
Québec	0.378
Newfoundland and Labrador	0.388
Ontario	0.393
Canada	0.395
British Columbia	0.405
Alberta	0.407

0.300   0.325   0.350   0.375   0.400   0.425

Source: Statistics Canada.

unemployment insurance, family benefits. Lastly, we must not forget what has been, historically, the social-democratic NDP base in the Prairies.

Québec, therefore, is not the champion we might think, but it is nevertheless more egalitarian than the other three large, industrialized and urbanized provinces: Alberta, Ontario and British Columbia, recently joined by Newfoundland.

If we compare Québec to a province that rather resembles it— Ontario—the effect of income distribution is evident. Examining family income, before state intervention, shows us that the degree of initial inequality is higher in Québec than in Ontario. The Gini Coefficient for Québec incomes is 0.517, higher than Ontario (0.512), but government transfers are higher in Québec as a result of provincial policies, yes, but with the help of Ottawa, and this pushes the Gini coefficient in Québec to 0.418, below Ontario (0.430). This is sufficient to restore our province to a more equal distribution of income. Taxes do the rest. Québec's Gini coefficient for after-tax income becomes 0.378, clearly lower than Ontario's (0.393).

We know that income inequality has been on the rise for three decades, even in Scandinavia, largely due to globalization and the tendency

WORLD INEQUALITIES
GINI COEFFICIENTS, 2010

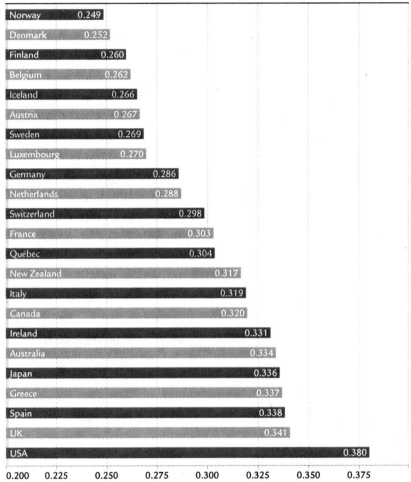

Norway	0.249
Denmark	0.252
Finland	0.260
Belgium	0.262
Iceland	0.266
Austria	0.267
Sweden	0.269
Luxembourg	0.270
Germany	0.286
Netherlands	0.288
Switzerland	0.298
France	0.303
Québec	0.304
New Zealand	0.317
Italy	0.319
Canada	0.320
Ireland	0.331
Australia	0.334
Japan	0.336
Greece	0.337
Spain	0.338
UK	0.341
USA	0.380

0.200 0.225 0.250 0.275 0.300 0.325 0.350 0.375

Source: OECD.

toward decreases in taxes, but this has not occurred in Québec. The Gini coefficient increased especially before the turn of the century, going from 0.345 in 1981 to 0.378 in 2001, although it has been relatively stable since, which is a good sign.

To sum up, although we are not Canada's champion and exception, we are nevertheless a relatively egalitarian society on the North American scale, more so than the rest of Canada on average and, not surprisingly, much more egalitarian than the US, the most unequal industrialized country on the planet. Still this comparison is somewhat less glorious when we look overseas to countries of the OECD which use slightly different data. Here Québec places 22nd, in the middle, with a Gini Coefficient of 0.304, just behind France at 12th with 0.303 and ahead of New Zealand at 13th with 0.317.

What is striking about this is that the industrialized world separates into two distinct groups. There are egalitarian societies, especially Scandinavia and the other northern European countries, which form a nearly homogenous group with Gini coefficients from 0.249 for the champion (Norway) to 0.288 for the Netherlands. All these countries, without exception, are Germanic, or at least linguistically so. This phenomenon is more sociological than linguistic, and it transcends political ideologies to a common culture and conception of society, manifestly coloured by Protestantism.

On the other hand, there are the less egalitarian countries with Gini coefficients from 0.317 (New Zealand) to 0.380 (the US). This group is homogenous. Here we find all the English-speaking countries without exception, plus Japan and the Mediterranean. In English-speaking countries—especially the US, and to a lesser degree, the UK with its former colonies, including Canada—income distribution is influenced by a culture that places a higher priority on individual initiative. In the poorer countries of the Mediterranean, there is a different dynamic of persistent and traditional social hierarchies.

Québec, with France and Switzerland, belongs to a small group with Gini coefficients of around 0.300, which are not in either camp. One might say that France has one foot in northern Europe and another in the south. In our case, the mix is still more complicated: a hybrid society, both North American and European, halfway between the individualism of the English-speaking world and the interventionism of welfare states, whether Nordic or Latin.

POVERTY

Solidarity depends not only on the sharing of income. We also need to observe what happens at the two poles, rich and poor. Here, at least, although it may not break any records, Québec does stand out—at the bottom of the scale, with Alberta and Saskatchewan. However, the prevalence of poverty here is weaker. This is determined by measuring the rate of income against the sample basket of consumer goods designed to meet basic needs.

Doing so reveals that, in 2011, 7.4% of Québec families showed clearly less poverty than the Canadian average of 8.8%. Only Alberta showed fewer families in need. The ravages of poverty are greater among those living alone, because aid mechanisms are less generous, and because it is in this group that distress is the most extreme in the fields of mental health, homelessness and isolation. The rate of low-income earners in Québec is 27.1%, 4th in Canada, but again well below the average in Canada (30.1%). For the population in general, Québec is 3rd behind Alberta and Saskatchewan, with a low-income rate of 10.7%.

How good is this? Well, it is never good, but we can say that Québec, lacking the prosperity of these two Prairie provinces, also with low rates,

RATE OF LOW-INCOME EARNERS IN CANADA
CONSUMER BASKET, 2011

	FAMILIES	PERSONS LIVING ALONE	TOTAL
Canada	8.8	30.1	12.0
Newfoundland and Labrador	8.9	31.8	11.8
Prince Edward Island	10.2	30.9	13.0
Nova Scotia	10.6	32.8	14.3
New Brunswick	9.2	27.9	12.0
Québec	7.4	27.1	10.7
Ontario	8.8	33.0	12.0
Manitoba	9.5	22.9	11.5
Saskatchewan	7.7	20.7	9.8
Alberta	6.8	24.6	9.4
British Columbia	12.5	36.2	16.5

Source: Statistics Canada.

does very well in its fight against poverty, a preoccupation that has been shared by all our governments. Politicians' efforts to combat poverty have borne fruit, and the low-income rate for families dropped from 8.5% in 2002 to 6.0% in 2009, a meaningful step forward . . . nevertheless interrupted by the crash, after which it rose to 7.4% in 2011. Notable also is the incidence of low incomes affecting children younger than 18, an absolutely crucial measure. Québec is again one of the two provinces with the greatest success—10.7%, not far behind Alberta with 10.4%. The Canadian average is much higher (13.7%), an unacceptable threshold reached by several provinces and passed at 20% by British Columbia and Nova Scotia. Other measures for poverty give Québec less desirable results.

A comparison with the industrialized countries allows us to claim a relatively enviable average. The OECD's concept of poverty is not based on need, but relative poverty among individuals in that portion of the population with incomes lower than half the median figure. This approach places the Canadian rate of poverty at 11.4%, just above the average of 11.3%, 21st out of 36, once again in the English-speaking group of countries, the Mediterranean and poor countries such as South Korea, Mexico or Chile. Québec, at 10.0%, is slightly below average at 18th, although a large number of countries in Europe show poverty rates significantly lower than ours: Germany—8.9%, France—7.2%, and Denmark—6.1%. These should be models for us.

THE "1%"

If Québec succeeds relatively well in the context of North America's struggle with inequality at the lower end of the spectrum, there is less excess at the top. We know how much income gaps (especially the disproportionate share of wealth in the richest hands) have been widely discussed, particularly in the wake of the massive "Occupy Wall Street" movement and its denunciation of the richest "1%."

Excessive income gaps give cause for considerable preoccupation to numerous economists like Thomas Piketty, whose book *Capital in the 21st Century* has stirred considerable controversy, as it has to the World Bank and the OECD, which published a vast study on the subject in 2014.[22] This study shows how far income gaps between the 1% richest

POVERTY IN THE INDUSTRIALIZED WORLD
% OF HOUSEHOLDS WITH LESS THAN 50% OF MEDIAN INCOME, 2009–2010

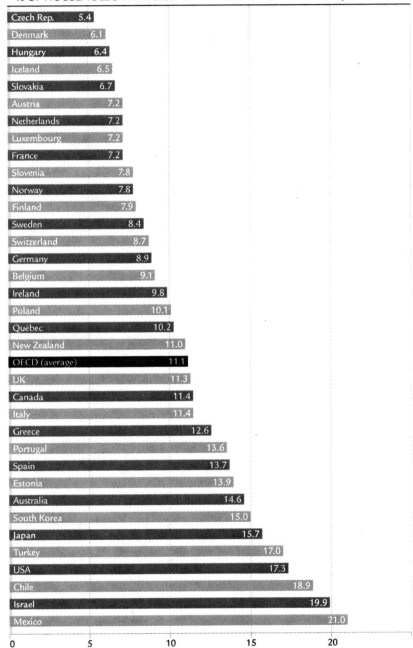

Country	%
Czech Rep.	5.4
Denmark	6.1
Hungary	6.4
Iceland	6.5
Slovakia	6.7
Austria	7.2
Netherlands	7.2
Luxembourg	7.2
France	7.2
Slovenia	7.8
Norway	7.8
Finland	7.9
Sweden	8.4
Switzerland	8.7
Germany	8.9
Belgium	9.1
Ireland	9.8
Poland	10.1
Québec	10.2
New Zealand	11.0
OECD (average)	11.1
UK	11.3
Canada	11.4
Italy	11.4
Greece	12.6
Portugal	13.6
Spain	13.7
Estonia	13.9
Australia	14.6
South Korea	15.0
Japan	15.7
Turkey	17.0
USA	17.3
Chile	18.9
Israel	19.9
Mexico	21.0

Source: OECD.

and the rest of the population increased markedly in most countries between 1981 and 2012, including Scandinavia. The phenomenon is still more evident in English-speaking countries: the income share held by the 1% more than doubled in the US, going from 8.2% to 19.3%!

In Canada, this group's share of income has increased less than in the US. According to Statistics Canada, this small minority's portion of income has gone from 7.6% in 1982 to 12% in 2011. In Québec, the increase has been a little more modest, but still noticeable, from 6.8% to 10.5%. In this respect, Québec is not Canada's champion of equality, but finds itself 5th ahead of the four Atlantic provinces and Manitoba, but behind the four rich provinces.

Still, some nuance is necessary. First, there is rich and richer. In Québec, the threshold for becoming part of the 1% is low: $174,600 in 2011. That is 21.4% less than in Ontario, where the bar is set at $221,600. Thus, in Québec, this small, select group includes millionaires, professionals and even some wage-earners, and if the entry requirements to the club of the very rich may be lower, their revenues are also: the median income of the 1% here is $241,000 against $319,700 in Ontario.

If Québec is more egalitarian than Canada as a whole, it still figures among those societies in which disparity in income is high. With 10.4% of all income held by the 1%, Québec overtakes Japan, Italy, Australia (10%), France, Spain and Norway (8%), Finland, New Zealand and Sweden (7%), Denmark and the Netherlands (6%).

Inequality in itself may not be dramatic, provided that poverty is kept low, and the situation of the majority remains comfortable, its status continues to improve, and gaps are kept in check, but the last quarter-century has seen them fall into excess, and the social contract broken. When the majority fail to benefit from economic progress, this poses a problem of social justice and calls into question the very foundations of societies like ours, societies that work on the principle that work must be remunerated adequately and that wealth creation must contribute to the improvement of society and living conditions.

AN EVER-PRESENT STATE

One cannot, in the light of all these comparisons, describe Québec as a haven of social justice in a sea of inequality as far as income distribution, poverty, and distortions favouring the rich are concerned. Rather, it is at the Canadian average. What does distinguish it are the means and practices it employs, which are unique on this continent. It has relied on a much larger role for the state, plus higher and more progressive taxes, to reduce inequalities. Public spending is higher as well, thus allowing for greater intervention to reduce the gap between rich and poor.

Public spending is equivalent to 47% of GDP—at all government levels, according to data from the Centre sur la productivité et la prospérité de HEC Montreal[23] (Centre for Productivity and Prosperity—CPP—at the HEC School of Advanced Commercial Studies at the University of Montreal). This level clearly surpasses the OECD average (39%), which also applies to Canada. It also goes farther than Ontario (38%) and all other provinces. On an international scale, Québec is one of the leaders, not far behind the champion in all categories: Denmark with 49%, and Sweden with 48%, equal with France.

By the same logic, fiscal revenue is also very high at 37.5% of GDP, even with Germany and the Netherlands, but still clearly behind Denmark (47.8%) and France (42.5%). Québec is also notable for the great gap between state expenditures and revenue. This can be explained by the fact that part of public revenue comes not from taxes, but from the profits of Hydro-Québec and also federal transfers coming from taxes in other provinces.

The result is the same, nevertheless. In his budgetary plan for 2014–2015, the Finance Minister estimated the level of Québec government expenditures at $11.3 billion above that of all other Canadian provinces combined.

It would be a serious error to believe that all of this $11.3 billion in extra spending makes up the envelope of Québec solidarity. A portion of it goes to servicing the debt—higher in Québec—to financing programs and organizations that do not exist elsewhere, to a ponderous public administration (a multiplicity of structures in health and education, for instance), to more generous business subsidies, not to mention the shameless cases of waste revealed in the wake of the construction scandals. Furthermore, Québec has adopted costly universal programs such as drug insurance and subsidized daycare, which bring about no form of transfer between the rich and the poor.

PUBLIC SPENDING
% OF GDP, 2009

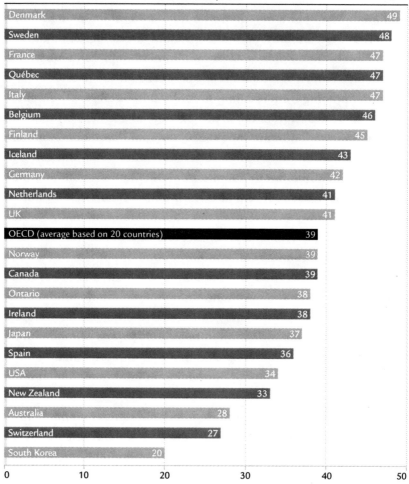

Denmark	49
Sweden	48
France	47
Québec	47
Italy	47
Belgium	46
Finland	45
Iceland	43
Germany	42
Netherlands	41
UK	41
OECD (average based on 20 countries)	39
Norway	39
Canada	39
Ontario	38
Ireland	38
Japan	37
Spain	36
USA	34
New Zealand	33
Australia	28
Switzerland	27
South Korea	20

Source: Centre for Productivity and Prosperity, HEC Montreal.

If the solidarity component in public expenditures, whatever its importance, is not always evident, it is nevertheless very much present in the area of fiscal policies, which are manifestly more progressive than elsewhere on the continent. Taxation is progressive when the rich, who possess a greater margin for manoeuvre, pay a higher proportion of their income than the poor. This notion is clearly difficult to calculate, although several indices point in this direction: for example, the fact that 37.2% of Québécois pay no income tax, or that the maximum tax rate is higher in Québec (49.97%), which puts it well above the OECD average (41%). Québec also counts more significantly on its income tax than any G7 country.

Université de Sherbrooke fiscalist Luc Godbout and his colleagues have developed a system of measures for Québec's net fiscal load,[24] a methodology refined by the OECD, that takes into account all taxes and charges, as well as monetary benefits, such as family allowances and refundable tax credits. Comparisons are made for differing family situations—couples without children, single-parent families, two-parent families—and for varying levels of average income. This approach has the advantage of including all fiscal charges and deductions (which are higher in Québec) but also what the population receives in exchange, thus giving a more precise picture of the real tax burden.

What these comparisons show is that Québec's tax load is the highest in Canada for those with large incomes, whatever their family situation, and lowest for families with weak or average incomes who have children, be they single-parent or two-parent. In other words, the fiscal system favours children at the expense of those with high incomes, a clear sign of progressiveness. On an international scale, and for the same reasons, Québec's tax burden for these categories is relatively low.

Another calculation from the same source shows that, with a rise in income, the rate of taxation grows more rapidly in Québec than in the G7 countries, which indicates that our fiscal framework is certainly more progressive.

IS QUÉBEC BEING GENEROUS?

Another way to measure the degree of solidarity in a society is by the generosity and selflessness of its citizens. This is not merely a digression; they are complementary aspects of a single reality. It is difficult to imagine a society in which collective solidarity does not project itself into an individual's life. Yet our somewhat hybrid nature seems to indicate that such a projection does not happen. If we measure Québécois by their charitable donations, they do not show themselves as generous.

In this regard, their behaviour is disappointing. In 2012, they gave $858 million to charity, barely 10.3% of Canada's $8.3 billion. The median donation was $130, which puts them far behind other Canadians. Everywhere else, median donations fall between $300 and $400. Thus, Québécois give two-and-a-half times less than New Brunswickers and three times less than Albertans. Québécois donors are just as numerous (20.7% according to Statistics Canada, working from fiscal data) compared with 23.5% in Ontario, for instance, but the amounts are much smaller.

One may look for explanations in various quarters. Perhaps, since they pay the most taxes, Québécois feel they have given enough through them and through state expenditures. Perhaps donations were once often funnelled through religious organizations, which are now far less present than they used to be.

Perhaps Québécois express their generosity toward causes that do not issue tax receipts and therefore do not appear in fiscal data. A study by the ISQ on non-receipted donations, shows that Québécois spent $1.2 billion on charitable organizations in 2010, much more than the amount

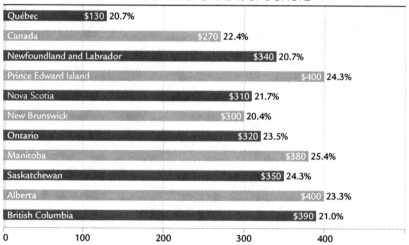

CHARITY IN CANADA
MEDIAN DONATIONS AND % OF DONORS

Québec	$130	20.7%
Canada	$270	22.4%
Newfoundland and Labrador	$340	20.7%
Prince Edward Island	$400	24.3%
Nova Scotia	$310	21.7%
New Brunswick	$300	20.4%
Ontario	$320	23.5%
Manitoba	$380	25.4%
Saskatchewan	$350	24.3%
Alberta	$400	23.3%
British Columbia	$390	21.0%

0   100   200   300   400

Source: Statistics Canada.

indicated by Statistics Canada, but there is nothing to rule out the same anomaly elsewhere.

Yet if, for the sake of argument, one accepts the explanation that Québécois are indeed less inclined to make cash donations because we pay higher taxes, this should not prevent us from finding time to contribute to the community, to those in need and to causes we believe in. But here, too, Québécois do not step up. In this case, fiscal arguments do not hold water. According to another study by Statistics Canada, 37% of us claimed we did volunteer work in 2010.[25] The Canadian average was 47%, although the figure is brought down by Québec. Everywhere else, the volunteer rate went from 48% in Ontario to 58% in Saskatchewan.

Québec's volunteers were clearly less numerous, and they put in far fewer hours to causes they supported: 128 hours on average, against 156 in Canada overall, 164 in Ontario, and 207 in Nova Scotia. What is the explanation? Are we just too busy? Not according to the statistics on hours of work. It is difficult to see any other reason than reduced commitment and lower awareness.

VOLUNTEERISM IN CANADA
NUMBER OF HOURS AND % OF VOLUNTEERS, 2010

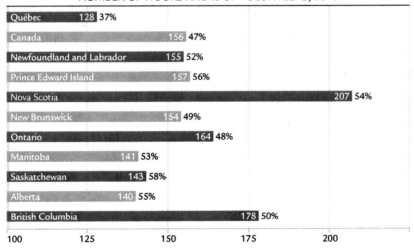

Source: Statistics Canada.

ARE WE OPEN-MINDED?

Solidarity is also a matter of showing solidarity to those who are different from us, that is, in being open to them. It is an attribute often associated with Québec, that of an open and hospitable society. This notion of a welcoming Québec takes a hit when we come to the debate around the Charte de la laïcité (Charter of Secularism), a proposed law presented by the Marois government in the fall of 2013, which uncovered an ethnocentric current of retrenchment and mistrust of others, and one which was stronger than we ever suspected.

We now know that Québec is distinct in that way. Forbidding the wearing of "obvious" signs of religion in the public service—the most litigious part of the project and also the Marois government's particular "branding"—is inconceivable in English Canada or in the US, both countries which define themselves by welcoming immigration. In this instance, we can hardly say our exception is a sign of modernity.

In this matter, Québec has been behaving like a minority, forgetting its obligations as a majority. It has also been acting as though it were a homogenous society, fearful of external threats, but forgetful that it, like the rest of the continent, has been an immigration entity since its foundation, rather than a homogenous European-style society. In fact, to validate its misdirection, Québec has had to resort to overseas examples, notably in France (a country coming to grips with its colonial past—National Front included) or the Nordic countries, where the discussion has been promoted invariably by parties of the extreme right.

The Marois government wished to present its proposed charter as an expression of openness and modernity and a defence of the grand principles of state secularism and equality between men and women, which explains its support from certain feminist groups. Yet we have also seen the PQ government pick up the baton dropped by the defunct ADQ in this matter and gaining considerable support in the less urban and less educated areas of Québec. A CROP poll published in *La Presse* in March 2014, clearly showed the Charter was supported by a majority of francophones, who expressed their unhappiness about immigration.

If 68% of francophones were for a ban on obvious religious insignia, 52% would tolerate the crucifix, but less so the kippa (37%), the hijab

(35%) or the Sikh turban (29%). We are thus motivated less by secularism than mistrust of non-Christian religions.

Fifty-nine percent of francophones found that "there are too many immigrants in Québec," and a little more (61%) supported the Charter. Thirty-two percent of non-francophones held the same opinion. A mere 53% of francophones said they felt at ease "in a neighbourhood where there are a large number of immigrants," and slightly fewer Charter supporters (51%).

As to the real fear of losing one's identity ("the immigrant communities weaken the unity of Québec"), this was expressed by 57% of francophones, but only 19% of non-francophones. The idea was stronger among partisans of the Charter (62%).

Briefly then, there is a clear correlation between support for the Charter and fear of immigration. One might say it exists in Europe as well, but this would be comparing apples to oranges. No European country is a haven for immigrants like the US, Canada and Québec. Francophone Québec seems to distinguish itself—and not favourably—from the rest of the continent to which it belongs.

Without wishing to caricature partisans of this charter, among them one does find a large number francophone Québécois outside the large urban centres who are still attached to Catholicism, and who display a certain fear of immigration, especially when it is Muslim.

In discussing this, we must remember another trait of the French-Canadian soul: a convivial society, little given to violence, who favour collective harmony and kindness in interpersonal relations. There is very little show of violent racism, no Ernst Zündel, no Front national, no Dieudonné (an Afro-French rapper widely condemned for his racism), no Tea Party.

This trait of character was measured well, in a Léger Marketing poll of Spring 2013, by asking if the refusal of a public sector employee to remove a religious symbol should be grounds for firing. Barely 35% of the population thought so, and 51% opposed. Among francophones, 40% were in favour of firing and 49% against. The more one enters into detail on this, the more the debate becomes difficult. Québécois, expressing a distrust of immigration, nevertheless do not care for a confrontation.

The proposed charter died with the defeat of the PQ in the April 2014 elections, but it still left scars.

WHAT KIND OF SOLIDARITY?

Québec, then, generally manages well with income distribution, though our performance is not exceptional worldwide or Canada-wide, and is even a little below the latter. We have also seen that Québécois are no more open or mutually helpful than other Canadians.

So we cannot really say that Québec is unique or constitutes a model; nor can we define it, as we often do, in terms of solidarity. In fact, there appears to be a disconnect between what we say—the claims of all political parties that it is a priority—and symbolic measures such as the poverty law adopted by the Assemblée nationale—and, of course, reality. Other provinces seem to do better, but with less talk. One also observes a gap between the monetary efforts made and tax revenues or concrete results. Why, for instance, does Québec, with taxes as high as Denmark's, not manage to be as egalitarian or to fight poverty as effectively? This is why it is important to try and understand what it is we describe as solidarity, its origins and its limitations.

I believe real efforts to reduce inequality do not necessarily depend on a political culture of the left, as in certain countries influenced by socialism. Politically, Québec lies within a very conservative tradition: no Paris Commune, no Spanish Civil War. Our DNA is more Duplessist than Socialist, and since the Quiet Revolution, our political culture has been challenged by the national question. The two main parties, who have swapped power to and fro for more than 40 years, are coalitions formed on a constitutional basis in which elements of left and right coexist.

Of course, other mechanisms help to explain the existence of a certain consensus, particularly in the fight against poverty, which has been waged constantly by all our governments, be they Liberal or Péquiste. These are, no doubt, communal reflexes in a minority society used to sticking together, for a long time held together by the Catholic Church, then, after it fell, by the state instead.

Québécois consider it normal for the state to help those in difficulty and expect to receive the same treatment themselves by establishing programs when necessary. Add to this the fact that the development of the state through the Quiet Revolution provided both a bulwark and a springboard for the success of the francophone minority. This created in us an attachment to our government, a tendency to lean on it and be wary of reducing its size, all feelings derived less from socialist leanings than reflexes of identity preservation. Québécois are not left-leaning, but rather statists. This defines us, the size, not the generosity of the state.

Note, for instance, that never, in public debates or in polls during election campaigns, do citizens prioritize questions related to inequality or poverty. We do not gather in the streets—except particular interested groups—to demonstrate for more social housing or an increase in social welfare. Furthermore, a report by the Conseil national du bien-être social[26] (Council on Social Welfare) revealed that, in 2009, the amounts of Québécois family welfare benefits in most situations were not more generous than in all Canada, but, in fact, rather average. Similarly, the minimum wage is not highest in Québec, but in Ontario, Manitoba and Nova Scotia.

The solidarity expressed by Québécois could best be described as passive solidarity, resting not on personal commitment or a willingness to sacrifice. In Québec, there is no tax revolt, as in the rest of Canada and the USA. Québécois accept tax increases more readily than other Canadians, and without complaint, knowing that the money will help the needy. This lack of revolt, it must be added, is in part due to a lack of mobilization that keeps us from voting with our feet. This passive solidarity can also be referred to as indirect solidarity. The absence of any tax revolt is also in part due less to the nature of our fiscal regimen (more progressive than in other provinces) and more to the fact that 37.2% of our citizens pay no income tax.

It is easier to be a spontaneous partisan of increased state intervention and an increase in the tax burden if we don't pay for it ourselves, but get others to do so . . . no irony intended. This is apparent from the CROP poll conducted for Cogeco in November 2013 showing 54% of respondents in favour of higher taxes for the rich, and 59% believing there is sufficient wealth in Québec, and we just need to distribute it better. To sum up, solidarity is for other people to practise.

There is another political mechanism in Québec which makes us appreciate social intervention. In most public discussions in favour of state support, citizens do not clamour for more aid to the underdog, but rather improvement or maintenance of services they themselves need. Perhaps this can be called "auto-solidarity." Québec's grand social battles have invariably been about universal programs which are not redistributive, but which aim to supply the same services or the same level of aid to all, and which do not provide more to the down-and-out than to others. This applies to low-cost daycare, university fees, access to health care or subsidized hydroelectricity rates. In each case, battles waged in the name of the less fortunate also benefit a majority of average wage-earners. Thus, it appears, well-ordered solidarity begins at home.

One last mechanism seems also to be in play, and that is the hybrid nature of our society, clearly evident in the international ratings on poverty and inequality. I said earlier that we are a mix of Europeans and Americans, of Latin and Nordic values, in our policies and social safety-net, but this synthesis is not always for the best. When we get things from here and there, we sometimes risk choosing the worse of two options, and thus it is with the principles of solidarity. We seem to be Scandinavian and collectivist as receivers, but rather North American and individualistic as givers, then Latin in our social behaviour.

What we are missing is the reciprocity which underlies societies that are truly solidarity-minded, those which expect collective support with social obligations in return. This essentially is the social contract. Québec has evident flaws in this respect. One is naturally in the scale of tax evasion among the rich, but also among others who tolerate working and paying under the table on a grand scale, bill-less purchases to avoid paying sales tax. Entire industries function this way, construction, for instance. The extent of collusion and corruption in awarding public contracts has made Québec more typical of countries bordering on the Mediterranean than on the North Sea. All these deviations shake one's faith in the social contract and cast doubt on the legitimacy of expenditures made with our money. We live in a fragile equilibrium, and Québec cannot become a Sweden or a Denmark in America if this problem is not solved.

CHAPTER 9

ARE WE HEALTHY?

The theme of health is a difficult one, because it touches not only on science, politics and public finance, but also on some very strong emotions. I am referring to illness, fear of suffering and death. Public discussion is already complicated and potentially explosive, and it becomes literally unmanageable if one adds prejudices and misconceptions to that. I am convinced reforming this system would be infinitely easier if people were better informed, and if governments were less paralyzed by unpredictable swings in public opinion. If we were a bit more lucid, these debates would spin less out of control and be more useful.

A ton of books has been written about our health system along with a phenomenal number of studies, plus piles of reports from commissions of inquiry. I certainly do not pretend to diagnose our system in detail nor propose solutions to get us out of the permanent state of crisis in which we find it. I have written about forty articles on the subject in the past three or four years, enough to fill half this book, yet I do not feel I have done more than touch on the subject. My objective here is much more modest: once again I shall confront preconceived ideas and myths with facts. If we were more clear-headed, discussion would not careen out of control and hence be more useful, so I shall comment on seven persistent myths.

The first grand myth, to which I shall devote only a few lines, is easily deflated: health care is free. It is not. It costs money, a lot of it, and we pay for it with our taxes, indirectly, not out of pocket. Using the term "free" has a pernicious effect, for it prevents us from being fully aware of the real costs of our system of health.

A QUÉBÉCOIS SYSTEM?

The second grand myth is that our health system is our own invention, something that incarnates our specific values—a showpiece of the Quiet Revolution—and hence important to preserve exactly as it is.

Historically this is false. It was created in two stages: first came hospital insurance in the 1960s. Then came health insurance in the 1970s. Both were initiatives of the government of Canada, which wanted all provinces to have access to a program conceived in Saskatchewan. It promised the provinces it would finance a large part of the plan. Health is constitutionally a provincial responsibility, each one creating its own formula while respecting the criteria established by Ottawa. In Québec, it emerged from the Castonguay-Nepveu Commission Report, one of whose authors, Claude Castonguay, became Health Minister in the government of Robert Bourassa so he could put in place the system he himself had planned. It was at first a variant of the Canadian system with a few notable exceptions for the time, including the creation of CLSCs.

The "Canadian content" in our system of health care is in the rules that underlie the provinces' actions, imposed by Ottawa as pre-conditions for federal subsidies. These were reinforced by the Pierre Trudeau government of the time and are enshrined in law—the Canada Health Act—overseen by the central government, which is responsible for it. It outlines five conditions that must be respected by the provinces in order to receive subsidies from Ottawa: public administration, comprehensiveness of the system, universality, portability and accessibility.

Behind this law is one overriding principle that must be staunchly defended: a citizen should never be deprived of quality care for lack of means. By enshrining this principle in law, and by framing it in five exact and immutable principles, the federal government postulated that there is only one acceptable way to reach this greater objective and manage a health-care system. From this, in turn, emerged three postulates: firstly, that justice can only be assured if the system is public, next that the service must be entirely free, and lastly that the creation of such a system was incompatible with the existence of private care.

These three elements led us to a system in which the only way to ensure social justice was seen as an obligation to offer identical services to all. This principle, an illusion, is that of single-tier medicine, and in Canada and Québec it has become an obsessive dogma.

We already know—we shall return to this—that the quasi-totality of industrialized countries which share our values have not chosen this formula to reach the same goals as we have. Such a framework is extremely rigid and not conducive to change. It becomes dogma, leaving little room for initiative and renewal. It has an additional drawback, enshrining a form of trusteeship by the federal government, which must survey the provinces in an area that is their own jurisdiction, which can punish them by withholding subsidies if conditions are not met, in fact, because they are the guardians of virtue.

This Canadian dogma draws strength from several misunderstandings. Firstly, referring to the law may falsely lead one to believe that any and all transgression is illegal. In fact, it is a *policy* promulgated by the former Trudeau government. There is nothing illegal about violating it; to do so means not conforming to the federal criteria of admissibility, and is no more than a moral obligation.

Why such rigidity? In Canada, the health system plays a role in our identity, just as language does in Québec. Health is a central element that English Canadians believe helps set them apart from Americans. Hence there is great fear among Canadian nationalists that any departure from the dogma will set them adrift toward a situation much like that in the US. Examples of emotional declarations about this are numerous. Roy Romanow, former premier of Saskatchewan, for example, and Canada's then Prime Minister Jean Chrétien, who had set up a commission of inquiry, declared, "We are at a turning-point in Canadian history, because insurance is just as essential to the unity and identity of our nation, as it is to our health." Again, Michael Ignatieff, then leader of the Liberal Party of Canada, criticized the notion of a deterrent user fee to discourage abuse—as proposed by Québec Finance Minister Raymond Bachand: "This is the spine of Canadian citizenship that is at stake." In other words, touch health, and you touch the soul of the country—Canada, it should be said, not Québec.

To sum up, the system of health care in Québec is Canadian, with a Canadian architecture and Canadian criteria. Conformity is the purview of the Canadian government. Even more astonishing is the fact that Québécois, even the most nationalist, including leaders of the Parti Québécois, have adopted values which are, in essence, at the heart of the Canadian identity.

A UNIQUE SYSTEM?

The Canadian system, like its provincial variants, is unique in the industrialized world. No other country has equipped itself in quite this way, locked down by five conditions and enshrined in law. Here, we are no longer talking about a myth. Under Canadian law, every other country's health system would be illegal, none would pass inspection by federal politicians, all of whom, without exception, defend the integrity of our own.

Any offence against it is subject to controversy: any user fee or private medical act, calls up the media and political spectre of what is called "two-tier medicine." Anywhere else, such practices exist without provoking inflamed discussion as they do here, nor do they prevent these countries from attaining a high degree of justice and equity in health, and they often perform better than we do. They accept practices that are absolutely forbidden in Canada, be they private hospitals, doctors who work in both public and private sectors, deterrent user fees, etc.

The OECD, in its "Economic Study of Canada, 2010," spent two-thirds of its 179 pages on the Canadian health system, nor was it an emotional apology for a model, but rather a proposal for profound changes to the present one.

Most interesting in this study was its description of our program. The authors first had to explain our system to readers in other countries. It is here that we see how difficult it is for a foreign observer to understand the system; it forbids financial participation by patients and relatives, and excludes private care. In this, it is not only atypical, but difficult to comprehend: for example, lively debate and denunciation of the coexistence between public and private medical practice. The media make headlines of doctors choosing to disaffiliate from the public plan, yet working in the same institutions as public doctors, almost as if there were some risk of contagion, or of specialists who move from purely private practice a few weeks a year, then return to the public sector.

The mix in which a doctor works in both the free public sector and the fee-for-service private sector, is forbidden in Canada, and even considered somewhat diabolical. The fear is that doctors who do so will shift "heavier" cases to the public system, or drain cases away from it to their private practices, thus weakening the former.

Less well known is the fact that Canada, alone among industrialized nations, prevents this. Instead of managing the problem, as others do successfully, we have opted for a juridical approach. This simple fact should give us pause.

The fear of two-tier medicine and mistrust of the private sector have also led to an odd provision that does not allow a citizen to buy insurance covering private care if the same treatment is available in the public network. This absurd measure keeps honest citizens from spending their money ethically. We can blow a bundle at the casino and spend money abroad, but we cannot invest a few thousand dollars to ensure our family's health. This bizarre monopoly is maintained even when essential services are unavailable, and transforms us into hostages of the public system.

Furthermore, the prospect of minimal user fees gives us the shudders, because we assume that we are paying for services that should be free, or that the less fortunate will be discouraged from seeing a doctor, since they are taxed for being sick. Several countries have user fees: in France and Belgium, it comes to 30% of the cost per visit. In Sweden, a social-democratic country, the cost is around $30. In Germany and the Netherlands, citizens covered by private insurance pay a deductible minimum.

Private clinics and hospitals exist virtually everywhere, sometimes alongside public ones. This is the case in France, Spain, Italy, Portugal, Belgium, the Netherlands, Ireland, Great Britain, Denmark, Switzerland, Sweden, Norway, Germany, Austria, Australia, Japan and New Zealand.

A myth still persists. It is true that our system is unique, but the myth consists in the belief that being so is a virtue, unless of course, the entire Western world is wrong, and we alone hold a monopoly on the truth.

A PUBLIC SYSTEM?

Even though it is exclusive to us, we could be proud of our system if it were purer, more public than the others, something important in the world of health. No, it is not! For all its rigidity and the grand principles it stands for, ours is actually one of the least public in the West! Quite a paradox.

In Canada, 29.9% of all health expenditures in 2013 were not assumed by the state, but by citizens themselves, either out of pocket or through insurance. Québec's proportion (28.7%) is slightly smaller, in the middle of the pack, since five provinces pay a smaller portion for private care.

Thus the private sector clearly counts for more than in most comparable countries. On average in most OECD states, the private share for

2011 was 26.6%, twice as much as the Netherlands (14.4%), Denmark (14.7%) and Norway (15.1%). The UK, despite Margaret Thatcher's reforms, also went less private (17.2%), as did Sweden (18.4%) and France (23.2%). Only two well-to-do countries spent more: Switzerland with 35.1% and the US—always in a class by itself—with 52.2%. Like the rest of Canada, Québec was above average at 12th place among 30 OECD countries.

Fascinating, is it not, a country on the prowl for any hint of privatization—an offence against its fundamental values—actually counts less on public expenditure than most countries to which it compares itself?

There is an explanation for this, but no excuse. The marked presence of private health care is due to the fact that, while hospitalization and medical treatments are nearly all assumed by the state, a great many services are not fully covered. Strictly speaking, the private sector is scarcely evident in the health network: 90.9% of Canadian hospital expenditures and 98.9% of doctors' fees are public, yet consumers, or their insurance, pay 91.9% for other professionals and 61.9% for medication.

Thus in reality, there are two parallel health networks in Canada. The first was created in the 1960s. This public one provides free and universal treatment, with doctors and hospitals confined to a strict legal framework. It is nearly perfect, the hardest and fastest in the Western world, with a minimal private presence, which is frequently decried if it goes too far. The problem is that the boundaries of this public regimen were drawn 30 years ago and have not changed to take account of any new development in the health-care situation.

The other regimen involves anything not covered, or imperfectly so, by the initial public one: medication, dental care, eye care, a considerable portion of psychological treatment, physiotherapy, several diagnostic tests and care of the elderly. Here, the private sector has a large role to play.

The average Canadian citizen has the inalienable right to be treated free for the flu or an anal itch, but if he has no money for expensive treatment or medication (except in Québec), if he loses his teeth, or if he needs rapid quality care for an aging relative, well, that is just too bad!

Here is two-tier medicine for you. Both the Canadian system and its

Québécois variant are schizophrenic. On the one hand, classic medicine is virtually Cuban, but the rest—dental care, diagnostics, glasses, medication, physiotherapy, elder care, psychology and psychiatry—is little or poorly covered by the public scheme and falls into the realm of American-style chaos.

Our situation, frozen in time, seems somewhat hypocritical. Yes, it is public and free, but not truly universal. We passionately defend its public essence, while conveniently forgetting that the state does not play its role correctly, and that coverage is less complete here than in most advanced countries. The recommendations of the OECD study on Canada, often labelled as right-leaning, called for the expansion of coverage to include "essential pharmaceutical products and, when the time comes, home care, a selection of therapies and nursing services." The OECD proposes that Canada expand its public system, not shrink it.

Nor is this all. It is easy to forget that an important share of expenditures made by the state go to financial activities outside the public sector, including doctors' remuneration—more than $5 billion of the overall $30 billion devoted to health. In general, doctors are not employed by the state, but independent professionals, more paid on the basis of fee-for-service, consultants and suppliers, often owners or partners in private clinics. The existence of a private network *within* one which is "public" seems to trouble no one, except when it comes to surgery.

There is considerable confusion over the way in which health activity is shared between the public and private spheres. If we are not clear on what is public and what is private, it is hard to have a calm and enlightened conversation on the subject.

AN EFFECTIVE SYSTEM?

This sharing between the private and public spheres would appear to be less troublesome if, owing to its unique nature, our system were the best in the world, but it is not, as numerous comparisons have shown. Overall, the Canadian system, not a bad one, is about average on the scale of the industrialized world, and so is Québec's.

About ten years ago, the Canadian government and the provinces opted not to upset their health system too much, but simply to inject a good deal of money in order to improve it. We can call this the "improved status quo," and within it, from 2003 to 2012, health expenditures in Canada went from $124 billion to $207 billion, or nearly three times the inflation rate. Québec's annual growth was 5.6%. What was the result of this $83 billion injection? Next to nothing.

So concluded Health Council Canada, an independent consultative body established by Ottawa to follow and measure the progress of our system of health after the federal-provincial accords of 2004: "A decade of reforms following these accords has led to only modest improvements in the area of health and health care. The expected transformation never occurred. It is time to reorient."[27] This is not a cry of alarm, but rather of despair.

The report compared Canada to 10 rich countries possessing similar institutions: New Zealand, the Netherlands, the US, the UK, France, Australia, Germany, Sweden, Switzerland and Norway. With expenditures equivalent to 11.2% of GDP, Canada is one of the countries that devote the most resources to health, along with the US, France and Netherlands. It is out in front on expenditures, but not for the performance of its system. This is the great Canadian paradox.

According to the report, Canada is in the median compared with other countries: for example, 5th of 11 in life expectancy, 7th of 11 in prevalence of multiple chronic illnesses, 7th of 11 in mortality due to cancer, but 2nd of 11 in cardiac illnesses.

The area in which Canada excels is in our *perception* of the quality of care. We are 3rd of 11, behind New Zealand, and equal with Australia. Canadians are satisfied with the care they receive, which is amazing, given other results. I believe this is an expression of national pride and the ongoing comparison with the US, which is by far the worst in Western health.

Once again, this is paradoxical, because Canada compares badly for the services afforded its citizens, where it is clearly out of the running: 9th of 10 for same-day or next-day appointments, 9th of 10 for care outside scheduled hours, 11th of 11 in wait times for elective surgery, 10th of 11 for unavailability of results at scheduled appointments, 7th of 11 for information-sharing between emergency clinics and doctors, and 9th of

10 for electronic filing. To sum up, the system is medically correct, but does not take an interest in patients themselves.

The Canadian Institute for Health Information, an interprovincial body, also performed a comparative analysis, which concluded: "No clear tendency emerges from the Canadian results. By numerous indicators, Canada finds itself in the middle group of performance averages (25th to 75th percentiles). Sometimes its performance is better, sometimes worse. Other OECD countries show varying results, but no country exceeds Canada on all indicators."[28]

These results are similar enough to those published by the Health Council of Canada. Canada stands out (over the 75th percentile) in cardiovascular deaths and for citizens' perception of the state of their health. It fares poorly (below the 25th percentile) in lung-cancer mortality, infant mortality and the prevalence of diabetes. For health determiners, it places well in the fight against smoking, physical activity and vegetable consumption, but not for obesity.

For access to care, Canada is clearly above average (75th percentile) for three operations —cataracts, hips, knees—targeted by governments, but it is below the 25th percentile for the diagnosis of breast cancer, dental care (not covered), visits to a family doctor, and worst of all, for consultations with a specialist.

A third study carried out by the Commonwealth Fund,[29] compares 10 countries with the US explicitly to show that Uncle Sam has fallen down on the job. It includes Canada, Australia, France, Germany, Belgium, the Netherlands, Norway, Switzerland, Sweden and UK.

The UK comes first, followed by Switzerland and Sweden. The US is dead last, 11th out of 11. What about Canada? We are third-last: 9th out of 11 for quality of care, 8th for coordination of care, 9th for putting the patient at the centre of the system, 9th for access to care, 11th for delays, 10th for efficiency, and—the supreme insult for a country enamoured of justice—9th for equity.

In brief, Canada is average among industrialized countries, with results (life expectancy, etc.) that are good but not exceptional, yet it finds itself lagging when it comes to access and "quality of service."

So what about Québec? It is similar to Canada, but worse. Interprovincial comparisons show us as average among provinces, but lagging behind when it comes to access! This we can glean from a study of the C.D. Howe Institute[30] (among others), which applies the Commonwealth Fund data to Québec and Ontario, and then compares the two provinces to four European countries (France, Germany, the Netherlands and the UK).

Fifteen percent of Québécois questioned had no family doctor, as opposed to 4% in Ontario and 5% in the four European countries. Sixty-eight percent of Québécois have difficulty obtaining care outside normal office hours, versus 58% for Ontarians and 46% for Europeans. Forty-two percent of Québécois and 40% of Ontarians can obtain an appointment the same day, compared with 62% in Europe. Resorting to the emergency clinic for primary care is much more frequent in both Québec and Ontario (24%) than in Europe (barely 6%), but, once in the emergency, 40% of Québécois had to wait more than four hours, against 23% in Ontario and 5% in Europe.

The Conference Board of Canada, for its part, published an analysis in 2013 comparing the provincial health systems in detail.[31] The three richest provinces, Ontario, British Columbia and Alberta scored A. Québec found itself in the middle with B, like New Brunswick and Nova Scotia. Québec stands out for factors linked to lifestyle (alcohol, excess weight, smoking, vegetable consumption, but not for physical activity, where it was alone in the D category). Québec obtained B for its state of health based on 30 indicators, A for health resources, C for productivity, but it alone scored D for placing the patient at the centre of the health system.

All such comparisons are necessarily imperfect. First, because data differ from one place to another. Second, because in many cases the results depend on factors unique to a country or region, like the Canadian offensive aimed at increasing the performance of certain specifically targeted operations. Third, because these results depend not only on the system itself, but also on factors which are social, genetic, lifestyle, social inequity and political effort in the area of public health. The impact of chronic illnesses, for instance, depends a lot on the prevalence of poverty. Life expectancy also depends on road safety and the crime rate. Some

COMPARATIVE ANALYSIS OF PROVINCIAL HEALTH SYSTEMS

PROVINCE	OVERALL PERFORMANCE	LIFESTYLE FACTORS (5 indicators)	STATE OF HEALTH (30 indicators)	HEALTH SYSTEM RESOURCES (8 indicators)	EFFECTIVENESS OF HEALTH SYSTEM (47 indicators)
British Columbia	A	A	A	C	C
Alberta	A	B	B	C	B
Saskatchewan	D	C	D	D	C
Manitoba	D	C	D	C	C
Ontario	A	B	B	D	A
Québec	B	B	B	A	C
New Brunswick	B	C	D	A	A
Prince Edward Island	D	D	D	C	D
Nova Scotia	B	C	D	A	A
Newfoundland and Labrador	D	D	D	A	D

Source: Conference Board of Canada.

indicators reflect the cumulative effects of several years: lung cancers due to decades of cigarettes; or inversely, the years it takes before the deterioration of a health system shows up in statistics.

What must be remembered about Canada, and even more about Québec, is that the problems of both are not attributable to the quality of care or to medical practice, nor to the competence of professionals, but to the organization of these two systems, to their philosophies and to their attitudes toward patients.

AN ECONOMICAL SYSTEM?

Now let us look at costs. Here we are once again faced more with a paradox than a myth. The Canadian health system and its Québec variant are roughly average in their performance and results. Their costs, however, are another matter entirely. Our health care is one of the world's costliest.

There are two ways of comparing health costs between societies. The first is to evaluate the portion of resources earmarked for health by examining total expenditures in relation to GDP. The second uses the total amount spent per person.

Strangely, the two measures can send contradictory messages. Québec expenditures are very high when measured in regard to GDP. Yet they are relatively low when we consider average expenditures per person. This is a result of the fact that Québec is relatively poor, and thus its GDP is less than other comparable societies. In order to spend the same number of dollars as Ontario, for instance, more has to be spent on health.

In 2013, Québec's expenditures on health in terms of GDP percentage (12.2%) were clearly above the Canadian average (11.2%) and that of Ontario (11.5%). This is a measurement that takes into account each province's ability to pay. Thus, Manitoba and the Atlantic provinces devote more of their resources to health (between 14% and 16%). Inversely, but for the same reason, the western provinces earmark less of their GDP to health (between 8% and 9%) not because they neglect the health of their citizens, but because the relative level of expenditures is less onerous than for other provinces.

If we look at expenditures *per resident*, however, the portrait is very different. Québec is the province where expenditures are the lowest ($5,531 per person). Only British Columbia ($5,775) and Ontario ($5,835) are likewise below the $6,000 mark. The national average is $5,988. The 8% lag behind the rest of Canada seems to indicate that Québec is highly effective, but half of this advantage is owed to the fact that Québec pays less well its doctors and its other health professionals and network personnel. This is partly because the weak continental mobility of francophones allows Québec to avoid raising salaries; there is simply no possibility of a large-scale exodus to other provinces or the US, as is the case elsewhere in Canada. Lower expenditure levels are also a function of rationing higher up the chain in Québec; this is evident above all in longer waiting lists.

From an international perspective, Canada is one of a handful of countries spending the most on health. The OECD puts the US in the lead with more of its GDP spent on health (17.7%) than anyone else. This

WORLD EXPENDITURES ON HEALTH
% OF GDP, 2011

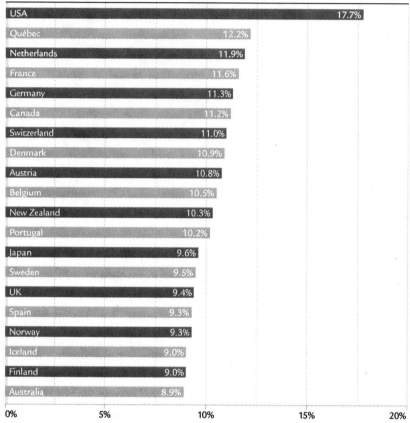

USA	17.7%
Québec	12.2%
Netherlands	11.9%
France	11.6%
Germany	11.3%
Canada	11.2%
Switzerland	11.0%
Denmark	10.9%
Austria	10.8%
Belgium	10.5%
New Zealand	10.3%
Portugal	10.2%
Japan	9.6%
Sweden	9.5%
UK	9.4%
Spain	9.3%
Norway	9.3%
Iceland	9.0%
Finland	9.0%
Australia	8.9%

Source: Canadian Institute for Health Information.

is enormous, a country beyond all norms, the only one without any real public system; yet it spends a fortune on health without really taking care of the population as a whole. Their contrasts are downright embarrassing, with private luxury medicine on one hand, and a much more extensive public network than one might suspect for the poor and elderly, but an enormous hole in the middle for citizens of modest income and those who are not eligible for insurance.

With this sole exception, the category of countries characterized by a high level of expenditure on health (between 10% and 12% of GDP in 2011) included the Netherlands (11.9%), France (11.6%), Germany

(11.3%), Canada (11.2%), Switzerland (11%) and Denmark (10.9%). Québec (12.2%) was obviously behind the US, but ahead of all the other industrialized countries, without exception!

Several countries have very good health systems with excellent results, and yet they clearly devote fewer resources to it, like Sweden (9.5%), the UK (9.4%), Norway (9.3%), Finland (9.0%) and Australia (8.9%).

The portrait changes if we view expenditures in dollars (2011 US dollars for now), and relating to data from the OECD (see the graph on page 148). The US is once again on another planet with $8,508. Next comes Norway with $5,669, Switzerland ($5,643), the Netherlands ($5,099), Austria ($4,546) and Canada in 5th place ($4,522). This is expensive compared with Sweden ($3,925), Australia ($3,800) or the UK ($3,405). We should recall that in the rankings of the Commonwealth Fund, the UK came first, Sweden was 3rd and Australia was 4th. This would appear to indicate a good system can be had for less.

In this comparison, Québec, with expenditures totalling $4,176 US, is in 10th place, ahead of France, Australia, the UK and Sweden, all countries that do better at lower cost.

Of course, some nuances are needed to better understand these rankings. For example, the UK National Health Service is not noted for luxury, and the French system is generous, but in deficit. Some countries, such as Sweden, depend a great deal on lifestyle habits to boost health and reduce dependency on health services. Less obesity, for example, means many fewer visits to the doctor. One cannot deduce conclusions mechanically from total expenditures for every country across the board and decide that, say, Québec can easily reach a level similar to Sweden's (9.6% of GDP). Still, these comparisons do show us other ways to improve the health of a population besides just pumping in billions more dollars, and that there is a way to control the explosion of costs without sacrificing quality.

SYSTEMIC SOLIDARITY?

It remains to be seen if Québec can do this. Let us review the basics. The province faces two problems. The first lies in the development of front-line care: access to a family doctor, ready access to a health professional, and wait times for emergency rooms. The ISQ estimates that 21% of

EXPENDITURES ON HEALTH PER CAPITA
IN 2011 US $

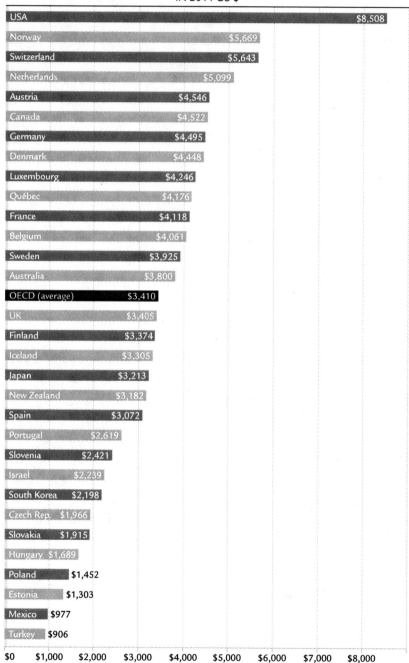

USA	$8,508
Norway	$5,669
Switzerland	$5,643
Netherlands	$5,099
Austria	$4,546
Canada	$4,522
Germany	$4,495
Denmark	$4,448
Luxembourg	$4,246
Québec	$4,176
France	$4,118
Belgium	$4,061
Sweden	$3,925
Australia	$3,800
OECD (average)	$3,410
UK	$3,405
Finland	$3,374
Iceland	$3,305
Japan	$3,213
New Zealand	$3,182
Spain	$3,072
Portugal	$2,619
Slovenia	$2,421
Israel	$2,239
South Korea	$2,198
Czech Rep.	$1,966
Slovakia	$1,915
Hungary	$1,689
Poland	$1,452
Estonia	$1,303
Mexico	$977
Turkey	$906

Sources: OECD, ICIS.

Québécois have no family doctor, even though Québec is the province with the most doctors per inhabitant after Newfoundland and Nova Scotia. The second problem is, as elsewhere, the explosion of costs. The natural growth of total health expenditures in Québec is 5.6% per year, and it is greater than economic expansion or the increase in government revenue. In fact, it will come to represent an increasing portion of overall government expenditures to the detriment of other missions, and continue to keep public expenditures in a deficit dynamic.

These problems are well known and well identified. What is more, the solutions are known already. They may not be easy to apply, but they can help, and yet we refuse to do so, or at least change so slowly that things continue to get worse. This reflects upon the rigidity of our system, its incredible inertia, and also on the reticence of the political class and society in general to approach health issues in an adult manner.

Québec has done well in initiating and developing its front-line, adding places in medical faculties in order to increase the number of doctors. We have also hit on the right formula for family medicine groups (GMF), an organization to allow general practitioners working in teams to see more patients and open their doors longer. Yet this reform has levelled out, partly because several GMFs have failed to respect their clientele objectives load, and because their implantation has been uneven. In outlying regions, it seems to be working, but in Montreal the problem is severe, because 51% of citizens have no family doctor, according to the Agence de santé et des services sociaux (Health and Social Services Agency) in the metropolis, due to the reluctance of doctors to organize themselves into GMFs. For 400 private clinics, there are barely 42 GMFs and about 30 network clinics on the island.

The development of front-line care also depends on multidisciplinarity, the creation of teams and delegations to allow doctors to share their responsibilities and free up more time for more patients. Thus the concept of clinical nurses, better trained and with more responsibilities, has been developed. This reform, though much less advanced than in Ontario, still meets with considerable resistance. The responsibilities of druggists in renewing prescriptions and dealing with certain problems have also been increased in order to free up doctors and offer greater access to health professionals. Here, too, Québec is behind the rest of

Canada, and is stalled, notably because the government refuses to remunerate pharmacists sufficiently. In both instances, resistance from medical personnel has ground things to a halt.

Behind the slow development of front-line care there is another problem. Reform is dragging, as is the growth of GMFs and the revised sharing of responsibilities associated with a change in the practice of medicine. If mistakes are to be avoided, the way in which doctors are remunerated must be changed, so they can be encouraged to modify their work habits and adapt to the altered nature of their activities. The best way to do this is to remunerate them according to their pool of patients, and not according to fee-for-service, as they are presently. This approach would facilitate the reorganization of work, the intelligent delegation of tasks, and use of the Internet. This essential reform is, at best, broached with great timidity.

As to cost control, the network has aimed at efficiency and efficacy for two decades, and has often been straitjacketed by the logic of accountancy dictated by budget cuts. The former Minister of Health in the Charest government, Yves Bolduc, relied heavily on the techniques of modern management, like the Toyota method. Most of the time, however, the network has been limping from one set of compressions to another, often responding with arbitrary measures.

There are, however, other ways of controlling expenses than by budget cuts. The most promising reform in this regard is not necessarily the most spectacular, nor the most visible to patients, but it will have a profound impact. It consists of rethinking hospital financing in such a way that the money follows a patient, as it does a doctor. At present, hospitals are subsidized on a historical basis, quite independently of the volume of their activities, except in the case of certain surgical operations. This mode of financing provides no incentive to perform better, and it may even penalize certain praiseworthy initiatives.

Financing by activity, on the contrary, encourages innovation and ongoing improvements. It has, in fact, become the norm internationally. Québec is very much behind on this point and will have trouble making up for lost time due to a lack of political will and an essential element in attaining that goal: a close knowledge of the costs of hospital activities.

A working group, run by McGill economist Wendy Thomson, submitted a report on this in February 2014 entitled "Money Follows the Patient: The Establishment of Patient-Based Funding in the Health Sector." It proposes pilot projects to make up for lost time. Well received by the finance ministers, it was not, however, by her colleagues in health. It remains to be seen if Québec will at last decide to move on this issue.

Another solution to improve the system, in terms of both cost and quality, is computerization and the use of information and communication technologies (TIC). Here, too, Québec is very much behind Canada and the world, despite having already spent a fortune on it. Thomson pegs Québec's expenses for these at $485 million in 2012–2013, yet the development of a computerized health dossier has become something of a tragicomedy from delays, cost overruns, etc.

After a decade of fruitless attempts, there are finally attempts to install, region by region, not exactly a true computerized file, but one which does give doctors access to test results. A full electronic patient file, already the norm in practically every other field of human endeavour, is still a long way off. This is no small handicap, and the symptom of a system living in an isolated bubble far from the regular laws of economics and incapable of making proper choices.

Cost control can also be achieved via the pricing of medication. Traditionally, Québec has offered better protection to the original products of pharmaceutical research companies, notably to encourage their development in-province. Our standards are robust, and they show more respect for international practices than those of Canada as a whole.

For generic copies which can be produced after patents have expired, however, Québec has been passive and contented itself with profiting from more vigorous initiatives from other provinces. This is all the more surprising, because Québec is the sole province to have installed a universal drug insurance scheme, thus disbursing more for medication. In all logic, we should also have been the leaders in cost control. The government of Québec, instead, has again been passive and ineffective in this, especially since it is the second most important item in the health budget after hospitals. The Auditor General, for example, has discovered major gaps between the prices paid by different establishments in the network, as well as a lack of harmonization with private insurers who cover half the population.

Financing hospitals and remunerating doctors by itemized act, the management of drug prices and computerization are all part of the solutions on which economists agree, and which the OECD recommended in its report on the Canadian systems in 2011. Moreover, there remain two other recommendations less likely to meet with popular approval. The first would be the installation of a deductible or user fee like those already applied in most countries, and as Québec has already done with drugs. Such a measure, forbidden by the Canada Health Act, was timidly alluded to in the budget by Liberal ex-Finance Minister Raymond Bachand, who was forced to abandon the idea even before debate could begin. The second recommendation was recourse to the private sector, not as a replacement for the public network, nor to deprive citizens of free and universal access, but rather in order to confer certain tasks on private clinics and thus stimulate competition and emulation, as well as unclog the network.

Experiments in this direction have been carried out, notably an agreement between Hôpital du Sacré-Coeur de Montréal and a private clinic, Rockland MD. Hospital surgeons rented space and support staff to the clinic in order to carry out surgical operations that the hospital could not accommodate, and by doing so reduced waiting lists and avoided regrettable delays for patients. It worked, and over eight years, 13,000 operations were carried out at an average cost of $2,456 rather than $2,679 before, and still respected the principles of free access and equity. The Couillard government nevertheless put a stop to this agreement subsequent to a veritable crusade waged by the Ministry and the Agence de santé de Montréal (Public Health Agency) against this pilot project.

Experiments like that of Rockland MD are not acts of privatization, but rather contracting out, in which the choices and financing continue to be public. The most important thing in health is not to know who does what, but rather who decides and pays what.

If we scrape off a few surface layers of this question, I believe the roadblocks will prove to be less a matter of ideology than symbols. Hospitals are the foundation of our public health system and the embodiment of its

quality. Shifting what are normally considered hospital activities elsewhere is seen as heresy, even though technology permits it, as does the
new architecture we wish for our network.

The traditional concept of the hospital enjoys huge support from hospital administrations, the health bureaucracy and unions. The sources of
resistance to this project and others reveal perfectly the forces that are
applying the brakes to change. First comes the potent corporatism of a
network that is not really a network, but an assemblage of non-commu-
nicating chambers. Corporatism is omnipresent among general practitioners, specialists, nurses, unions and the administrations themselves.
There is still another corporatist pole in the health landscape: the caste of
bureaucrats, who play an important role in the inertia of it all.

The second source of resistance derives from a dynamic fostered by
the Canada Health Act, rigid and non-responsive, which was also
assimilated by Québec. The explanation is that Canada (and Québec,
which, in this case, is in no way distinct) is the only country in the world
that has no overriding principles, no common objectives or traditions
defining the parameters of the system, but simply the Act. Thus, unavoidably, all structural change must be approached in legal terms with
lawyers, judges, etc.—even the Supreme Court, in the Chaoulli decision
(where the Court decided that the Act was illegal in that it caused excessive wait times that violated the Québec Charter of Rights and Free-
doms). This then brings us to moral questions of right and wrong as well.
Instead of wondering whether a certain measure will improve care or
not, we have to ask if it is legal.

In addition, this law and the principles behind it have fuelled a patho-
logical phobia of the private sector, which, for example, explains why the
Ministry has such difficulty coordinating insurance and pharmaceutical
companies, plus druggists, because these agents, with their mercantile
activities are not seen as partners, but foreign bodies.

Defending this system and its underlying principles has serious consequences very well identified in international comparisons. Every country
with a health system in crisis is searching, changing and experimenting
in order to improve care. Yet here, invariably, the first question we ask is:
"Is it legal? Does or that conform to the law?" We should, instead, be

posing the only questions that matter: "Is this good for patients? Will this improve our health?" The title I used for the article on Québec's decision to terminate its agreement with Rockland MD summed it up: "System 1, Health 0."

What is our health system for? Who is supposed to benefit from it? Bureaucrats? The network? A certain conception of society . . . or rather the welfare of patients? This is exactly what ex-Minister Claude Castonguay said in his own report. The first of his 13 proposals for reform was about re-orienting the system toward people. This might seem obvious, but what a revolution it would be to turn around a network originally built for the needs of its founders rather than those it was meant to serve. This would constitute a radical overthrow of the finality and workings of the system.

Being forced to defend the values of the system itself, instead of thinking about people, one ends up making decisions that go against their interests, forces them to wait, or inflicts on them a levelling down to the lowest common denominator. Thinking of the network rather than the patients forces a system supposedly imbued with a sense of justice to compromise its accessibility and to end up being less and less socially cohesive and supportive of the population.

CHAPTER 10

ARE WE "GREEN"?

On March 29, 2014, at exactly 8:30 p.m., the lights in Montreal's City Hall went out. It was our way of taking part in the worldwide Earth Hour movement. On this occasion, monuments across the globe—notably the Eiffel Tower, the Sydney Opera House and the Burj Khalifa in Dubai—were all plunged into darkness for one hour, at 8:30 p.m. respective to each time zone. The reason is not hard to guess. It was a small gesture to economize energy and reduce greenhouse gas emissions: symbolically, a moment in the dark to reflect on global warming. Despite its apparent nobility, this gesture was hollow and admirably summed up Québec's relationship with the environment and energy.

This initiative sought to remind us that small acts in our day-to-day lives can have repercussions on the environment. The French, for instance, largely count on electricity generated by nuclear power plants. Many countries, such as the US, Sweden or Great Britain (as well as several provinces of Canada), derive their electricity from thermal sources (gas, oil or coal) and these, of course, produce greenhouse gases.

Such is not the case here, for our electricity is solely produced by using renewable resources, hydro in particular, as well as a little wind power. When we douse the lights then, it has no impact whatsoever on greenhouse gas emissions. At most, it can be said that lower energy consumption would add to the water level in reservoirs and dams, thus permitting us to increase exports to American states where our energy would replace the dirtier kinds. Such a link, however, is very indirect, and this is why we can safely say that Mayor Denis Coderre's finger on the switch is hollow symbolism.

Still, it could be said we must not approach these things literally, and by extinguishing certain lights in Montreal, Sherbrooke, Trois-Rivières, Rimouski or elsewhere, we are making a useful symbolic gesture as part of a worldwide movement, and are giving voice to our preoccupation about the high stakes involved. But symbolic gestures are not neutral, and the effect might at times even be perverse. In this case, no sacrifice is required, and there is no concrete effect, especially if it gives those participating in this ritual the impression they have done something useful for the planet and a feeling of reassurance that their duty is done. There conscience is still satisfied the next morning when they climb back into their SUVs.

We are very much given to such symbols and empty gestures, if not to real change and results. There is a dichotomy between Québécois pride, persuaded as we are that we are an environmental model, and our backwardness in adopting behaviour that would make ours a green society. In this, we are almost all talk and no action.

I have already written a great deal about this, that our successes are largely due to our geography. Unlike Albertans, we are not sitting on massive oil and gas reserves or tar sands, but we do boast a part of the Canadian Shield with scattered lakes and rivers of colossal hydroelectric potential. This same electricity affords us a better environmental record than our neighbours, but the fact that we emit fewer greenhouse gases than Canada or the US is the result of geographical good fortune, nothing we can pat ourselves on the back for. Of course, we are ecological during the census time, just not in our daily lives.

My colleague at *La Presse*, François Cardinal, has written a very enlightening book on this subject, *Le mythe du Québec vert*[32] (*The Myth of a Green Québec*), which takes apart the image we have of our environmental performance and shows our behaviour and choices to be anything but green. We are not reinventing the wheel here. His demonstration dates from 2007, and it remains true, as recent data show.

THE UNIQUENESS OF QUÉBEC

Thanks to Manicouagan, but especially Churchill Falls (huge dams in northern Québec and Labrador, respectively), and of course James Bay, Québec has at its disposal a significant quantity of hydroelectricity which has had a major impact on our energy habits. In addition, it has encouraged the development of electricity-consuming industries, such as aluminum smelting plants, drawn by competitive pricing. It has also induced consumers to use electric heating, an anomaly in North America.

Thus, in 2009, electricity made up 40% of all the energy used in Québec, scarcely more than petroleum, which counted for 39% of our consumption. Natural gas was 13% of the total, and biomass, such as wood residue, 7%. Coal was a marginal 1%. In all, 47% of the energy we consume comes from renewable sources (electricity and biomass), while 53% is fossil fuel (coal, gas and oil).

The accompanying table, the Energy Report, is radically different from that found elsewhere across the globe, for fossil fuels represent 81%

of consumption, renewable energy barely 13%, and nuclear energy 6%. Our record on energy also stands out from that of Canada as a whole, with 33.2% for natural gas, 32.5% for oil, 21.6% electricity and 7.8% of coal (omitting electricity, we have a total of 73.5% for fossil fuels).

Québec further stands apart in the way we produce electricity. To us, this means water and also a little wind in the past few years, especially now that our only nuclear generator, Gentilly-2, is closed and our gas plants barely matter. This adds up to electric and renewable energy being synonymous, which is not the case elsewhere. Ontario has shut down its coal-powered generators, and derives 59% of its electricity from hydro power, with 11% from gas. Only 28% of its electricity comes from sources which are renewable. In Alberta, 40% of electricity production comes from coal, and 41% comes from gas.

Hydro-Québec's abundant energy production—one of the largest renewable energy producers in the world—has strongly affected consumer habits. Most Québécois heat with electricity, a situation found only in Iceland and Norway. This, of course, has effects, since heating counts for 64% of household consumption and hot water for 12%. Eighty-five percent of Québec households heat with electricity, which puts us in a class apart. Ontario and the West are almost entirely heated by gas, whereas the East prefers oil.

A CLEAN QUÉBEC

All of this has consequences. Québec can afford to be relatively clean, thanks to all this hydro power, which cuts greenhouse gases. Without too much effort—though we should not discount the ambitious efforts toward reducing emissions undertaken by the government—we can come up smelling sweet.

This has allowed Jean Charest and Pauline Marois to respect the Kyoto Protocol and preach to English Canada, despite having an easier time of it than Albertans, who are well aware that their prosperity relies on the production of petroleum.

It allows Québec a certain international standing, particularly considering how sensitive we are to praise from abroad. US ex-Vice President, Al Gore, himself recycled into globe-trotting for the environment, once said: "Québec is the conscience of Canada when it comes to the environment." At the Nairobi Summit in 2011, French Energy and Sustainable Development Minister Nelly Olin denounced the inaction of Canada, declaring: "I am pleased to note that not everyone is following this path, and we can look to Québec, which is committed to a very strong policy, and I salute both their policy and their courage. [. . .] It must be said [. . .] 'bravo' for them. They have understood and will take the lead over others."

This awareness is evident in numerous polls, where Québécois express their environmental preoccupations. We are not far off from other Canadians, except on the tar sands. In 2012, this energy received the support of only 36% of us, but 63% from Canadians. It is one more example of what I call our "baby seal syndrome," because nothing is easier than denouncing the ways of others.

In fact, as the graph below shows, Québécois do emit fewer greenhouse gases than other provinces. Nevertheless, Québec, a large industrialized province, still managed to put out the equivalent of 80 megatonnes

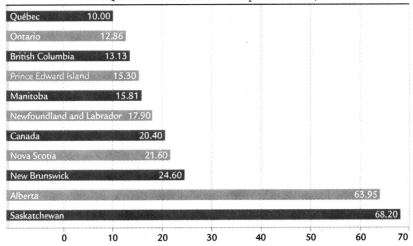

GREENHOUSE GAS EMISSIONS IN CANADA
IN EQUIVALENT TONNES OF CO_2 PER CAPITA, 2011

Québec	10.00
Ontario	12.86
British Columbia	13.13
Prince Edward Island	15.30
Manitoba	15.81
Newfoundland and Labrador	17.90
Canada	20.40
Nova Scotia	21.60
New Brunswick	24.60
Alberta	63.95
Saskatchewan	68.20

Source: Environment Canada.

of carbon dioxide in 2011, the 3rd highest in Canada, although our emissions per inhabitant are clearly the lowest in Canada—10 tonnes—half the national average, six times less than Alberta or Saskatchewan.

Given our energy record, these weaker emissions are not, in themselves, very impressive. Neverthelesss, Québec has managed to reduce emissions significantly over the past two decades—all the more difficult because it cannot count on simpler methods such as, say, Ontario, which can shut down its coal generators.

Between 1990 and 2012, Environment Canada estimates Québec reduced its emissions of greenhouse gases by 6.8%,[33] thus exceeding the objective fixed by the Kyoto Protocol, by which signatories agreed to reduce their emissions to 6% below their 1990 levels.

This success was attributable to the government of Jean Charest, not noted for his support of the environment. This is partly explained by allowing the reduction of oil consumption, both industrially and residentially, plus the slowing down of the economy after the 2008–2009 crisis and the weakening of energy-consuming sectors such as pulp and paper. Overall, however, the goal of the exercise, reducing the intensity of emissions, i.e. their importance relative to economic activity, has decreased by 30% since 1990.

The contrast with Canada is striking: its emissions increased 18.3% over the same period, despite being a signatory to Kyoto. Canada next announced a new, more modest target for 2020: a reduction of 17% below 2005 levels. The eastern provinces reduced emissions slightly below the 1990 level. Ontario, with a drop of 5.6%—largely due to the closing of coal plants—did nearly as well as Québec, whereas provinces farther west saw their emissions rise from 1990.

Still, before crowing, we need to see how Québec stacks up on the world scale. A source document for the Commission sur les enjeux énergétiques du Québec (Québec Commission on the Energy Stakes), published by the Marois government in 2013, asserted:

> It goes without saying that the level of energy consumption affects reports on greenhouse gas emissions. Thus Québec's emissions are still twice as important (10.5 t CO_2) as those of Sweden (5.3 t CO_2), a country with many similarities.

This documented imbalance reveals only a part of the truth.[34] Data from the OECD indicates that Québec, were it a distinct country, would be among those emitting the least greenhouse gases, as the graph on the following page shows. We actually do better than Scandinavia, often seen as a model for us, except for Sweden, the all-around champion. Québec places 7th out of 19. Countries boasting better emission controls constitute the large mature economies in the south of Europe—France, Italy, Spain and the UK. Relatively speaking, our record is a good one.

A GREEDY QUÉBEC

That said, things could be still better, because if Québécois, relatively speaking, are "clean," they are still greedy consumers of energy. We are among the biggest consumers on a planet which invests more and more in conservation and lifestyle changes.

Worldwide, the World Bank, the International Energy Agency and the OECD evaluate consumption in Canada as equivalent to 7.4 tons of oil per inhabitant. The Environment Canada Energy Statistics Guide sets Québec's share at 86% of pan-Canadian consumption (6.4 tons of oil). If we restrict our comparison to industrially advanced countries, Québec would be in the 5th place out of 20, behind Iceland, a country outside any norm with triple our consumption, as well as Luxembourg, another abnormal country, plus the US and Canada as the graph on page 163 illustrates. It also shows Québec equal with Finland and just ahead of Norway (5.7 tons of oil per inhabitant). Sweden is not far behind, at 5.2, while most European nations remain below 4.

What can we deduce from this? Well, Québec consumes a lot of energy, like the rest of North America, and Nordic countries consume more (Québec is comparable with Finland, consuming only 12% more than Norway). The large energy-producing nations consume more than others who pay a lot for it, like France or Germany (who suffer cruelly from a lack of energy resources). The poorer ones consume less (such as Spain at the top of the graph), and others I have not included, who consume still less (i.e., Portugal or Greece).

The same pattern of thinking holds true for electricity consumption, in which we are the manifest champions. In 2010, according to the

WORLD GREENHOUSE GAS EMISSIONS
IN EQUIVALENT TONNES OF CO_2 PER CAPITA, 2011

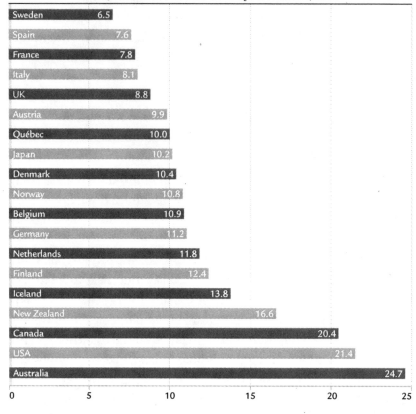

Source: OECD.

Ministry of Natural Resources, total consumption of electricity in Québec was 179.7 terawatt-hours (TWh), equivalent to 22,663 kilowatt-hours (kWh) per person. According to the World Bank, this puts Québec in 3rd place among rich, high-consuming countries, behind Iceland (52,370 kWh per person) and Norway (23,174 kWh per person). Québec consumes more electricity than the rest of Canada (16,406 kWh per person). Finland and Sweden follow with 15,738 and 14,030 kWh, respectively. Consumption in most other industrialized countries is much lower, three or four times less than in Québec (5,000 to 8,000 kWh per person).

I must add here that the argument most frequently used to make us feel guilty is that the other Nordic countries, with similar climate and

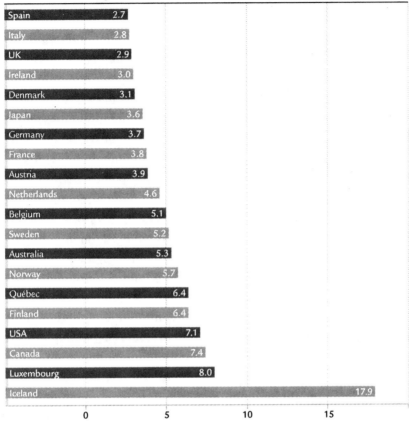

WORLD CONSUMPTION OF ENERGY
IN EQUIVALENT TONNES OF OIL PER CAPITA, 2012

Spain	2.7
Italy	2.8
UK	2.9
Ireland	3.0
Denmark	3.1
Japan	3.6
Germany	3.7
France	3.8
Austria	3.9
Netherlands	4.6
Belgium	5.1
Sweden	5.2
Australia	5.3
Norway	5.7
Québec	6.4
Finland	6.4
USA	7.1
Canada	7.4
Luxembourg	8.0
Iceland	17.9

Source: World Energy Agency.

geography, consume much less. Firstly, it is false to assert that their consumption is far different from ours, with the exception of Denmark. Next, it is likewise false to claim that climatic conditions are the same. The January night-time temperature is –6.8°C in Oslo, compared with –14°C in Montreal. Knowing that 64% of the energy consumed by households in Québec goes for heating, we get a different picture. The vastness of our territory also seriously increases our transportation needs.

I say this not to justify our behaviour, but to situate it as precisely as possible for the sake of fact, not urban legend. There is nothing spectacular about our record in this. From 1990 to 2009, consumption increased

11% here, keeping pace with demographics. There has been no real change per capita in the past 20 years, despite Kyoto and global warming and all that has been done to change our behaviour.

It is still more worrisome when we get into detail and take a closer look at four principal sectors. Residential consumption remained stable between 1990 and 2009, while demand in the commercial and institutional sectors shot up 43% over the same period, notably due to development in the tertiary economy. Industry's share decreased, especially from difficulties concerning pulp and paper, as well as petrochemicals. The real problem, however, was transport—a 29% demand—and worse still, its explosion continues. Here, energy demand has augmented by 30% per person in 20 years (up 15%). Contrary to other countries, transportation is our main generator of greenhouse gases (44% emissions). This explosion stems from the increased number of cars and SUVs on the roads, no matter what their energy efficiency. The burgeoning of just-in-time distribution rests on strong growth in the trucking industry, as well as a strong increase in demand.

Québec's industrial needs hardly justify this energy gulf, for they are falling steadily. The abundance of electricity has been a stimulus to development of such energy-consuming industries as aluminum, but this strategy has consequences, notably on what is called energy intensity: Québec consumes a lot of it to stimulate economic activity. To increase our GDP, we must consume much more energy than certain other countries—60% more than the US and 50% more than Sweden. It is a high cost for fewer results at a time when most countries are trying harder to reduce their consumption in order to boost their economies.

Thus, despite its green image, Québec is a great consumer of energy and has not succeeded in restricting demand or modifying its consumption.

WATER-DRINKERS

Pretty much the same dynamic governs our relationship with the source of life—water. The ways we use it, consume it and pollute it constitute one of the most important measures in evaluating a society's care of the environment.

A study published by Environment Canada in 2009 indicates that Québec is one of the provinces which consumes the most water: 706 litres per inhabitant a day.[35] Québec is 3rd behind New Brunswick and Newfoundland, but well above the Canadian average of 510 litres. In Ontario, a highly industrialized province, consumption is a mere 409 litres. This is a considerable gap: Québécois consume 72.6% more water than Ontarians.

One might think this is due to industrial structure or some sort of specific need—agriculture, for instance—but no, this is not the case. Québec again comes 3rd behind New Brunswick and Newfoundland for home consumption, too, at 386 litres—well above the Canadian average of 274 litres. Here again, the contrast with Ontario gives us a jolt, for the average domestic consumption is only 225 litres a day (71.5% less than Québec).

So why is this? Do we have more swimming pools? More lawns to water? More asphalt driveways to hose down? Cars that need washing more often? Is there some obsession with personal hygiene? Not a bit of it, except the archaic state of our aqueducts. Leaks are a normal part of water distribution. According to Environment Canada, they account for 14% of all the water distributed in our large cities and 7% in smaller municipalities. In Québec, however, the rate of leakage has risen to 22.1%.

This is part of the answer. The rest lies in our consumer habits. There is no specific reason—geographic, economic, social or climatic—to justify this difference . . . unless it be that we simply care less. There is a simple cause for this too: a lack of metering and hence of billing. It is all free, or so we think, and therefore it does not matter.

In principle, the mechanism of control by pricing should not be necessary if, naïvely, we believe that this is not needed for a change in behaviour. In this case, it may be that an abundance of fresh water invites citizens to treat water as an inexhaustible resource which imposes no need for economy. True, our water reserves are not threatened, and our lavish consumption hardly ever empties our water tables or lowers the level in our waterways. Montreal's water comes from Lake Saint Louis, Rivière des Prairies and the Saint Lawrence River. The water that fills our needs is only an infinitesimal part of what flows into the Gulf of Saint Laurence and the Atlantic Ocean. That is not the problem; the cost of transport and filtration for water that we waste, sewage treatment and its effects on nature . . . these indeed are.

According to OECD data relying on another concept—management of water samples—Canada is the 5th biggest world consumer of water after Chile, the US, Estonia and New Zealand. A simple rule of threes can give us an idea: Québec consumes 38% more water than Canada, is 3rd in the world with a colossal consumption that is 3 times more than Denmark, 3 times more than France and 4 times more than Germany.

This is huge, but a certain nuance is called for, as in the case of energy: in a location replete with water, it is understandable that we would consume more water, use the resources at our disposal (unless it harms the environment), and penalize ourselves with prohibitive costs for them, but in this matter it is clear that Québec is quite simply negligent and, once again, not very green.

MASTERS OF OUR OWN TRASH?

The volume of our garbage is yet another important measure of our sustainable actions. We know that Canada produces 25 million tons of garbage a year. These same data from Statistics Canada show that Québec produces 5.8 million tons, or 11 tons a minute.

In Canada, then, Québec places 2nd in its volume of waste, being the second biggest province in the country. We are 5th in production, with 733 kilos per person a year, slightly above the Canadian average of 729 kilos, overwhelmed by Alberta and Saskatchewan, the two biggest producers of industrial waste.

However, if we stick to domestic waste—a better indicator of citizen behaviour—Québécois, with 356 kilos per person, are in a class of their own. Their production is above the Canadian average of 272 kilos, and 2nd to Newfoundland among the provinces. Our neighbour, Ontario, churns out 242 kilos, 50% less than Québec, a huge gap.

We might want to console ourselves with the fact that we are beginning to cut back. Recyc-Québec, a public organization, records an important drop in the average household's production of garbage from 872 kilos in 2008 to 746 kilos in 2011.

In the "garbage world," there are two major considerations: the quantity of garbage produced—closely tied to consumer habits, from needless waste to packaging and what we do with it—and the proportion of rejected materials we manage to reuse, rather than choke dumpsites or resort to incineration. In 2010, Canada recycled eight million tons of refuse, 24.5% of the total amount. Québec's rate of recycling, using slightly differing data, was above that with 28.7%.

A devastating documentary *La poubelle province* (*Trashcan Province*) broadcast on Radio-Canada in 2012 described us as a champion of wastefulness. International comparisons are difficult to establish for production of refuse and even more so for recycling. Nevertheless, a study by the Conference Board of Canada published in 2009 estimated that Canada was the biggest producer of municipal garbage from a sampling of 16 countries. The data we have tells us that Québec, were it a country, would be 1st, ahead of Canada.

CARS

There is an environmental area where we are not "champions": cars. Our environmental actions here are nothing to brag about. Québec is below the Canadian average for ownership with 0.59 of car per person—if they could be carved up that way! Québec is 6th, equal with British Columbia and Nova Scotia. Two provinces stand at the high end of the scale—Alberta and Saskatchewan—with Ontario near the bottom. In the number of vehicles per household, Québec is truly at the very bottom with 1.35 automobiles per family, well below the average of Canada at 1.47. These results obviously depend on a multitude of factors which are beyond individual control: geography, urbanism and the availability of public transit. Still, Québec fares better.

Such a comparison can at times mask a phenomenon we observe here as well as elsewhere: the troubling increase in the raw numbers of vehicles. In 1987, the first year of data collection on public transit, there were 3,649,979 vehicles in circulation in Québec, according to the SAAQ (Québec Automobile Insurance Agency). This swelled to 5,985,463 in 2011, an increase of 2.3 million vehicles in more than 24 years: a phenomenal increase of 64%. Yet the increase in population was only 18%. The number of vehicles had thus increased 3.5 times faster than the number of citizens. This rose with the quality of life and with changes in behaviour.

Still more astonishing, this process has accelerated even more in recent years. These data count for nearly a quarter-century, beginning at a time when it might be said environmental consciousness was not what it is now, and the population was not yet aware of the impact of greenhouse gases, and so the increase in the number of automobiles could be set down to ignorance. In fact, however, the biggest rise in the number vehicles was reached in recent years, when one could no longer help being aware. Half the increase was registered over the past 10 years.

There is, however, one positive note: Québécois consume less gas than Canadians elsewhere—an average of 9.9 litres per 100 km, as opposed to an average of 10.7 across Canada. The best results are Nova Scotia's, where lower consumption is nevertheless explained by the price of gas, which is higher in Québec, and by different choices of vehicles, despite the increased number of SUVs and other large vehicles from 29% in 2003 to 35% in 2011.

Québécois' favourite vehicles are in effect less energy-consuming. *Protégez-vous* (*Protect Yourself*, a consumer protection magazine published by the Québec government) lists the top-25-selling new vehicles, and four of the leading five are compacts: Honda Civic, Hyundai Elantra, Toyota Corolla and Mazda 3—but only one truck, the Ford Series 3, which is in 3rd place. In Canada, however, the logic is quite the opposite. Two vehicles are far ahead of the competition, and both are trucks: the Ford F series and the Dodge Ram. Why? Is it because Québécois are greener, or they are less rural?

What is clear is that less of our population lives in the country; our culture is more oriented toward the automobile, a plague when it comes to the environment, and it continues unshaken—so another illusion bites the dust.

CONSUMPTION DOES IT

With dozens, even hundreds, of small, everyday gestures, we could make ourselves be more "green." The most symbolic is certainly to abandon plastic bags in stores.

This, at least, has been a veritable success in Québec. According to an Environment Ministry study in 2012, we have decreased the use of our plastic shopping bags by 52% from 2007 to 2010: there were 2.2 billion of them in 2007; in 2010, there were 1 billion. Their numbers dropped by 60% in the purchase of everyday goods. Business has voluntarily joined the program, and consumers have followed happily, urged on by a price $0.05 per bag.

This seems to have made Québec the champion of reusable bags within Canada: 95% of Québécois use them, far more than the average Canadian (74%), and ahead of Ontario (77%), Manitoba and British Columbia (66%). The western provinces are more resistant, perhaps because plastic bags are made with petroleum derivatives.

It is the kind of environmental practice that Québécois adore: a fine gesture not requiring much effort. If we take a closer look, however, we cease being champions when it starts to cause discomfort. Statistics Canada's household survey asked many questions about sustainable behaviour. By and large, Québécois are fairly average in behaving responsibly—lowering thermostats at night, using energy-saving bulbs and certified appliances such as Energy Star, etc.—and above average for shower heads which reduce water usage, plus buying locally.

How does one classify all this? L'Observatoire de la consommation responsable (Responsible Consumption Index) at the University of Sherbrooke, with the collaboration of the magazine *Protégez-vous*, has created a sustainable consumption index from 49 indicators and a complex algorithm, which shows how entrenched some habits are: more than 80% of respondents say they practise recycling, and 60% reduce energy consumption by buying locally more often. Alternative transit, is still not popular: 39% walk or cycle, 28% carpool, and only 28.2% use public transportation.

Our immediate neighbours in Ontario (68.9% in 2012) do better than us (62.3%). Ontarians also win out in composting, sustainable transportation, de-consumption (reduced consumption out of concern for the environment), civic consumption and protection of the environment. It is not necessarily recycling and consuming locally that allow Québécois to do better, for in the latter case, we cannot be sure if environmental factors provide the motivation as opposed to concerns connected with identity and cuisine.

GREAT HYPOCRISY

Québécois do not pay for the water they consume, and this helps determine their level of consumption. It is evident that the same holds true for electricity. The low price is a decisive factor in our high consumption of electricity, in which we are world champions, and hence, huge energy consumers.

This makes no sense environmentally, because low prices, by definition, encourage over-consumption and discourage efforts to attain energy efficiency, thus counteracting every current tendency. It is similarly nonsensical in economic terms, because the price charged by our state company is lower than elsewhere. This pricing policy amounts to a subsidy and leads to a poor allocation of resources, depriving its principal shareholder, the government, of significant revenue that could go toward debt reduction and program financing. This lost income (for Hydro-Québec and, thus for the government, which owns it) is colossal. If residential rates were doubled in order to reach a level we can call "normal," then the company's annual revenue would increase by $4.6 billion, completely changing the state of public finances. Depriving ourselves of our collective income, knowing how great Québec's needs are, makes absolutely no social sense.

In documents and on its Web pages, Hydro-Québec shows great pride in its low prices. Their figures show how great the gap truly is. The residential consumer living in Québec during 2013 paid 6.87¢ per kWh before taxes. Our immediate neighbours, who often buy their electricity from us or are interconnected with us, generally paid almost double: 12.48¢ in Toronto, 12.39¢ in Ottawa, 15.45¢ in Halifax, 11.82¢ in Moncton and 16.50¢ in Boston. In New York and San Francisco, consumption of 1,000 kWh/month was three times more expensive. Thus, the electricity bill for Québécois families is the lowest in North America, according to Hydro-Québec data. In fact, it may be the lowest in the industrialized world. Can this be normal?

To answer the question, I looked at Norway, another large producer of hydroelectricity, although it produces less than Québec: their per capita production is 30,000 kWh, more than our 24,000 kWh. Despite this abundance and similar production costs, they paid 86.4 øre (14.84¢ per kWh) in late 2013—twice what we paid in 2014—with a rate of 89.3 øre (a rise of 3.2%) in three months, plus 7.5% in 12 months.[36]

Sweden produces nuclear energy and hydroelectricity, and is integrated into the North Pool network with the other Scandinavians and Poland. It is here they negotiate energy exchanges.

Consumers pay a "spot" price, which can vary from hour to hour. The price of electricity may fluctuate considerably, depending on demand or

MONTHLY ELECTRICITY PRICES
RESIDENTIAL CLIENTS, 2013

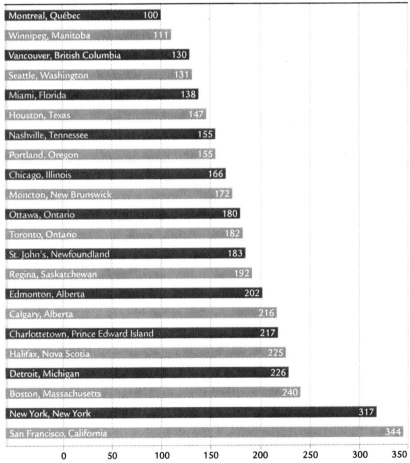

City	Price
Montreal, Québec	100
Winnipeg, Manitoba	111
Vancouver, British Columbia	130
Seattle, Washington	131
Miami, Florida	138
Houston, Texas	147
Nashville, Tennessee	155
Portland, Oregon	155
Chicago, Illinois	166
Moncton, New Brunswick	172
Ottawa, Ontario	180
Toronto, Ontario	182
St. John's, Newfoundland	183
Regina, Saskatchewan	192
Edmonton, Alberta	202
Calgary, Alberta	216
Charlottetown, Prince Edward Island	217
Halifax, Nova Scotia	225
Detroit, Michigan	226
Boston, Massachusetts	240
New York, New York	317
San Francisco, California	344

Source: Hydro-Québec.

weather conditions. In 2012, according to Eurostat, the price per kWh was €0.134, that is 20¢ (three times) higher than here. Denmark, with few electricity resources, needed to pay €0.298 (45¢). France, with important nuclear resources, commanded €0.102 (15.3¢).

Throughout the world, countries prosper from their resources. The best recipe for wealth is obviously to "hit the jackpot" by finding oil on one's territory. How do such regions succeed in becoming rich with black gold? Not by giving it away or selling it off cheap, but by getting the best price possible and profiting as much as they can from any price rise.

Québec, in its own way, is one of those sheiks ... with its "blue oil." Despite the small size of our economy, we are a great producer of it (190 billion kWh per year). This makes us 4th in the world, behind giants like China, Brazil and the US. And what do we do with this fabulous wealth? We sell it so cheaply that we almost give it away. We alone in the industrialized world have this pricing policy, just one more piece of economic nonsense that has an environmental impact.

Wind power (6.87¢/kWh) does not pay, nor do most of our other measures in favour of energy economy. Yet not one environmental organization has demanded a rise in hydro rates to help curb consumption. Why not call this the "great hypocrisy"? A society that knowingly chooses to sell its chief energy source cheaper than anyone else cannot seriously claim to be green.

Our position on hydro rates and the environmental stakes involved can be summed up as just so much bluster and contradiction.

CHAPTER 11

ARE WE HARD-WORKING?

In 2006, former Premier Lucien Bouchard dropped a small bombshell on the political landscape of Québec by challenging the idea that we are hard-working. "First," he said in an interview on the TVA network, "we've got to work harder. We aren't doing enough. We do less than Ontarians, and infinitely less than the Americans. We've got to do more!" He was right. We are no longer the valiant heirs of the settlers and explorers like Louis Hébert (widely believed to be the first European farmer in Canada in the early seventeenth century).

Reaction was, to say the least, lively, especially from the great union federations, who unanimously denounced the former premier: "Slavery is in the past," said Roger Valois, Vice-President of the CSN (Confédération des syndicats nationaux: Confederation of National Trade Unions, CNTU), and President Claudette Charbonneau, called the analysis "somewhat superficial." Québec suffered from a problem of sharing—rather than creation—of wealth, she said. Henri Massé, President of the FTQ (Fédération des travailleurs du Québec: Québec Federation of Labour, QFL), retorted that the solution lay not in a stronger work ethic, but in research and innovation: "I find Mr. Bouchard very disturbing. Perhaps he should take a walk in the real world. His declaration has offended pretty much everyone in the day-to-day world of Québec."

Even former Premier Jacques Parizeau, having a few accounts to settle with his successor, set aside his background as an economist to mount the political battle horse. "Once again, we Québécois have disappointed Mr. Bouchard. What a pity."

If Mr. Parizeau had looked at the figures, he would have seen that Mr. Bouchard was right. Québécois do work less than their Ontario cousins. This can be measured and checked against data that leave no room for doubt. The real question is not "Do Québécois work less?"—which is a fact, but "Why?" and "What are the consequences?" and "How much of a problem is it?"

THE HEIRS OF LOUIS HÉBERT?

The data are quite clear. In 2012, we worked on average 35.4 hours a week: less than the average Canadian (36.6 hours), and behind all other provinces, without exception, and very far behind Alberta (39 hours a week). Ontario, the principal partner with which we usually compare ourselves, works 36.5 hours a week . . . just one hour, not much, it might be said, but 1.1 hours make for a 3% gap, and this is not negligible. In one year, this totals a difference of 57.2 hours, nearly two weeks' work.

Of course Mr. Bouchard's style tends to amplify the reaction he received. His crushing tone and bursts of moralizing have led many to misinterpret his point and to see them as a personal attack, as if he had accused them of being lazy, when they were convinced they were hard workers. His ideas have also been distorted by an additional confusion (very current in public debate) between subjective effort and objective productivity. This reaction no doubt also relates to the image Québécois have of themselves.

The history of Québec is one of settlers leading a hard life, having had to establish themselves from nothing, clear the landscape, survive and feed their large families. Some exiled themselves farther west, in the Abitibi or the US, and worked still harder. Québec, then, is Louis Hébert, a hardy people: an image Québécois have always had of themselves, although down through the years, they may have changed and their lives become easier. Up to 1976, Québécois worked harder than Ontarians,

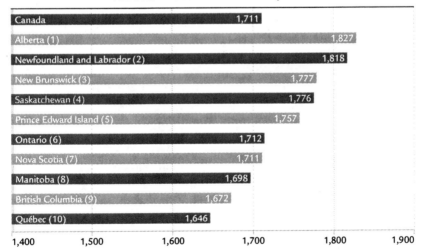

HOURS WORKED PER YEAR, 2012

Canada	1,711
Alberta (1)	1,827
Newfoundland and Labrador (2)	1,818
New Brunswick (3)	1,777
Saskatchewan (4)	1,776
Prince Edward Island (5)	1,757
Ontario (6)	1,712
Nova Scotia (7)	1,711
Manitoba (8)	1,698
British Columbia (9)	1,672
Québec (10)	1,646

Source: Statistics Canada.

but this has not been true for nearly 40 years. Now they tend to be unionized workers protected by collective agreements.

Another way to measure the same thing, and most often used in international comparisons, is the average number of hours worked in a year. This, among other things, takes into account days-off and holidays. With this measure, the gap between Québec and the rest of Canada is even bigger. Québécois work 1,646 hours a year, below the Canadian average of 1,711 hours. The gap with Ontario (1,712 hours of work) is 3.9%, and in the US, the number is 1,790 hours, so we cannot say that Québécois work hugely less, but still the 8.1% gap is significant.

We stand out not only for the number of hours worked each year, but also over a lifetime. The average retirement age in Québec is 60. In Ontario, it is 62 years, and in the US 65. The proportion of the older working population on the labour market—whether employed or not—is thus much lower here than elsewhere in Canada. For the overall population, with an activity rate of 65.2% at the end of 2013, Québec came 6th in the country, slightly below the Canadian average of 66.5%. Participation in the labour market is likewise slightly lower than in Ontario (66.4%)—our habitual basis for comparison.

This gap grows markedly with age. For 60–64-year-olds, the rate of activity is 46.3% here (10th in Canada), far behind Ontario (54.9%). For 65–69-year-olds, still fewer work here (18.8%), as opposed to 27.4% in Ontario and still more in the Prairies. Briefly then, many Québécois have stopped working at a time when, elsewhere in Canada, those of the same age continue to be professionally active. This is not good news, for it increases the impact of an ageing population on the economy.

Still more interesting in the debate provoked by Mr. Bouchard's outburst, was the incredulity of so many Québécois when faced with assertions that were nevertheless so rigorously correct. When he dropped this little bomb, a mere 39% of Québécois questioned in the Léger Marketing poll agreed with Mr. Bouchard and felt, with him, that we should be working harder. Forty-three percent disagreed. Only 29% of the young people (ages 18–34) agreed. Was it because they work harder, or because they do not want to? History does not say.

Such gulfs between myth and reality appear in other indices. A vast

2006 study by Statistics Canada—a general social study on time management—showed that Québec had the biggest proportion of people who considered themselves workaholics (28.5%) as opposed to the Canadian average of 23.8%!

A CROP poll in 2006 ordered by the Ordre des conseillers en ressources humaines agréés (Order of Certified Human Resources Counsellors) showed that 23% of respondents estimated their workload as too high.

It should be noted, however, that data on the activity rate show that there are more Québécois on the labour market than Americans, for instance. Nor does this mean that they work harder. Less work carried out does not mean fewer workers. Such a rate of activity can be influenced by several factors having nothing whatsoever to do with the desire to work: poor economic conditions that discourage job-searching, for instance; or the fact that in certain countries, the presence of women on the labour market is weak, as in Japan.

Moreover, no one, to my knowledge, says that Québécois work less than other Occidentals, but rather that they work less than other North Americans. It is well known that the work week is, in fact, short in some other countries, notably France with 35 hours.

IS WORKING LESS REALLY SO BAD?

Comparisons on an international scale can lead us to an even more interesting discussion. They show that shorter work weeks do not necessarily lead to disaster . . . far from it. We are witnessing throughout the industrialized world a gradual shortening, a phenomenon rightly associated with economic and social progress, along with the search for a better quality of life. We want more leisure time for family life: no more being a slave to work, no more wear and tear on mind and body, especially those confined to physically exhausting work or repetitive, undignified tasks.

Not so long ago in 1946, just after the Second World War, the Québec people worked 42 to 44 hours per week. In 1976, the work week dropped to 38.9 hours. In 2012, the limit was 35.4 hours, a decline of 3.5 hours in thirty years, nearly 10%. This reduction in the work week was the product of a time when the level of life was improving. It emerged from value changes, union pressures and laws, but also the benefits of prosperity.

Such strong forces do not appear to be letting up. The increasing presence of women on the labour market, notably in Canada and Québec, has forced a discussion on reconciling work and family. Young people also seem to be adopting work values different from those of their elders. The same thing is happening worldwide.

There is a very clear link between the length of the work week and relative poverty in a country: the poorer the country, the more people work. Among OECD countries, while Canada has a workload of 1,710 hours a year, this comes under the threshold of 2,000 hours in countries like Chile (2,029), Greece (2,034), S. Korea (2,090) and Mexico (2,226).

It should be noted that several advanced economies work much less than Canada or Québec: Belgium at 1,574 hours, Denmark at 1,546, France at 1,479, Germany at 1,397, Netherlands at 1,381, and Norway at 1,420 hours. In fact, Canada rather resembles other English-speaking countries: the US, the UK, Australia, New Zealand, where the tendency is to work quite a bit more. Still, in Québec, once again, we are more like the Europeans.

Several high-performing countries have short work weeks, so there is no cause-and-effect linkage between amount of effort required from workers and economic success. This is because another variable comes into play: in countries where the workload is lower and where fewer hours are worked, in fact, the whole economy performs better, for prosperity requires that the contribution of each hour be greater, that it produce more. This is obvious, of course: for a greater economic activity to involve working less, the work must be more enriching. This is the very definition of productivity measured by GDP, the value added by each hour worked.

There is an observable constant: less work coincides with greater productivity: quite a simple law really. Quality of life, measured by GDP per inhabitant results from a certain number of factors: the number of workers, proportion of them whose work is measured by the employment rate, the number of hours worked and the value added by these hours.

The French example speaks to this eloquently: the government made a hotly contested decision to reduce the work week by law—the notorious 35-hour week—but the organization in production made up for the reduced contribution from labour. This is also apparent in all European countries with shorter work weeks than Québec, where productivity is nevertheless much higher. All right, one cannot have one's cake and eat it too: if workloads are to come down, there must be modes of production that assure the same level of revenue. This is where half-European Québec has a problem: copying European work routines, but with no compensatory improvement in productivity.

THE PRODUCTIVITY GAP

When it comes to productivity, we have a big problem. The productivity of labour in Québec (i.e. GDP per hour worked) was $43.70 in 2012, putting us 5th behind (in order) Alberta, Newfoundland (pumped up by its oil), Saskatchewan and Ontario, and below the Canadian average of $47.80. Québécois, working fewer hours than other Canadians, also showed weaker productivity per hour of work.

Comparing internationally shows the true scale of the problem. If Québec does not perform well in relation to Canada, the country as a whole does not perform well on an international scale, and this places Québec at the tail end. Canada, with an hourly productivity of $47.30 US, obtains results which are modest by international standards: 15th among OECD countries, far behind leaders such as Norway, where the hourly productivity of labour is nearly double ($86.60). This can be explained partly by petroleum production, but several other countries still succeed in achieving higher productivity without it: Ireland ($71.20), the US ($64.10), Netherlands ($60.20), France ($59.50) and Germany ($58.30). Québec, at $43.20, is still lower—in 17th place between Italy and Iceland.

It must also be said that, for the moment, there is no way out. Not only is work productivity lower in Québec than in Canada and the OECD, but the growth in productivity is weaker, so much so that the gaps are increasing, not declining—this according to data presented by the CPP (HEC Montreal). Annual productivity between 1981 and 2011 was 1.08% in Québec, 1.26% in Canada and 1.94% for all OECD countries.

Weak productivity is heavy with implications. Not only because it does not allow one to make up for fewer hours of work; productivity is also the main determinant in quality of life. An insufficient level in Québec explains, as Chapter 12 will show in detail, why Québec has not attained the level of prosperity it could aspire to.

Introducing the concept of productivity into this discussion may have brought an element of confusion, because evoking it can be interpreted as a sort of reproach or accusation. This would be unjust, for if productivity is low, it is not the workers' fault. If personal choices (type of job, attitude with regard to overtime and retirement, preference for part-time jobs, values, unions, etc.) can exert a certain control on the length of the work week, they are hardly responsible for the level of productivity. Most determinants of productivity are beyond the workers' control.

Québec's weak productivity rate is not due to workers sleeping on the job or slowing down their machines. This can, of course, happen, but only indirectly, for instance, when unions or workers reject structural transformations or any other type of change or are resistant to training and retraining. With all this, the chief responsibility for a rise in productivity is not theirs. An increase in productivity depends largely on the structure of industry—the weight of traditional sectors, the ratio of small and average businesses. It also depends on business strategies, the quality of management, the tendency to innovate, the organization of work and, especially, the level of investment. This in turn depends on the fiscal context, market conditions, political climate, etc. Collective choices also play a part, such as investment in education, the harmful effects of certain industrial policies, for instance, which favour job creation over added value.

Still, the results are there to see: with less work and productivity, our situation is fragile, and does not procure an adequate standard of living or impressive salaries. We may say that this is a social choice we have made—leisure, quality of life, a balance between work and family—and the choice to work less and earn less needs to be respected. Have we truly made this choice as a society? Do Québécois really work less by choice? If so, have we done so with full knowledge of the outcome? I believe this to be far from the truth.

Several factors might explain why the work week is much shorter in

PRODUCTIVITY IN THE WORLD
GDP PER HOUR WORKED, IN 2012 US $

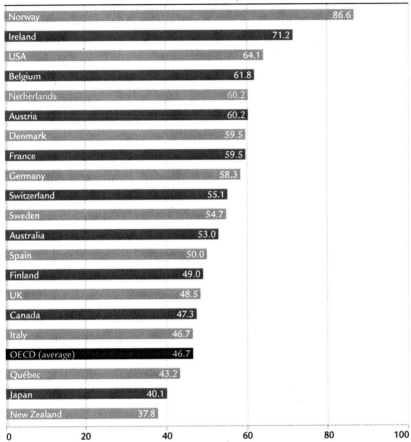

Country	GDP per hour worked
Norway	86.6
Ireland	71.2
USA	64.1
Belgium	61.8
Netherlands	60.2
Austria	60.2
Denmark	59.5
France	59.5
Germany	58.3
Switzerland	55.1
Sweden	54.7
Australia	53.0
Spain	50.0
Finland	49.0
UK	48.5
Canada	47.3
Italy	46.7
OECD (average)	46.7
Québec	43.2
Japan	40.1
New Zealand	37.8

Source: OECD.

Québec. First comes the weight of the public service, higher than in other provinces where working conditions are better than in the private sector, notably shorter work weeks, more holidays, days off, sick days and, especially, earlier retirement. The second factor is greater regulation in certain industries—construction for example. The third factor is the higher rate of unionization—39.9% in Québec to 31.1% in Canada, 28.2% in Ontario and 23.5% in Alberta—because a frequent union demand is the reduction in the number of hours worked per week. Unions also ask for time and a half or double time for overtime, as well as early retirement or the ability to leave the labour market as a result of economic or institutional factors, not from personal choice. This includes layoffs in manufacturing, which penalizes older and less mobile workers in particular. It also includes employers who encourage workers to take early retirement to reduce personnel, or the increasing weight of the public and para-public sectors in Québec, another reason for early retirement.

I am far from certain that such a decision is fully conscious. Belonging to a union is rarely the result of personal choice. Of course, citizens choose when they vote or react to what politicians and others do. Public reaction, in fact, has been fostered by public debates, which encourage the process that contributes to reducing the work week, but it is frequently an indirect consequence of which they were not necessarily aware. Several studies and polls have shown that Québécois express a greater preference for leisure time than other Canadians, and exhibit a greater propensity for *la joie de vivre*.

In order to find out if we are truly talking about our choice as a society, we would have to be directly and clearly faced with it, the question being put one way or another: do you wish for less professional activity, and do you accept reduced remuneration as a result? Do you also accept the resultant standard of living and an increased tax burden if the same level of public services are to be maintained, barring a reduction in these services? That would be a real choice.

This question is not one we can ask ourselves as long as we are convinced that we work as hard as, or harder than, others. This exemplifies a myth which blinds us to reality and prevents us from asking the correct questions . . . and getting answers to them.

CHAPTER 12

ARE WE PRODUCTIVE?

Whatever calculating or statistical methods we use, the conclusion is invariably the same: Québec, in terms of economic performance, is significantly behind most societies we like to compare ourselves with. It has to be said and reiterated that our growth is weak, and our standard of living inferior to that of our neighbours and partners.

A dozen or more years ago, researchers, economists, politicians and journalists began comparing our performance with that of other societies and measuring our standard of living. I was part of this current, with *Éloge de la richesse* (*In Praise of Riches*) in 2006. The manifesto *Pour un Québec lucide* (*Clear Heads for Québec*), launched by Lucien Bouchard, also took this approach.

The conclusion of all this—whatever the methods and statistics used—was invariably the same: Québec, in terms of economic performance, was seriously behind most of the societies we compare ourselves with. Growth is weak, and our standard of living is inferior to our neighbours and partners.

Such an approach stirred up lively reaction and interminable discussions. The very principle of these comparisons: proposing statistical calculations and interpretations which presented Québec in a less than perfect light than if one cherry-picked figures, periods, and measures—removing this and adding that, always trying to make the figures say what they did not—in order to conclude that the situation is not so bad (or sometimes preferable to that of our neighbours) is striking in that it generally reveals the two sides are not speaking the same language.

Expressions such as "in solidarity" are levelled to counter "clear-sighted" on the turf of "social justice." There is a refusal to speak of "wealth-creation," denying conclusions arrived at through performance measures such as GDP and preferring to opt for "sharing" or invoking measures of well-being instead. It can lead to statements like, "We may have less income, but we have daycare," or, "Maybe we are poorer than the Americans, but we have a better health-care system," each time comparing apples and oranges.

To avoid this confusion, I propose another way, which consists of carefully separating our reflections on economic performance from those on the financial situation in our homes. These two realities are obviously linked and influence one another, but we are not discussing the same things. I have devoted a chapter on the performance of our economy, its capacity to create wealth, and another on the way this economic context influences our well-being. The very clear conclusion is that Québec is definitely less prosperous than most comparable societies. Chapter 13 will show that Québécois, despite everything, manage relatively well—at least so it would appear—when it comes to purchasing power and standard of living.

Confusion between the two approaches arises in large part because the measure most often used: GDP per inhabitant is considered synonymous with "standard of living." The latter expression is at the root of several misunderstandings, because it implies financial ease for our citizens, individual prosperity. This is not the case, at least not directly.

GDP allows us to measure the volume of economic activity as whole revenue, or overall expenditures by consumers, governments and business, which gives the same results. It is a measure of production. It is also a measure of economic dynamism when we examine rate of growth. If we divide this GDP by the population, we can obtain data which allow us to compare economies. It is still an indicator of production, in this case, an indicator of production per capita, which allows us to evaluate the performance of the economy rather than the personal comfort of its citizens.

This is even more apparent when certain elements enlarge GDP without having much effect on citizens' day-to-day lives: petroleum revenues, for instance. Louisiana has a higher standard of living than Québec, even though the state is, in several respects, a Third World enclave within the US. This is also true for Newfoundland, with a per-capita GDP higher than Québec's, yet this is not reflected in the daily lives of its people.

All this does not mean it is a measure deprived of real meaning. It tells us about growth in a given economy, its dynamism, the power of its punch, its potential and its current performance. This is no small thing, and clearly Québec is no champion in this category.

THE ONTARIO EXPLOSION

So, how does Québec manage? Let us begin by comparing ourselves with Ontario, our neighbour and competitor for decades, also a benchmark and point of reference. As noted, we normally use GDP per capita to compare two economies, but in doing so, a portion of reality is not taken into account—demographic change, for instance. By comparing our per capita GDP with that of Canada and the US, we observe that the Canadian standard of living is slightly lower than that of the US, but these figures give no indication that one of these two former British colonies has exploded to become the principal economic force on the planet, with 320 million inhabitants, but the other, with only 40 million, is a relatively minor economy, just barely a member of the G8.

The same could be said of our two neighbouring provinces. When I began my career as a journalist in 1976, Montreal was still more populous than Toronto. Today, the Queen City is the great metropolis, fourth in size in North America with 2.8 million inhabitants, almost double the population of Montreal, which has 1.6 million. In 35 years, we have witnessed a considerable turnabout and a veritable explosion which must also be taken into account. Toronto has drawn more immigrants than Montreal, plus more citizens from other provinces (including Québec), as well as capital. This has meant more houses being built, more offices, more plants, and this dynamism has spread over the province. Economically, Ontario, not much different from Québec several decades ago, is now much more powerful, much more populous and wealthy, with a much greater power of attraction and, of course, far greater tax revenues. Between 1971 and 2013, the population of Ontario went from 7.8 to 13.5 million. Québec's, not very far behind at first (6.1 million), is now only 8.1 million. Our population growth rate was 32.9%, less than half that of Ontario at 72.5%!

This demographic fact contributes to the success and power of Ontario. This is why initially I wish to measure the true dynamism of these two provinces simply by examining overall GDP, rather than GDP per capita. This is a method not normally used, but which deserves to be put into service more often, because it allows us to measure economic trajectories more precisely.

ONTARIO'S ECONOMIC EXPLOSION
QUÉBEC AND ONTARIO GDPs, IN 2012 $

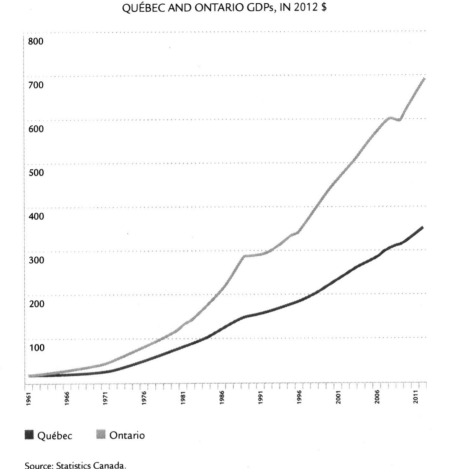

■ Québec ▨ Ontario

Source: Statistics Canada.

In 1961, the GDP of Québec was $10.6 billion. Ontario's was higher at $16.7 billion. In other words, our economy was equivalent to 64.3% of Ontario's, a gap of slightly more than one-third. In 2012, the GDP of Québec was $357.9 billion to Ontario's $674.5 billion. Ours was now no more than 53% of theirs, just over half.

The graph above is striking. In two curves, it sums up the economic history of our provinces. Québec and Ontario have gone different ways, and their economic trajectories are noticeably different. There has been an explosion in Ontario, but not in Québec, and this should be borne in mind when we compare per capita revenue, for it omits this particular dimension.

TOO SLOW CATCHING UP

Even though the size of Québec's economy has not kept up to Ontario's furious pace, the overall lot of its citizens has improved, happily enough for Québec's standard of living (GDP per capita) to have played catch-up with its neighbour.

STANDARD OF LIVING: QUÉBEC'S SLOW CATCH-UP WITH ONTARIO

GDP PER CAPITA IN QUÉBEC AS % OF ONTARIO'S

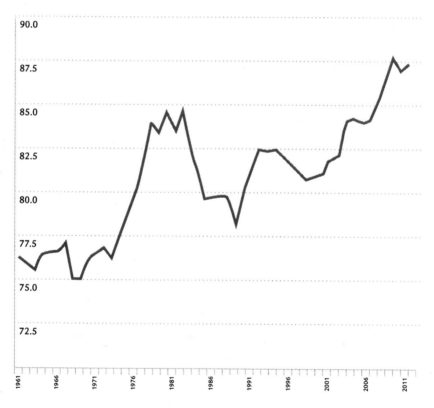

Source: Statistics Canada.

In 1961, the standard of living was equivalent to 76.2% of Ontario's. In 2012, the ratio was 88%, and the 24% gap with Ontario shrank to 12%, in other words, 50% less in 51 years. Not bad. Clearly, this is good news. The Québécois standard of living in 2012, was $44,267, only $5,512 less than $50,290 in Ontario. If Québec had not progressed during those decades, the gap would have been $11,970. While this is cause for contentment, the graph facing shows it is possible to see just how hard this catch-up was. Our recovery was slow and punctuated with failures. It is possible to discern several phases:

- The status quo—from 1961 to 1973, the GDP per capita in Québec stabilizes at around 75–76% of GDP per capita in Ontario.
- An initial leap, bringing the ratio to 83–84% between 1974 and 1982.
- A drop from 1983 to 1989, in which the standard of living in Québec went down to 78–79% of Ontario's.
- A second period of status quo, from 1990 to 2002 of about 81–82%.
- Another leap, from 2003, when the Québécois standard of living climbed to 85% that of Ontario by 2008, followed by more progress to the level of 88% in 2012. This essentially resulted from the crisis in Ontario.

This catch-up then is laudable, but the most spectacular aspects have more to do with Ontario's misfortunes than real progress in Québec. The period is also a very long one that extends over half a century, two generations. This should be sufficient time for a society to catch up completely, as certain European countries have done. Consider, for instance, Ireland or Spain. The latter's standard of living was only 72% that of France in 1980, but by the dawning of the crisis in 2008–2009, Spain had almost equalled the French standard of living at 97.4%. Why them and not us?

ONE OF THE LAST IN CANADA

The first indication that our catching-up with Ontario—especially in recent years—has more to do with Ontario's decline than our dynamism is that their GDP per capita is below Canada's. Historically, Ontario has been a rich province, richer than average. In 2003, its standard of living was 105% that of Canada as a whole. It is now at 96%, owing to the crisis and the impetus of other provinces—Alberta, Saskatchewan and New-foundland—grounded in natural resources.

The second indicator shows that Québec now lags behind the rest of Canada. In 2003, the per capita GDP of Québec was 15% lower than 9 other provinces. In 2012, the gap expanded to 20% ($44,267 in Québec to $54,822 for the rest of Canada), no small matter at $10,555. In 1961, our GDP per capita was 4th in Canada behind Ontario, Alberta and British Columbia. In 1980, it fell to 5th place, then 6th in 2000, and then 7th. This is definitely a slow decline.

If we look at the data for 2012 in the graph below, we see a GDP per capita of $44,267, superior only to that of New Brunswick, Nova Scotia and Prince Edward Island. Newfoundland, thanks to oil, has clearly out-stripped us, and New Brunswick is rapidly catching up. Their standard of living was 87.5% of ours in 2003. Now it is 94.1% (2012). Manitoba overtook us in 2006, and other provinces are closing in.

Why, then, does urbanized Québec, over-equipped with universities, with cutting-edge industries and a diversified economy, show economic results barely ahead of the Atlantic provinces?

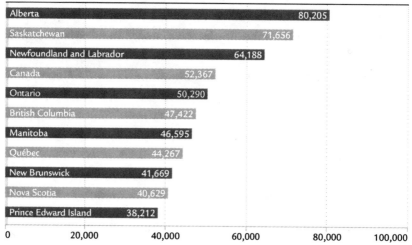

STANDARD OF LIVING IN CANADA
GDP PER CAPITA, IN 2012 $

Alberta	80,205
Saskatchewan	71,656
Newfoundland and Labrador	64,188
Canada	52,367
Ontario	50,290
British Columbia	47,422
Manitoba	46,595
Québec	44,267
New Brunswick	41,669
Nova Scotia	40,629
Prince Edward Island	38,212

Source: Statistics Canada.

ONE OF THE LAST IN NORTH AMERICA

It is possible to perform the same comparison with states in the US. Of the 60 jurisdictions, Québec and the Atlantic provinces come in last. Over the years, and depending on specific conjunctures and variations in purchasing power, the GDP per capita in Québec stands at about 55th. This exercise becomes redundant after a while: the upshot is the same— the US constitutes a rich and powerful economy, and this power is reflected in every state, even the poorer ones, just as the relative weakness in Canada's standard of living is reflected in all provinces but Alberta.

The comparison is still useful to show how far we have to go to fill the gap separating us from the neighbouring states, our competition. It can also compare us to cities like Boston that are, in some respects, our models. This tells us who we are dealing with, and the enormous gap in living standards between Québec and the states helps to measure the strength of our principal partner. For this, I will use a compilation by the Institute for Competitiveness and Prosperity,[37] an Ontario organization, which limits the comparison to 14 pairs of states, including those with which Ontario does business and can reasonably compare itself, including Québec. The reason for the latter is not clear: perhaps because our presence makes their economy look better!

Ontario ranks low, with a per capita GDP of $49,900 CAD, ahead of Florida and Québec, both at the tail end. The revenue gap between our rich neighbour and the American states in the analysis is significant. Ontario is far behind New York's $76,000 and Massachusetts' $73,000, or Illinois' $68,000. While there may be much resemblance between Montreal and Boston (their history, architecture, universities, knowledge economy), that is where the similarities end: Québec's average income ($44,267) is less than 60% of Massachusetts'.

THE POOREST AMONG THE RICH COUNTRIES

This exercise is much more troubling when we compare Québec with OECD member countries, because some of them, in size and values, are much closer to us. (We cannot reject such comparisons with the back of our hand, as might be possible with American data if we believe that their standard of living is the product of a model we reject.)

STANDARDS OF LIVING IN THE INDUSTRIALIZED WORLD
AS GDP PER CAPITA, IN US $
PURCHASING POWER PARITY, 2012

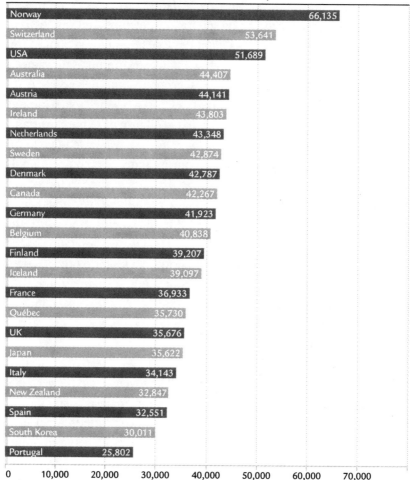

Norway	66,135
Switzerland	53,641
USA	51,689
Australia	44,407
Austria	44,141
Ireland	43,803
Netherlands	43,348
Sweden	42,874
Denmark	42,787
Canada	42,267
Germany	41,923
Belgium	40,838
Finland	39,207
Iceland	39,097
France	36,933
Québec	35,730
UK	35,676
Japan	35,622
Italy	34,143
New Zealand	32,847
Spain	32,551
South Korea	30,011
Portugal	25,802

Source: Institut de la statistique du Québec.

The results are staggering. Québec once again trails badly. It places 17th in a selection of 24 rich countries in the OECD with $35,730 US in purchasing power, a standard of living barely more than half Norway's ($66,135), which, it needs be remembered, has been pumped up by oil. Québec is also 18% behind the Netherlands ($43,348), 20% behind Australia ($44,407), and France ($36,993), despite the latter's economic quagmire. Québec is closer to Spain ($32,551), a mere 8.9% ahead of it, and it trails Belgium by 12.5% ($40,838).

In fact, Québec is 16% below the average per capita GDP of all 24 countries ($42,280), even all 34 OECD members ($36,276), despite the organization being dragged down by emerging countries like Mexico, Chile and Turkey, plus the economies of former Soviet bloc states like Estonia or Slovenia.

It is worthwhile to list all those ahead of us: Luxembourg, Norway, Switzerland, the US, Austria, Australia, Ireland, Netherlands, Sweden, Denmark, Canada, Germany, Belgium, Finland, Iceland and France.

It is even worth turning the knife in the wound to cite those that Québec has managed to outstrip: Japan (in permanent crisis), the UK (temporarily, because it has since recovered its strong growth), Italy (in its own quagmire), New Zealand, Spain, South Korea and Portugal . . . not to mention emerging countries and those of Eastern Europe.

This much is striking, however, as noted by the CPP in its report for 2013, not so long ago. Québec was for a long time average (in 1981, the standard of living was equal to that of the richer countries of the OECD). So in the past 30 years, either Québec has lost ground, or other countries have grown faster. Whichever we choose, the result is the same: a gap of 16% that did not exist several decades ago.

THE REASONS FOR LAGGING BEHIND

How do we explain that our performance has dropped so much in relation to others? According to the 2012 plan of the CPP, 90% of the growth in Canada's standard of living since 1981 is due to an increase in labour productivity. Hence, it maintains that growth in productivity is the "powerhouse of war."

This research group's preoccupations and positions lean to the right according to traditional definitions, but its analysis of productivity was enough to shake Jacques Parizeau early in 2014 and convince him that Québec needed a major remedy. Nicolas Marceau, Finance Minister in the Marois government, again relied on this analysis in a brochure on investments accompanying his first budget:

> It has been shown over the past 30 years that an increased stan-
> dard of living depends essentially on the growth of labour pro-
> ductivity. Other factors—labour intensity, the employment rate
> and demographics—are, as a group, marginal in the long term.
> Québec, however, always lags significantly in labour productivity,
> compared with other areas.[38]

The standard of living, according to classic theory, is the result of several
forces: the number of people working (size of active population and rate
of activity), work effort (hours worked) and the outcome of their work
(production per work-hour), a simple measure of productivity. Québec,
however, can no longer count on the first two factors, because the active
population has begun to decline due to ageing, and because it would be
unrealistic to believe we can convince Québécois to work more. The sole
factor over which we can exercise some control is productivity.

We have already seen in the preceding chapter that productivity is
lower than in Canada and the average industrialized country: 9% below
the Canadian level, 24% behind Germany and 33% behind the US. It is
also increasing less rapidly than elsewhere. The CPP, for whom this is a
central concern, describes this growth as "anemic."[39] Since 1981, annual
growth in average productivity has been 1.78% in OECD countries,
1.25% in Ontario, 1.16% in Canada and 1.07% in Québec.

This leads us to a second question: why are we less productive? The
productivity lag can be explained by two orders of factors. First, there are
global factors: insufficient effort devoted to the main determinants of
productivity, which play a role in all economies. Next, there are local factors, specific traits of Québec society not conducive to a growth in productivity.

If we examine how certain countries arrived at a higher level of productivity, we notice that three elements contribute to their success: investments, education and innovation. I will insist especially on investments, because the two other factors have been dealt with in previous
chapters.

Investments play an important role, not only with regard to economic
growth, but also growth in productivity. To begin with, they contribute
to creating economic activity, and next, they can modify the way we do
things, with new technologies, new procedures, and more modern and

effective installations. This is why not all types of investments play an important role in productivity. Those we do need are private investment, because productivity in an economy does not derive from the public sector; more precisely, investment in production equipment, be it machines, tools, software, telecommunication materials, or be it in the industry or in services. This scheme has been analyzed in detail in a report by Pierre Fortin, who in 2008 presided over a work group on investment created by the finance minister at the time, Monique Jérôme-Forget.[40]

Our problem, as you will have guessed, is that the level of private investment is too weak and public investment is too strong—one cannot compensate for the other because they are fundamentally different. The private share of investment in the GDP, according to Québec budget documents, was 8.8% in 2011, as opposed to 11.7% for Canada. It is possible to measure the size of investments another way, by examining how much this represents per worker. The level of investment per worker in 2011 was $10,000, versus $11,200 in Ontario and $15,000 for Canada as a whole—results influenced by the size of the natural resources. Québec's investments in machines and materials were $5,000 per worker, far behind Canada ($7,500) and Ontario ($7,600). This gap continues when we compare ourselves with the rest of the world.

The consequences are most important according to the Finance Ministry: "If private investments had the same relative importance in Québec as in the whole of Canada, they would have been 33.5% higher, by $10 billion."[41]

Two other major tools for improving productivity are education and innovation. In the case of education, Québec has constructed a high-level network which, nevertheless, has certain drawbacks, and these can have an economic impact. There exist multiple links between education and productivity: managerial and professional needs, flexible and creative manpower capable of fostering change and adapting to it. Factories, machines and programs without humans to invent and use them will not go far. In fact, Québec, as we have already seen, still has work to do in order to increase university graduation rates that currently prevent far too many young people from exploiting their potential to the maximum. Moreover, the struggle with illiteracy is far from over.

Another aspect of education—manpower training, which is crucial for productivity—still has a long way to go. It is one of the indicators used by the Conseil du patronat (Québec Employers Council) in its Bulletin de la prospérité du Québec (Québec Wealth Bulletin) in 2013. According to the CPQ, in 2008, the proportion of adults who had undergone job-related training was 28.2%, far behind the Canadian average of 36% or Alberta's 43.3%, but let us recall that education in Québec is not in crisis, nor lagging behind. Instead it seems to be doing rather well, but more investment would be most welcome in this sector, as would some fine-tuning to allow it to perform better.

The link between innovation and productivity is obvious. New ideas, products, procedures, entrepreneurs, and researchers are needed for an economy to improve its methods, the essence of productivity, which depends heavily on intelligence. The challenge here for Québec, as already shown, is the transition from research to concrete innovation, from labs and research centres to offices and plants.

This brings us to a third question. The standard of living is lower when productivity is reduced, and if productivity goes down, it is largely the result of weak investment. Given the considerable efforts of government to attract foreign investments and subsidize business, why does Québec not succeed?

There are a number of explanations: a hidebound industrial structure, still leaning on weak technology centres, often made up of small and middle-sized businesses, such as furniture and food production, which invest and innovate very little; fiscal policy which discourages some businesses; the heavy hand of the state and its red tape; relatively high labour costs, especially when the Canadian dollar is strong; linguistic restrictions; the political context, which comes into play at certain moments; well intentioned but badly aimed economic policies, like all the job-creation programs, particularly in outlying regions which, by definition, do not favour productivity; costs tied to a dysfunctional construction industry; unfortunate strategic decisions, such as the Marois government's crusade against the mining industry.

Behind these considerations is a culture which does not always encourage growth, research, or economic performance, and which exhibits a relatively weak entrepreneurial spirit along with a mistrust of business and the private sector, as well as little appetite for risk. There is no consensus on the importance of making ours a more high-performing economy. This lack of consensus constitutes a serious block.

YES, IT IS SERIOUS

What to make of this avalanche of figures and graphics? Well, the conclusion is clear: the GDP per capita is weaker than those of the other provinces and states, and of other developed countries. Québec trails behind OECD nations and finds itself definitely among the less rich of the wealthy countries—a paradox, for ours is not a backward society.

On the contrary, it is modern, urbanized, civilized and educated, with a university network of high calibre, a remarkable cultural life, cutting-edge industries and businesses which are extremely dynamic. Yet Québec does not fully succeed in transforming all this into wealth-creation. I have the profound conviction that we can easily do better, exploit our great potential even further and become a model economy without selling our souls.

We may not like these figures and reject per capita GDP as an imperfect measure, but it is a common one used all over the world. Obviously, standard of living has its weaknesses and does not give us a full picture of the economic situation in a society, but it does well in showing us its performance, its vigour and its competitive ability.

We cannot deny the existence or the gravity of this problem. Arguments which seek simply to devalue the concept are nevertheless incapable of refuting this reality, attempting rather to show that our average family income is reasonably close to that of Americans, or that Canadian purchasing power is nearly equivalent, which is true. A 16% gap in standard of living with countries of the OECD does not necessarily mean a great difference in purchasing power. We will go into this in greater detail in the next chapter.

Let us just say for now that it is beside the point. Relative well-being does not lessen the fact of Québec's economic weakness, its low performance and the serious results this engenders. A low standard of living matters. It has consequences: it reflects weaker growth, and is accompanied in general by less vigorous job creation, signifying less revenue, savings, profits, tax revenue for the state, individual and collective resources.

Unconsciously, a large number of Québécois react to this dilemma by posing the imperatives of economic development in opposition to social justice. We must make a choice, we are told, and Québec's is made. We may be less prosperous than our neighbours, but we are more egalitarian.

This argument is attractive, but it is false, because, if we look around us, it is possible to see perfectly well that one does not exclude the other—we do not have to sacrifice either. In this case, yes, we can have our cake and eat it too. It is enough if we observe what is happening in northern Europe and most of the advanced European countries. These countries, as we have already seen, without exception, have higher standards of living than we do, and still afford a social safety net at least as good as ours, and a far more just distribution of income.

This tells us two things. First, if we put ourselves to it, Québec could have a higher standard of living without compromising social justice. The myth that one threatens the other is a tenacious one, but it simply does not hold up.

Second, there are no rules. It is possible to be egalitarian, and thus interventionist as a state, and still be high performing, just as surely as we can be high performing and inegalitarian, like the US. Similarly, it is possible to be both inegalitarian and ineffective too. No one has yet made the obvious choice, which is to be in solidarity and *also* high performing . . . no one.

It is true that Québec, as seen in Chapter 8, divides up the pie better than elsewhere in North America, and this compensates partly for our lower standard of living. What we often forget to add is that our pie is smaller, and that brings a crowd of consequences, such as our permanent fiscal crisis. It would be more intelligent to produce a bigger pie and continue to share it out well.

CHAPTER 13

ARE WE RICH?

In the preceding chapter, we have seen that the economy of Québec is less prosperous than those of most comparable societies, but per capita GDP—the classic yardstick for standard of living—is an imperfect tool for evaluating people's concrete financial situation, buying power and, even more, their happiness.

The GDP per capita includes elements that do not necessarily affect the personal situation of citizens. For instance, the fact that the per capita GDP of Denmark is $7,311 higher than ours does not mean that a Dane has $7,311 more in his pockets each year, or that the Larsen family, with two children, has $29,244 more to spend than the Bouchard family.

Similarly, the way in which petroleum swells Norway's GDP, as it does in the Persian Gulf, does not mean their citizens are swimming in money. The same holds true for Louisiana, with a standard of living higher than Québec, even though the state often resembles a developing country. Closer to home, even though Newfoundland has overtaken Québec according to many indicators (on paper), this Atlantic province is still, in several respects, a poor province, because the benefits of petroleum have not yet reached the population.

These global statistics reveal another important flaw: not taking income sharing into account. In countries where all the wealth is in the hands of a few, a strong GDP does not reflect a high standard of living.

Finally, people's economic well-being depends on many other factors, notably cost of living and, with it, actual purchasing power. It also depends on taxation and on state programs which, in a society such as ours, procure services that the citizen would have to pay from his own pocket, such as health care in the US.

All such elements must be considered when comparing it with other societies if we are to have a clear vision of the true standard of living and power in a population. We are reminded that, as with other complex realities, there is no set of magic figures to sum it all up and still retain essential nuances. This is the case with pre-election opinion polls: one can easily jump to conclusions too rapidly by retaining the simple percentage of support for each party. One must also see the rate of change in their favour, their linguistic and regional distribution, the rate of satisfaction with the government, etc. Sports fans know how complex the handling of statistics can be.

The same can be said for our reflection on the incomes of Québécois: a variety of indicators must be used which do not describe exactly the same thing, but clarify different facets of the problem. These complementary elements allow us to obtain a better final portrait of the situation. With all these nuances, our conclusion will be clear enough: Québécois have lower incomes than their neighbours, yes, but the actual gap is less great than indicated by per capita GDP. Workers' and families' incomes make Québec essentially "a bigger Atlantic province." Such a comparison with our neighbours and partners shows that we can do better and deserve as much. Above all, there is no reason to be satisfied with the present state of affairs.

JOLLYING OURSELVES ALONG

All this goes to say that to deal properly with this complicated question, we must tread carefully. I did not see this caution in the process put forward by Jean-François Lisée, then columnist for *L'actualité* (a news magazine roughly resembling *Maclean's*, though with a higher level of journalism) and strategic thinker for the Parti Québécois before becoming a minister in the Marois government, then Opposition member. With the help of economist Pierre Fortin, he suggested an indicator quite different from per capita GDP. To help deal with fiscal data, he included revenue declared by Québec and US citizens, with the exception of the 10% highest earners, arguing the huge disparities of income in the US for this top layer include a major part of overall income (50% in the US, 37% in Québec). This imbalance also artificially increases the average and misleadingly raises the apparent standard of living for all.

With this approach, 90% of "ordinary" Americans have an average income of $17,061, to $16,820 for Québécois, a gap of barely 1.4%. This leads to the assertion that the average Québécois does no worse than an American, an interesting conclusion, no doubt. It throws a useful light and proposes an element that needs to be included in the overall puzzle, while enriching our reflection on the subject. I do not contest this approach, but rather the abusive use that the journalist-turned-politician puts it to. It is worth taking the time to show why this is incorrect, because it reflects a current of opinion very much present in public discussion.

Firstly, it is my contention that Jean-François Lisée and Pierre Fortin have pushed their argument a bit too far in comparing the work and income of Québécois and Americans. Chapter 11 has shown that the former work fewer hours than the latter. This has led them to recalculate the income of Americans in the supposition that they effectively work fewer hours. The equation thus gives us a net advantage for an income of $16,820, ahead of the much reduced income of Americans ($14,890). The exercise, however, is highly artificial and arbitrary, a bit like a Mercedes driving slower than a Toyota if equipped with a Yaris engine.

What is more, Jean-François Lisée has chosen these figures as justification for a crusade, one he has led for many years against those he upbraids for criticizing the Québécois model. His calculations, published in *L'actualité*, were re-used in an essay, or rather a pamphlet, entitled *Comment mettre la droite K.-O. en 15 arguments* (*How to KO the Right in 15 Arguments*), published in 2012. He reproached this "right" for abusively citing the dips in GDP:

> The American standard of living is at least 21% higher than Québec's. François Legault [leader of the CAQ and former PQ Minster of Education] has gone so far as to assert that this difference was as high as 45%. Once again making the much-repeated mistake of spreading misinformation.

This was an amazing attack. Being preoccupied with Québec's being economically behind its partners is a reflection of neither political right nor left. This reasoning contains several errors. The first is conceptual, and it consists of placing two approaches in apparent conflict with one another—standard of living as measured by GDP per capita, and the population's fiscal revenues—as if the two approaches were incompatible: one true, the other false. These two notions are not opposed, but rather complementary.

A further mistake included in Jean François Lisée's attack lies in regarding the Québec model as a success on the basis of his calculations:

> Our society successfully assures a superior quality of life to a greater proportion of its inhabitants than the world's superpower. It does so despite a lower generation of gross wealth. This, it seems to me, is a considerable exploit.

It was imprudent to arrive at such a rigid conclusion on the strength of calculations which, however interesting they may be, can only be approximate. This demonstration does not permit a conclusion confirming the success of our model, and the failure of theirs, which is not at all the same thing. It also underscores the consequences of America's disorientation and ever-increasing income disparities. To demonstrate the effectiveness of the Québécois model, it would be necessary to compare the income of Québécois with those of other Canadians or other societies sharing our values. Otherwise, we are charging down a blind alley.

A more recent study documents very well the dead end the US is rushing into. In its April 22, 2014, issue, the *New York Times* headlined: "The American middle class is no longer the world's richest." The daily went on to say, "the average after-tax income in Canada, significantly lower than the US in 2000, now seems to be higher." This dossier analyzed median disposable income for households in 20 countries over a period of 35 years, beginning with a study of Luxembourg. Available income took into account revenue from transfers and taxes. Using median income allowed separation of the population into two groups equal in number: those with income above the median, and those with income below it. This was a way of avoiding the problems associated with an average income artificially pumped up by the very highest incomes.

According to this study, Canada, by 2010, would have caught up with the US, while a large number of countries, such as Norway, would not be far behind. This would be explained by incomes, which have increased by 19.7% over the last decade in Canada and barely 0.3% in the US, due to both the perverse effects of its unequal income distribution and the effects of their crisis, notably in construction.

The last mistake is by far the most serious. Mr. Lisée's way of showing how Québec carves up the pie has numerous advantages, but it underestimates the consequences of its being too small in the first place. This is no mere detail and is heavy with implications. The effort to spread the belief that all is just peachy, that Québec shines by its accomplishments, makes it very difficult to invite people to help with the size of the pie. In this sense, it is a modern version, varnished with a layer of sophistication, of the old way of thinking, "born to be poor" ("né pour un p'tit pain," a traditional phrase to describe Québec's lowly status and expectations, an admonition not to be "uppity").

It is worth asking why, because, in fact, when dealing with income, work and performance, we often find ourselves faced with a new wave of boosters, always emerging from the political left and more often than not, the sovereignist left. And why is this? Permit me a double explanation. To begin with, it is important for the sovereignist current to present Québec in its most favourable light to inspire pride and self-confidence, thus reducing fears that Québec has neither the aptitudes nor the abilities to become a country. Next, the Québec model must be defended because it connects the PQ and the left, especially unions.

BACK TO BASICS

After this long detour, let me deal with something less simple, less clear and more tortuous, where we shall examine various ways of measuring income, so as to answer more correctly the following question: do we live well?

To begin at the beginning, i.e. salaries, which, for most of us are the basis of our income. We are among those who earn the least in Canada. In January 2014, the average weekly wage was $836.85, 7th in Canada, far behind the $932.28 earned in Ontario. This difference ($95.43) represents a gap of 11.4%. Québécois also earned less than Newfoundlanders, who were beginning to profit from the oil boom. Québec was not progressing, but on the contrary, regressing. Ten years earlier, in 2003, we were 4th in Canada for wages. Since then, Manitoba, Saskatchewan and Newfoundland have overtaken us.

The average hourly wages were at about the same level for Québec, at $23.39, 6th in Canada, ahead of the Atlantic provinces and Manitoba.

Another basic statistic is the taxable income declared to the federal government (supposing that we are all telling the truth): $36,563 for Québécois and $42,583 for Ontarians, a gap of 15%, and the rest flows from this, since salary is the basis of income. Québécois earn lower wages. They work fewer hours. With a below-average employment rate, there are fewer of them working than in higher-performing provinces. There are no two ways about it: it is hard to be richer, then, isn't it?

The figures are clear and simple, and they tell us one basic thing: we earn less than all the others, except the traditional Atlantic three. With these figures, the rules of the wealth-sharing game do not apply, because the very rich are not wage-earners. We can hardly call this an accomplishment, and yet it is the only boast we can make of our model. This again is why, if we wish to evaluate the Québécois model, it is wiser and more logical to begin by comparing the rest of Canada.

QUÉBEC 9TH OUT OF 10

There is still another classic way of measuring wealth: disposable household income. This is the macroeconomic measure available from the national accounts, although it excludes elements which are not, in fact, part of people's real income. This includes all types of income accruing to each household, including government transfers—welfare, for instance

DISPOSABLE HOUSEHOLD INCOME IN CANADA
IN 2012 $

Alberta	38,761
Saskatchewan	31,363
British Columbia	30,474
Newfoundland and Labrador	30,461
Canada	29,907
Ontario	28,745
Nova Scotia	27,063
Manitoba	26,995
New Brunswick	26,793
Québec	26,347
Prince Edward Island	26,115

Source: Institut de la statistique du Québec.

—from which taxes and other payments are made to governments. This is household income for consumption or savings, real money in their pockets. This better describes their financial situation than per capita GDP, and it gives a better overall measure, including several elements that reflect the true prosperity of an economy rather than that of its citizens alone.

In 2012, the per capita disposable income of households was $26,347 in Québec, far behind the Canadian average of $29,907, a gap of 12%. If one compares Québec instead with the nine other provinces in the rest of Canada, it widens to 15%, and there has been no catch-up. On the contrary, in 2007, the income gap between Québec and Canada was 8%, and with the rest of Canada it was 12.5%.

As the graph on page 205 shows, we place 9th in Canada, behind all provinces and territories, except tiny Prince Edward Island. Here are the figures in descending order: Alberta, $38,761; Saskatchewan, $31,363; British Columbia, $30,474; Newfoundland, $30,461; Ontario, $29,745; Nova Scotia, $27,063; Manitoba, $26,995; New Brunswick, $26,793; Québec, $26,347; Prince Edward Island, $26,115. Thus Québécois have less money than most other Canadians.

Such data are disturbing, and rightly so: is it normal for Québec—with all its riches, talent, cutting-edge industries, cities and culture—not to succeed in converting all these into financial resources for its citizens? Is it normal for Québécois to be poorer than New Brunswickers? Nova Scotians? Manitobans?

Well, yes it is, completely, and it is important to talk about this again and again until we collectively get it and do what must be done to reverse this tendency, for there is indeed a tendency ... downward. For five years, from 2007 to 2012, household income growth in real terms was 5.3% in Québec and 8% in the rest of Canada.

In 2007, Québec came 7th, overtaken by Newfoundland in 2009, thus falling to 8th. In 2010, New Brunswick and Prince Edward Island overtook us, dropping us into last place. Optimists might rejoice, saying we have managed since then to outrank the land of *Anne of Green Gables*.

How to explain all this? In part, but only in part, this is due to higher taxes here than anywhere else, but even without this factor, we would still place 8th. Resource and oil wealth plays a part in propelling provinces in the West and in providing a new start for provinces like Newfoundland and, to a lesser degree, Nova Scotia.

We have no oil, and our economy is chronically anemic. Investment is inadequate, and our entrepreneurial fibre is generally too weak to transform our resources into wealth. No strategy will allow us to adjust if we do not liberate ourselves from reflexive denial, and if we do not stop fooling ourselves that all is well in the Kingdom of Québec.

FAMILY INCOME

It is also possible to consider things from another angle, one based on declared income. We can look at median family income rather than average income, and thus avoid the distortions tied to income inequity that come with using an average. Here, too, family incomes in Québec are below those in Canada. Across the country in 2011, the total median income was $72,240 versus $68,170 in Québec, a gap of 6%, more drastic than we have found with other measures, but it still places Québec 6th, ahead of the Atlantic provinces. With this measure, Newfoundland, situated as one of the leaders with other measures, finds itself in 9th place, which shows that oil riches are not fully reflected in the quality of life.

Here, too, it is possible to note a specificity in Québec, and the news is both good and bad. Median income statistics allow us to distinguish two-parent and single-parent families. In the case of single-parent families, where the parent most often is a woman, Québec does very well. With median resources of $39,700, Québec single-parent families rank 2nd in Canada, right behind Alberta, and well above average ($37,900), which reflects on our social and fiscal policies. Among two-parent families, still in the majority, the prospect is less rosy. Two-parent families in Québec receive $74,060, which puts us in 8th place, with a gap of 7% in relation to $79,530 for Canada.

MARKET INCOME

The Canadian Income Study is the tool most used by economists, based on information obtained from direct study of households. It specifies three types of income. First is market income, the total inflow from economic activity. Next is total overall income, including the aforementioned plus government transfers: unemployment insurance, pensions, etc. Finally, there is net income after taxes, what is actually left in our pockets.

The CIS reveals roughly the same things as other studies. The market income for Québécois families in 2011 was $55,700, which is 7th in Canada, behind the Atlantic provinces, except Newfoundland, as might be expected. Québec income is $10,200 lower than the Canadian average of $65,700, a significant 15.6% gap. With Ontario this rises to $13,900 (20.1%). And why even mention Alberta's $88,400?

Next, what happens when the state intervenes? First, if we include transfers, our income increases by $9,800, a huge leap to a $65,300 total. This might tempt us to take a positive view of the Québécois model, but it would be a mistake, for the same phenomenon is present elsewhere in the country: transfers are above $10,000 per family in the four Atlantic provinces. Ontario resembles those of Québec, though slightly less ($8,000–$9,000), as do the four western provinces. What does this mean? It means that redistributive justice is a Canadian phenomenon and is the backbone of federal government transfers.

Finally, net income after taxes—real income—is second lowest in Québec because of the amount of taxes, as we know, which are higher here, equal with New Brunswick and ahead of Nova Scotia. This is nearly as high as Québec's market income, because transfers almost equal direct taxes.

This figure is, I believe, more reliable. Net income for a Québec family is $54,000. This means a gap of $8,800 with the Canadian average (14% less) and $12,300 in relation to Ontario (18.5% less).

We need to underline the fact that a Newfoundland family has $4,500 more to spend than a Québec family, a PEI family has $800 more, Ontario $12,300 more, Manitoba $4,200 more, Alberta $14,600 more, and British Columbia $7,000 more. Well, since it is the Québécois model we are discussing, this raises our level of income to that of New Brunswick and beyond that of Nova Scotia by $300. Quite a triumph.

Nor is it just a matter of ranking, for there are also dynamics. In 2012, before becoming Chairman of the Treasury Board, Martin Coiteux (Québec Finance Minister in 2014) was a professor at the HEC Montreal.

He analyzed the evolution of these incomes since 1978 in a study for the CPP, titled "Le point sur les écarts de revenu entre les Québécois and les Canadiens des autres provinces" ("Update on the income gap between Québécois families and those of the other provinces"). Mr. Coiteux noted that the gap with richer provinces grew more, while poorer provinces were catching up with us. All provinces made gains in relation to Québec, especially in recent years. He calculated that, between 2005 and 2009, Newfoundland succeeded in catching up by $5,573 per adult in a sample family, the Atlantic provinces caught up by $2,231, while Ontario increased its advance by another $693, the Prairies by $4,862, Alberta by $9,560, and British Columbia by $4,640.

THE PURCHASING POWER ARGUMENT

Let us sum up: regardless of which yardstick we choose, Québec lags behind other less wealthy provinces. Historic data also confirm that this gap is widening.

What we now need to know is how gaps between incomes impact our lifestyle and purchasing power. Several attenuating factors could be reducing the real impact.

The first factor is income apportionment. Gaps between rich and poor are less marked in Québec. In his study, Martin Coiteux noted, for instance, that the income difference between Québec and other provinces is nearly non-existent for the first quintile of income—the 20% poorest —and the gap widens as income increases. This is not good news, because Québécois in the higher quintiles continue to lag behind those in other provinces. Nevertheless, it tells us that, for 20% of us, the income gap is nil.

The second factor is cost of living. If it is lower in Québec than the rest of Canada, families need less money to afford the same quantity of goods and services. They are certainly less rich, but their purchasing power is comparable to that of other provinces.

We have no official statistics on the range of purchasing powers. Consumer price indices do not allow us to measure these differences. It is possible, however, to have an intuitive sense of price differences, notably for housing. House prices are generally lower in Québec than elsewhere.

THREE MEASURES OF HOUSEHOLD INCOME
IN 2011 $

	TOTAL MARKET INCOME	TOTAL INCOME	NET INCOME AFTER TAXES
Canada	**65,700**	**75,000**	**63,000**
Newfoundland and Labrador	58,100 (6)	70,600 (5)	59,700 (5)
Prince Edward Island	52,800 (9)	64,600 (8)	55,000 (7)
Nova Scotia	53,800 (8)	63,900 (9)	53,900 (10)
New Brunswick	52,100 (10)	62,900 (10)	54,200 (8)
Québec	55,500 (7)	65,300 (7)	54,200 (8)
Ontario	69,400 (3)	79,100 (2)	66,500 (2)
Manitoba	61,600 (5)	69,900 (6)	58,400 (6)
Saskatchewan	69,600 (2)	77,800 (3)	65,200 (3)
Alberta	88,400 (1)	95,400 (1)	78,800 (1)
British Columbia	62,100 (4)	70,800 (4)	61,200 (4)

Source: Statistics Canada.

In March 2014, according to the Canadian Real Estate Association, the average house cost was $320,558 in Montreal, $264,197 in Québec City, but $557,604 in Toronto, $462,994 in Calgary and $801,543 in Vancouver. Elsewhere, however, the differences are not as great: in Ottawa, houses cost $359,286, not much more than Montreal. In the Prairies or the Atlantic provinces, less again. Canada, of course, is not merely Toronto.

There are all sorts of indirect measures, which are hotly debated among economists, and the cost of living would account for the real gap in purchasing power between Québécois and other Canadians. There are differences of opinion about the Québec model. Martin Coiteux, a strong critic, estimates from the normal basket of consumer goods and services that the cost of living is 5% higher in Ontario and 9% in Alberta. These differences are much less than in the year 2000, and they continue to shrink. Economist Pierre Fortin indicates an 8.8% gap with Ontario and 6.1% with Canada overall.

Whether it be 5% or 8%, this cost-of-living gap with Ontario will do nothing to erase an income gulf of 18%. The question of cost of living figures less in several provinces and regions of Ontario, where the cost of living does not match the great urban centres.

There is a certain circularity in demonstrations that aim at shrinking income disparities by referring to cost of living. If life is less costly in Québec, it is largely because housing costs are lower, and if houses are more affordable in Québec, it is essentially because the standard of living is not as high, demand is weaker, and residences fewer and more luxurious. Briefly then, it costs less to live in Québec because it is poorer. Is this an occasion for rejoicing? Is this a plus for us? Life in Portugal is cheaper than in France, but this is no measure of success. Real estate prices are lower in Québec, but they also have a negative long-term effect on our heritage.

There is another attenuating factor of the effects of income disparity: despite their more modest income, Québécois have access to more "free" public services subsidized by other Canadians, by virtue of a greater state presence, notably electricity, sold at half the price charged elsewhere. Overall, these services, like subsidized daycare, benefit only a portion of the population, and this reasoning rests mainly on the unconvincing hypothesis that the heavier we are taxed, the fewer additional services we need to pay out of pocket. These high taxes, however, serve in large part to pay for more expensive infrastructures, a heavier debt service, activities not available in other provinces and from which citizens do not benefit, such as the "triplication" of administrative structures in health (Ministry, regional agencies and centres of health and social services).

THE ELEPHANT IN THE ROOM

There is another basic dimension which is easy to neglect. Efforts to minimize the fallout from a lower income level contain an individualistic logic, which is astonishing when one realizes that the most vigorous interventions come from those claiming to represent the left.

It is possible that the average Québécois, despite an income weaker than Ontario's or Manitoba's, does not do so badly in the everyday, because it costs less to live, even though, as we have seen, this does not seem to be the case at all. This arises from a logic which is at once microeconomic and individualistic.

The average Québécois does not live in a bubble but, in fact, in a society. The important determinants of his quality of life depend on state services and programs. If the average Québécois makes less money than elsewhere, he will also have more difficulty paying taxes. Our level of income, however one may calculate it—per capita GDP, median income, household income, weekly salary—indicates that the larger fiscal envelope which determines revenues is smaller in Québec. Individually, these weaker receipts can be compensated for without too much harm to the family. Collectively, nevertheless, there is a major impact.

I shall use a rule of "threes" to illustrate. Federal fiscal statistics from 2010 tell us that the total average income of Québécois was $36,353, compared with $42,583 in Ontario on blanket declarations. What would happen if incomes in Québec were as high as those of their neighbours? Suppose total declared income was not $227.6 billion, but $266.6 billion, a difference of $39 billion. If the same taxation rate were applied to average income in Québec for 2010, the government of Québec would recuperate at least $4.7 billion more in taxes, taking into account the progressive nature of the tax tables, which would increase the average tax rate. With this additional amount, who could dare speak of a financial crisis in Québec?

Similarly, the 10% richest individuals—subtracted from comparisons with the US because of the bias they exert on the average—pay taxes from which Québec cannot benefit because the richest among us are, on the whole, less rich. The richest are excluded from such calculations and comparisons. They are useful in evaluating level of real income for ordinary citizens, but, in doing so, we sweep aside the notion that these rich people pay taxes, when, in fact, here, they truly pay more than others. Those with incomes over $200,000 count for 0.79% of all taxpayers. In 2008, they declared 8% of all income and paid 17.27% of the taxes. There is a certain progressiveness in this.

In searching for a thousand-and-one ways to bolster a model in which the rich are fewer and average citizens do relatively well despite reduced incomes, we completely remove the fiscal dimension, the ability of the state to pay for services and ensure continuity. This is an inconceivable omission for left-leaners who firmly believe in the state. Scraping by with reduced revenues is no praiseworthy exploit. It is a handicap.

CHAPTER 14

ARE WE HAPPY?

Of course we are! Québécois are probably one of
the happiest peoples on the planet, and just maybe,
to stretch a point, the happiest of all! Amazing
but true. You would not know it to see our bloody
debates, our social movements, our "red squares"
paralyzing the streets, the state's financial crisis,
budget cuts, our mediocre economic performance
and our collective self-flagellation in front of the
Charbonneau Commission (Commission of
Inquiry on the Awarding and Management of
Public Contracts in the Construction Industry).
We may be "crybabies," but we have an intense
political life, and we are the happiest Canadians,
just as sure as Canadians themselves are among
the happiest on the surface of the earth. Clearly,
we are at the summit of the happiness pyramid!

All right, so happiness is hard to define, and even harder to measure. This must be why it has for so long been left to the philosophers, psychologists or priests (at least in the great beyond), but for several years now, economists have begun to explore the question as well. The final outcome sought by economic science is to optimize the level of satisfaction in a society, so it might be well to try and define "well-being" to understand what we can expect.

As has been seen, many have decried the limitations of GDP as a measure of society's success and happiness. This macroeconomic point of reference is too general and rather a blunt object, nor does it take many factors into account, beginning with income inequity. These criticisms came from populist movements often opposed to the current economic model, for whom money does not equate with happiness, and who—somewhat naïvely—wished to replace gross national product with gross national happiness. This, in turn, has steered us toward more austere economists and toward political initiatives such as those of French ex-President Nicolas Sarkozy, and Joseph Stiglitz, Nobel Prize winner in economics on this very question.

Briefly, this is an extremely complicated field of research, and two major approaches are used to measure the level of happiness in a society: i.e. the well-being and satisfaction of its citizens. The level of happiness may be analyzed from within or without. The first approach, interior, consists of asking people what they are feeling: for instance, if they were happy the evening before, or if they are generally satisfied with their life. This is a subjective measure of happiness which may seem quite tenuous, because responses can vary from moment to moment, from culture to culture, and according to one's definition of happiness. Nevertheless, a great many studies carried out by economists and psychologists show that these subjective experiences can, in fact, be measured and may provide us with useful information. The second approach, exterior, consists first of defining what may contribute to well-being, and next to verifying to what extent these determinants of happiness are present in society.

There is an obvious link between happiness and material comfort, especially for those who suffer from low income, hunger, discomfort and exclusion. At the bottom of the scale, happiness obviously increases with incomes, but at the other extremity, additional income provides fleeting satisfaction, and incurs a number of undesirable effects that affect happiness—such social ills as anorexia, the stress associated with success, anxiety generated by maintaining social status, or overwork. Inversely, we are intuitively aware that many other elements contribute to happiness, such as street safety, quality health care or the future of one's children.

In the wake of this reflection, in 1990, the UN developed an index of human development which added two other measures to income, life expectancy and educational level. This imperfect, but more complete index placed Canada first in the world, affording Prime Ministers Brian Mulroney and Jean Chrétien great satisfaction.

To underline its 50th anniversary in 2011, the OECD launched a much more complicated index called "Better Life Index" to measure, not happiness—which is ineffable—but more modestly, well-being.

Such an exercise was most welcome after the shortcomings of GDP. This appears in the case of Newfoundland, whose oil production has boosted per capita GDP, thus making it the 20th richest economy in North America, far ahead of Ontario. Yet, this new-found paper wealth has not yet translated into tangible prosperity for Newfoundlanders.

The difficulty with these new approaches is first to define well-being, then to find reliable data to measure and compare various societies. The OECD index includes about twenty indicators from crime-rate to pollution, health, employment and income.

THE SUBJECTIVITY OF HAPPINESS

Let us begin with the subjective measures of happiness. In 2012, my eye was caught by an article in the *Globe and Mail*: "Quebeckers are happier than the rest of us." This article, sounding somewhat astonished, revealed the results of a report from the Centre for the Study of Living Standards in Ottawa (CENEV).[42]

It was based on data collected by Statistics Canada over a number of years and excerpted from a larger poll on public health. To the classic questions on lifestyle, they added another, which asked if respondents were generally satisfied with their lives on a scale of 0 to 10. In 2003, 91.3% of Canadians declared themselves satisfied or very satisfied with their lives. By 2011, this proportion had risen to 92.3%, a significant increase, according to the authors. This study also ranked levels of satisfaction by province.

Using the average responses from 2003 to 2011 (in order to eliminate fluctuations from one year to the other), Nova Scotia ranked first with 94.1% satisfied or very satisfied. Québec was second with 93.2%, well above the Canadian average of 91.8% and Ontario's 91.0%.

The level of happiness had increased more in Québec than anywhere else over this period, to the extent that, in 2011, it was first, with a satisfaction rate of 94%, well above the Canadian average of 92.3%. This superiority in the quest for happiness is confirmed by results in urban centres: four out of five cities with the highest rates of happiness were in Québec: Québec City, Trois-Rivières, Gatineau and Saguenay. The fifth was Peterborough, Ontario.

Since the publication of this CENEV study, Statistics Canada has released more recent data for the year 2012 (see the graph on the facing page). Québec, with a rate of 93.6%, now finds itself in 2nd place behind Prince Edward Island, and still well above the average for Canada and Ontario (92.4%), Alberta (92.8%) and British Columbia (90.1%).

This happiness in Québec is striking enough for economists John Helliwell and Shun Wang to mention it in an imposing document, *The World Happiness Report*, noting:

> Québec residents, especially francophones, have, in the decades following the Quiet Revolution, felt increased satisfaction with their lives in comparison with residents in the rest of Canada. This cumulative difference is both important and statistically significant.

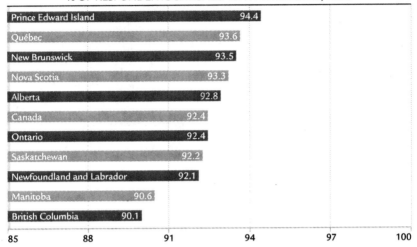

HAPPINESS IN CANADA
% OF RESPONDENTS SATISFIED WITH THEIR LIVES, 2012

Prince Edward Island	94.4
Québec	93.6
New Brunswick	93.5
Nova Scotia	93.3
Alberta	92.8
Canada	92.4
Ontario	92.4
Saskatchewan	92.2
Newfoundland and Labrador	92.1
Manitoba	90.6
British Columbia	90.1

Source: Statistics Canada.

The authors see the growth of happiness in Québec as equivalent to a doubling of their income, which shows, they say, that "social changes may have influenced well-being markedly."

Moreover, the Canadian study also presented comparisons with foreign countries, starting with data gathered by the Gallup World Poll, which studied 155 countries, asking respondents to evaluate their quality of life on a scale of 0 to 10 (the Cantril Scale). Canada placed 2nd worldwide with 7.7, just behind Denmark (7.8), but ahead of Norway, Switzerland and the Netherlands. France, the country of eternal malcontents, was far below (6.8).

Québec itself does not appear in the international ranking, but from what we already know about our lead in Canada and the size of that advantage, the simple rule of threes allows the deduction that we would obtain a score of 7.8 on the Cantril Scale and be out in front, beside Denmark (see graph on page 218). These measures are, of course, imperfect, and it is possible, for instance, that our attachment to "la joie de vivre" allows us to be more easily satisfied than the Danes, but Québec is one of the happiest places on the planet.

THE BETTER LIFE INDEX

The OECD approach, though quite different, still leads us to essentially the same conclusions. The Better Life Index includes 11 criteria employing 24 indicators, rated from 0 to 10 (10 being applied to the country placing first). Three of these criteria concern the material conditions of life: housing, income and work. The eight others deal with quality of life: education, health, social links, environment, civic involvement, satisfaction, security and a balanced work life. The resultant indicator thus takes into account a great many factors that contribute to well-being.

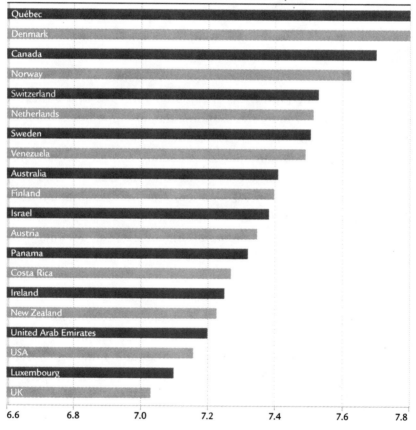

HAPPINESS IN THE WORLD
INDEX OF SATISFACTION WITH LIFE, 2012

Source: Gallup World Poll.

The Better Life Index takes care not to rank countries, because the rank does not derive solely from the results obtained in each category, but also from the importance given to each one. The OECD goes so far as to propose a tool allowing each person to create his/her own Better Life Index weighted by his/her own weightings.

And the result? In 2011, Canada won again, just behind Australia, not far ahead of three Scandinavian countries, Sweden, Denmark and Norway. Why? All of them score well for health, education, safety and communal life, although we are set back by rate of voting in elections and reconciling work with family. Also, Canadians are in the lead, just behind Danes, as we have just seen, in subjective measurement of well-being.

In fact, writing in *Québec Économique 2011*, published at CIRANO, Luc Godbout and Marcelin Joanis decided to calculate the Better Life Index for Québec, something I had set my sights on for this book, though with fewer resources at my disposal.

Their hypotheses are cautious, because one may not always have exactly the right data for Québec, but they assert that Québec would be first, just ahead of Australia and Canada, among the 38 member-countries of the OECD.

We will review their calculations in order to understand how an economic organization can measure happiness and see where we are in relation to Canada and the rest of the industrialized world.

Housing: the criteria here have two indicators. First comes the number of rooms per person. Canada, with 2.5, is highest, well ahead of the average for OECD countries (1.6). Québec shares 2nd place with Australia. The second indicator is the proportion of housing without basic sanitary installations, such as toilets per family. In fact, for Scandinavian countries, the proportion is zero. Canada is in the middle with 1.1%, almost certainly dragged down by conditions on native reserves. There are no data specific to Québec, but the authors suppose them comparable with Canada.

Income: the yardstick used for income is how much is available per inhabitant after transfers and taxes. In 2008, Canada placed 10th with purchasing power equivalent to $27,015 US. Québec, with $24,078, is

17th, slightly above the OECD average. The second measure, financial holdings per inhabitant, sees Canada at 9th, while Québec, with 20% less, places 11th.

Employment: the first indicator used is employment rate, or the proportion of the population of working-aged 15–64-year-olds who actually hold a job. Canada's employment rate of 71.7%, puts it in 10th place. Québec is just behind, with 71.1%. The champions are in Scandinavia and in Oceania. The long-term unemployment rate, the second indicator, is very low in Canada at 1%, one of the best. Québec does still better, with a rate of 0.8%.

Education: the indicators in education are as mentioned in Chapters 3 and 4. In Canada, the proportion of our population holding a high school diploma stands at 87.1%, compared to 85.0% in Québec. Canada and Québec are thus 6th and 11th respectively. Reading competence is measured starting with PISA test results, and Canada is up with the best at 524, with Québec just behind at 522.

Health: Canada's life expectancy is 80.7 years, ranking 10th, and Japan is highest with more than 82 years. Québec is not far behind Canada, with a life expectancy of 79.2. The second indicator is the subjective state of health. The same study that asked Canadians about their satisfaction with life also asked about their health. Québec responded positively at 89.1%, the OECD's second highest, behind New Zealand (89.5%), and ahead of Canada (88.1%). We are not told, however, whether this describes real state of health or simply Canadians' irrepressible optimism.

Community Life: what is evaluated here is the quality of the support network as measured by the Gallup World Poll, which gives Canada 7th place at 95.3%. The authors expect Québec would have obtained results comparable to Canada.

Environment: the indicator used here is air quality, measured by concentration of fine particles. Canada does not do well and stands in 24th place. The study supposes a similar situation in Québec.

Governance: here the rate of participation in national elections is used. Canada does poorly here, too. Our rate of 59.5% is clearly below the OECD average (72.3%), placing us 30th, while Québec, with a rate of 61.7%, places 28th. This also takes into account the degree of consultation on the process itself, and here Canada heads the list. Once again, the authors estimate Québec would have obtained a similar result.

Subjective Well-being: we have already seen that Québec shares 1st place with Denmark for subjective well-being. We have noted the index of 7.8 according to data from the Gallup World Poll, ahead of Canada (2nd with an index of 7.7).

Security: the indicator used for security is the homicide rate per 100,000 inhabitants. The homicide rate in Canada is 1.7—below average for OECD countries, compared with 1.1 for Québec. As to rates of aggression, a large Gallup study assigns Canada a rate of 1.4, best of all. Specific figures are not available for Québec, but if we regroup them with Statistics Canada data, it is possible to give Québec a score of 1.0—above Canada.

Work-Life Balance: we can look here at the proportion of employees who work long hours. The rate for Canada is low (3.8%), placing it 10th. Québec comes 4th with 2.1%. This includes the rate of employment for women with young children. Québec, with a rate of 80.3%, fares better than Canada (78%), ranking 2nd and 4th respectively. Finally, Québec comes off slightly better than Canada for leisure time, with 15.3 hours, in contrast with 15.0 for Canada, but comes in only 20th, clearly below the average OECD country.

On balance, Québec comes out ahead of the average among OECD countries 18 times out of 20. Sometimes it is above Canada, and sometimes below, but rarely is there much difference between them.

In compiling the results, Luc Godbout and Marcelin Joanis scored 82.1 for Québec with an equal weighting for all 11 themes. Thus, Québec is 1st, ahead of all OECD countries for quality of life, ahead of Canada (81.8) and Australia (81.4).

Calculated differently, so as to give equal weight to all 20 indicators, Québec remains in the lead with 80.5, while Canada (79.9) and Australia (79.3) follow. Another measure assigning different weights to a variety of indicators—3 for material indicators, 2 for health and education, and 1 each for the remainder—instead put Canada in front with 78.9, followed by Québec (78) and Australia (76.4).

These figures were done for the year 2011. Since then, other indicators have been added: water quality, years of education, work remuneration and housing costs. If we then re-calculate with more recent data from 2014, one notices that Canada has lost some of its shine, and is now 5th in the OECD. Australia leads with 81.2, followed by three Scandinavian countries, Norway and Sweden with 79.8, and Denmark with 79.5. Canada now places far behind with 78.4. This more recent ranking means Québec, supposing it is still slightly ahead of Canada, from here on, finds itself 5th.

However, a strong helping of nationalism aside, this is not very precise. There are too many hypotheses which could change the results, too many variations from year to year, too many differing impacts on weighted indicators. Worth retaining is that, as far as well-being is concerned, Québec shows results similar to Canada's, although certainly better. This makes it part of a very select club of countries with the best quality of life and a high degree of happiness. It is even ahead of the G7 countries, and, of course, the US, which is in 7th place, the UK in 11th, Germany 13th, France 17th, Japan 19th, and Italy 21st.

THE QUÉBEC ANOMALY

The preceding chapter showed us that income gaps between Québec and the rich provinces are significant, that the poorer provinces are catching up with us, and that Québec, in an industrialized world, is not performing well, nor very rich. So how is it possible to be both a goof-off and head of the class at the same time? The two views are not contradictory, but rather make up two facets of a single, complicated reality, with elements wholly different in nature, which must be taken into account for a proper diagnosis of the economy and society.

Overall measures of wealth, based on GDP or market income give us an idea of how large the pie is. A rich society is not necessarily a happy one. Well-being depends on any number of elements: the way the pie is divided up and how we count the slices. We must bear in mind that most elements that go into this index of well-being depend on the individual and collective resources available to a country. This is why richer countries are out in front and poorer ones bring up the rear. In this sense, of course, it is true, money does make happiness.

The initial mistake often made in this discussion is to see wealth and well-being in opposition to one another, like two antagonistic concepts demanding that we choose between them. Generally, those countries which offer a higher quality of life are the richest, with Québec as something of an exception, because resources are what is most of all required for quality of life.

The second error is in concluding that Québec's successes reflect a model which is unique and must be preserved. There are two reasons why this is not quite true. It is no coincidence that Canada, too, is often at the head of the pack, for our success comes not only from our own specificity, but also from the context of Canada. Ontario, British Columbia and Alberta would also lead in the Better Life Index, and if Québec, being poorer, manages to offer a good quality of life, it is also because we can rely on Canada's resources.

Every comparison with other countries that we have drawn so far contains an anomaly. As we have seen, a country's wealth does not guarantee that we will manage to build a harmonious and happy society. The US serves as a constant reminder of that. Still, this line of thought does not work in reverse. If wealth does not guarantee happiness, it does not necessarily follow that a poor society can be happy. All countries with a high level of well-being are rich, and their living standard is also high. The five countries leading in the OECD's Better Life Index are all, without exception, rich: Australia, Sweden, Norway, Denmark and Canada. This is because quality of life is costly, very costly. It requires a good system of education, health care, social programs to combat poverty and ensure social harmony, as well as housing and leisure. Standard of living allows us to measure the capacity of a society to pay for all this.

Did I just write "without exception"? In fact, there is one: Québec, in a category all by itself, with a below-average standard of living and a clearly above-average quality of life. Could this be the Québec miracle? Have we found the magic formula for obtaining well-being at a low price? Well, not really. There are explanations for the exception.

The Québécois system, with its programs and taxes, is not bolted to any pedestal to assure its stability. To use an imperfect image, let us take a circus performer, who, rather than having his feet firmly planted on the ground, tries to stay upright on a ball with crutches to keep him from falling.

This ball is the system of public taxes and expenditures which are the trademark of the Québec consensus. We succeed in offering our population the services that ensure our collective well-being by taxing them more than all our neighbours and in devoting a greater part of our resources to public expenditures.

Like the ball, this can be pumped up—in this instance, with outlays that never stop increasing—but, like any ball that gets too big, it can explode. The crutches here are the tools Québec has used to pay for services it cannot afford. Crutch number one is debt—indebting future generations for today's advantages. Number two is federal transfers by which citizens in richer provinces contribute to footing the bill.

We must stress that measures of well-being like those of the OECD are snapshots, portraits of a precise period, but by no means completely up-to-date, as in, say, a poll. They relate to past facts, not future ones.

The results that a society records as its level of well-being often depend on steps that were taken over a number of years. If conditions deteriorate, they do not show up right away, and a society can rest for quite a while on its laurels. This is the threat that faces Québec and Canada, which are neither progressing at full throttle nor at the peak of their glorious performance.

Such studies reveal nothing of our capacity to maintain these gains; in fact, the future requires us to maintain the policies that allowed us to reach this level. They cannot measure the viability of a model. Yet, in the case of Québec, this is the very question forced on us by the financial crises that successive governments have grappled with in vain. The results obtained so far by Québec are significant, but will be under very serious threat if the economic and financial rudder is not firmly steered toward the means we need to stay afloat.

The ball holding up our entire system has been overinflated and may blow up, splintering the crutches along with it. This is what we will turn our attention to in the following chapter.

CHAPTER 15

ARE WE VIABLE?

All's well that ends well, or so it seems. We may
not be as rich as some, but several things about
us stand out: the place of women, the relatively
egalitarian nature of our society, our dynamic
culture, our system of education, and to top it
all off, our high level of well-being compared
with other industrialized countries. What a nice
balancing act . . . why nitpick (as I so often do)?
Why criticize the model if it gets such good
results? Why change a winning formula? Don't
our neighbours in all directions say, "If it ain't
broke, don't fix it"? Yet this relative success is
built on a weak foundation, and the building is
unstable, sufficiently unstable so that we can say,
without passing for nay-sayers, that what we call
the "Québec model"—more properly called the
Québec consensus—is under threat. Let us go
further and say it will not be viable if we stand
by and do nothing.

The balance for Québec has long been a fragile one, but several interrelated factors will, in the next few years, contribute to making it non-viable. Public finances have reached the point of no-return, and this has been aggravated by a more marked demographic shock than elsewhere and more modest prospects for economic growth. All this is enough for us to say that it will not be possible to maintain this model for the future. We already see signs of wear as we move from one financial crisis to another, with a long string of freezes and decompressions, along with the deterioration of services. Let us take a closer look at the threats to our model.

CRISES IN PUBLIC FINANCES

The government of Québec, like governments all over the industrialized world, was mauled by the recession of 2008–2009. A weakening of revenue and the obligation to stimulate the economy by increasing public spending have plunged us once again into deficit after a decade of balanced budgets. Five years on, however, we discovered that, even though the economic crisis had affected us less than our neighbours, the crisis in public finances it provoked was more severe because of our precarious budget situation.

Starting in 2012 or 2013, the political world discovered, or was forced to acknowledge, what economists and research centres had known for years: the deficit being fought by the government was structural rather than merely incidental. The latter is brought on by the vagaries of the economy and erases itself when growth returns to cruising speed. The former, however, can be explained rather by an imbalance in public finances due to the long-term natural increase in state spending when it outstrips revenue and the economy.

This situation forces finances ministers to go from one contortion to another, in order to avoid falling into the red. In 2012, the structural nature of our deficit left us completely without control. When the recession of 2008–2009 hit us, Finance Minister Monique Jérôme-Forget fixed an ambitious target for return to a balanced budget by 2014. Her successor, Raymond Bachand, continued with her plan in 2012–2013, and managed to close in on the target, but the government of Pauline Marois and Finance Minister Nicolas Marceau, stuck with a slowing economy and a heavy financial inheritance, could not maintain the pace. Not only did they abandon the goal, but, in a series of revisions, let the deficit climb to $3.1 billion.

For 2014–2015, the new Liberal government promised to level off the deficit at $2.35 billion, then shrink it to zero the following year. The effort required for this would be colossal: spending cuts of $2.7 billion in 2014–2015 and $2.4 billion the following year, to which personnel constraints had to be added. These measures ushered in a period of budgetary austerity like none Québec had known since 1996–1997, under the government of Lucien Bouchard.

Economists used to following these things closely would say this return to a balanced budget, however necessary, can solve nothing. The deficits will recommence their explosion in coming years, because the structural factors responsible for deficits continue to exist, unless we revise in depth our programs and their pertinence. In addition, we need to refigure how our basket of consumer services are dispensed and financed.

This should not surprise us. Already, a consultative committee on the economy and public finances, created in 2009 by Minister Jérôme-Forget, had reported to her successor Raymond Bachand in 2010, that it foresaw this. The four university members on this committee, Claude Montmarquette, Pierre Fortin, Luc Godbout and Robert Gagné, asserted that the Liberal government's recovery plan was a "partial response," and they expected "a rapid reappearance of the structural deficit."[43]

According to the authors, Jérôme-Forget's scenario, aiming for a return to balanced budget by 2013–2014, would have created only a short period of relief, and, in fact, the target was later abandoned. As early as 2014–2015, the deficit would have reappeared to reach $4.8 billion 10 years later, with consequences on the debt. According to their projections, the gross accumulated debt would reach $251 billion in 2025–2026, an increase of nearly 33% in a decade. An analysis by the Conference Board of Canada suggested the same thing.

More recently, in 2014, an exercise on budgetary sustainability, participated in by fiscalist Luc Godbout and economist Pierre Fortin, put forward fresh projections. In this study, the status quo would bring forth a deficit that risked reaching $3.7 billion in 2020 and $8.4 billion in 2025, then exploding to $17.1 billion in 2030.[44]

When sounding the alarm for a recurring state of imbalance, one might use terms more often associated with the environment: durable, viable or sustainable. This study cites the OECD's definition of this concept: "budgetary viability is a multi-dimensional concept including solvability, stability of economic growth, fiscal stability and intergenerational equality. The implications are not only financial, but also social and political, and are linked to both present and future generations." They refer also to the definition offered by the Auditor-General of Canada: the capacity to finance present and future needs, to maintain growth, to properly finance future commitments without a heavier fiscal burden, and to procure for future generations the advantages which are no lower than at present.

Several months later, the Institut du Québec (Institute of Québec), a new think-tank, presided over by former Finance Minister Raymond Bachand, emerging from an association of the Conference Board and the Centre for Productivity and Prosperity, published another report on public finances in Québec, which pointed in the same direction.[45] With forecasts based on the analytic model of the Conference Board, this report, supposing the government would respect its recovery goals for 2015–2016, expected that, following the achievement of this short-term goal, the level of deficit would be $5 billion in 2028 and $10 billion in 2032. This document, however, proposes another scenario. Should the government succeed in curbing the growth in health spending from 5.2% to 4.2%, this would be sufficient to maintain balanced finances. The conclusion of the report is unequivocal:

> Short-term recovery is necessary to eliminate the deficit, but [...]
> Québec has, in fact, been regressing to a situation of structural
> deficit as soon as spending gets back to the status quo rate of

increase. The message is clear: short-term recovery alone will not do.

These are not forecasts, for it is obvious that no government will allow public finances to deteriorate that badly. They are rather projections, based on cautious hypotheses which attempt to measure budgetary sustainability, to see what will happen if the government of Québec keeps to its present budget policy, with services and the tax plan remaining unchanged. The goal of this exercise is to see whether present budgetary choices are viable or if they sentence us to excessive debt, preventing future generations from having a right to the same services.

These projections, which will not come true because governments are bound to act, are nevertheless useful, because they sound the alarm and give us a good idea of the efforts required to return us to equilibrium.

They remind us that the efforts to keep us afloat financially are going to be more and more painful. They further remind us that for years to come our public finances will be in a permanent state of crisis, replete with their string of emergency measures: blind cuts that wear out both citizens and public employees, and the hollowing out of programs. From one set of cuts to another, we already find ourselves with schools invaded by mould and tighter access to health services. Furthermore, the moment we drop our guard—we have seen this already with explosions in the deficit under Marois—the crisis returns double-quick.

This crisis-in-waiting is not so new. What is new are the factors that can do nothing but aggravate it. On the one hand, this will be because the demographic shock has changed the rules of the game and, on the other, because the crutches and other tools we once had to balance things, more or less artificially, are no longer there. The emergency exits are interlocking.

THE DEMOGRAPHIC SHOCK

The first threat our economy and our public finances face is the demographic shock, which some cautiously refer to as a "demographic transition." All advanced societies are being struck by important transformations of their populations due to a weaker birth rate, a prolonged lifespan and displacement of the age pyramids, such that young people are proportionately less numerous, and older persons more so. This phenomenon of ageing is more marked in Québec than in most other industrialized societies due to our unusual habits of reproduction. Québec showed a very high birth rate after the war, part of the baby boom. Fifteen years later, the reversal was spectacular, making us one of those societies with the lowest birth rate.

The result of this double record was that Québec found itself with a bigger contingent of baby boomers reaching a richer retirement than elsewhere, while the cohorts that followed them were less numerous. The result was that the proportion of those over 65 increased markedly: 5.8% in 1961, 8.8% in 1981, 13% in 2001, 15.7% in 2011, and will increase to 25.6% in 2031 and 27.7% in 2051, according to government projections.[46]

This transition is much more rapid than elsewhere, to the extent that it will provoke a greater shock than most other societies will experience. This is apparent in the number of years needed for seniors to go from being 12% to 24% of the population. In Japan, the country most severely affected, it will take only 22 years. Québec, with a transition of 33 years, is far behind Canada, which will have 42 years to absorb the shock. Germany will have 60 years, and France, 70 years.

We also know that these senior citizens will live longer than before, thanks to scientific progress and changes in lifestyles. This prolonged living, here as elsewhere, is striking. We most often speak in terms of life expectancy from birth, but this definition of longevity gives a poor accounting of the effects of ageing, because this will be affected by other factors, such as our successes against infant mortality or traffic accidents. We know that life expectancy is 84 years for women and 79 years for men.

The crucial data concern the number of years a person can expect to live *past* 65. It is 19 years for men and 22 years for women. This means that, on average, a man of 65 has a 50% chance of living to at least 84, and a woman has a 50% chance of living to at least 87 years. This life expectancy increases by 2.3 months every year. Thus, every five years, life expectancy gets a year longer. We already know, for instance, that one Québécoise out of 20 at age 65 will live to be 100.

On the other hand, Québec will have fewer young people. The 0–19-year-olds, who were 44.3% of the population in 1961, are now proportionately half as numerous—21.6% in 2011—a ratio which will remain stable far into the future.

The most significant result of this double process—and which best describes the effects of an ageing population—is the ratio of working-age people to those in retirement. In 1971, there were 9.4 persons aged 15 to 64 for each one aged 65 or more. This has now become 4.1 in 2013, and will sink to 2.1 in 2050.

This reality has all sorts of impacts on public finances. An ageing population puts enormous pressures on health spending, even though this is not the sole cause of increased costs. Consider the growing use and cost of medications as well as new technologies and more frequent diagnostic testing. These additional expenditures are replaced by the savings occasioned by ageing, for instance, in education or in public security.

These projections derive, among others, from the fact that the costs of health services clearly increase with age. According to data from the Institut Canadien d'information sur la santé (Canadian Institute for Health Information, CIHI), cited by the Godbout-Fortin study, average annual spending on health for those aged 35–39 is $1,692; it remains stable for those aged 45–49 at $1,960; it begins to climb to $3,057 for 55–59-year-olds, and to $3,521 for 60–64-year-olds, increasing exponentially thereafter: $5,175 for those aged 65–69 years, $8,485 for 70–74-year-olds, $12,598 for 75–79-year-olds, $14,919 for those aged 80–84 (more and more numerous) and $25,037 for the 85–89-year-olds. Will these levels of expenditure be similar for baby boomers reaching retirement better educated and in better shape than their elders, but with much greater demands on the health system than preceding generations?

There are other expenditures linked to an ageing population, notably financial support to workers ill prepared for retirement, long-term care, home care, and something we rarely speak about: adapting public services and households to this older population, much as we did for young people in the 1950s and 1960s.

Yet it is health that will exert the greatest and least bearable pressure on public finances. According to projections in the Godbout-Fortin study, annual growth in average expenditures will be 4.9%, up from a 44.3% total outlay in 2013 to 51.8% in 2030. The Institute of Québec prefers to speak of growth at the rate of 5.2%.

There are multiple consequences. Even though the share of other budgetary items like education will increase less rapidly, the impact of health will add to public spending faster than the economy can grow, hence an impasse. Governments, in order to finance the insatiable needs of the health network, will be forced to sacrifice other objectives or reduce spending elsewhere. Even if we succeed in slowing the growth of costs in health, their weight will deprive governments of any room for manoeuvre. In fact, in all cases, this consequence of demographic shock seriously threatens what we have called the Québec model, unless we can find ways to contain the exploding costs of health care.

AN ECONOMIC EFFECT

The demographic shock has another, even bigger impact, though less often discussed: its effect on the labour market. Due to an ageing population, the number of people leaving the labour market for retirement will be greater than the number of young people joining the workforce. The number of those of working age will decrease. When will this phenomenon reach us? Now! The year 2014 was the first year in which the active population began to decline.

Five years earlier, the arrival of young people added a further 30,000 a year to the labour pool. In 2013, the rise had been skimpy—7,800 more workers. The historical peak in active population was in July 2013, with 5,427,000 on the labour market. In 2014, the dip began modestly, with a loss of 4,500, which will then accelerate to 20,000 a year in 2020. According to the 2014–2015 Québec budget, the active population will have diminished by 0.2% a year between 2014 and 2018, while nevertheless increasing by 0.4% in Canada and 0.3% in the US.

These drops in working population pose a problem which is both quantitative and qualitative, and the first effects have already been felt in certain regions and certain industries, where the necessary labour is unavailable. This is a puzzle which can only get worse, as we find ourselves possibly with an army of underqualified workers who cannot find work, as well as thousands of vacant jobs.

These days, when the minister in charge of employment wakes up in the morning, the problem is no longer how to create jobs for the unemployed, but how to find the manpower for all the available positions. This is not simply a figure of speech: between 2011 and 2020, according to government projections, 1.4 million jobs will have to be filled in the province. A quarter of these will be new jobs resulting from economic growth. The other three-quarters will simply be replacements for those going into retirement. That is a lot of jobs.

To make matters worse, due to ageing, the rate of active labour will drop as more and more retire, a notable phenomenon, especially in Québec. According to a study by the Institute of Québec titled *Pour un contrat social durable* (*For a Sustainable Social Contract*), the rate of employment will reach around 66% in 2008, and 61% in 2032.

Thus the "relief" will be inadequate, bringing with it major consequences. Economic growth depends on all sorts of factors, such as investment and productivity. It is still, however, dependent on the number of workers contributing to economic activity. Therefore, due to demographic shock and its effect on labour, according to projections by the Conference Board of Canada and cited by the Institute of Québec, after an average growth of 2.1% over the past 20 years, Québec will enter a phase of annual economic growth of 1.6% for the next 20 years. The same phenomenon will hit Canada, but less markedly: average growth will reach from 2.5% to 1.9%, according to the Godbout-Fortin report. Annual economic growth, at 2% on average for the previous 30 years in Québec, will decline to 1.4%.

In point of fact, all these cases come with the same consequences: weaker growth drags down fiscal revenues, because the level of fiscal returns is closely tied to economic activity. Hence, just when Québec needs growth to fill its financial needs and regain balance the most, the exact opposite will be happening. Needs will grow, and resources will shrink. Thus the other door closes.

INCREASE TAXES?

When a government has no room to manoeuvre financially, it can always turn to taxpayers and increase tariffs and taxes. This is the road that has been largely followed by governments in Québec over the years, so much so that the well has run dry. I do not believe that the government of Québec can count much on this to resolve its financial impasse any more.

In the area of public finance, there are some verifiable and unavoidable facts—near mathematical realities, such as the health spending curve, the structural nature of the deficit, and the inevitability of an ageing population. Yet the fiscal stakes are not only financial and economic. There is also an important ideological aspect to our fiscal choices. The question of how far it is possible to augment taxes is not only a scientific matter. This is why it is difficult to define the optimal level of the tax load, especially since there exists no law or rule to set a clear correlation between this and economic performance. Certain countries tax their citizens heavily and still maintain a dynamic economy, as is the case with northern Europe. Others tax lightly and are in bad shape, like Japan.

I believe that we have reached our limit and can go no farther. If several revisions are without doubt possible at the top of the income scale for reasons of fairness, their impact would be too slight to make much difference for the budget, mainly because the tax burden in Québec is higher than that of all its neighbours: "1.11 times higher than Ontario, 1.15 times higher than the average for Canada, and 1.61 times higher than the US," according to the 2013 CPP report.

The budget for Québec in 2014–2015 showed one astonishing fact. According to calculations by the Ministry of Finance, the government of Québec "imposes an additional tax burden of $1,410 on each inhabitant . . . which represents $11.3 billion overall." What these figures tell us is that, if Québec taxed its citizens at the average rate of all Canadian provinces, the amount would be $11.3 billion less. This is quite a drop.

On a global scale, Québec is among the economies with the highest tax revenues, as the graph facing indicates. Fiscal revenues total 37.5% of Québec's GDP. We are not the most expensive, and quite far behind the two champions, Denmark and Sweden with 47.8% and 46.6% respectively, but we are still in the highest bracket, and closer to such European countries as France, Italy, Norway or Finland—around 42%—than we are to Ontario (33.7%).

We are not in northern Europe though. From a strictly geographic point of view, our immediate neighbours are not Finland and Norway,

WORLD TAX BURDENS
FISCAL REVENUES IN PROPORTION TO GDP, 2009

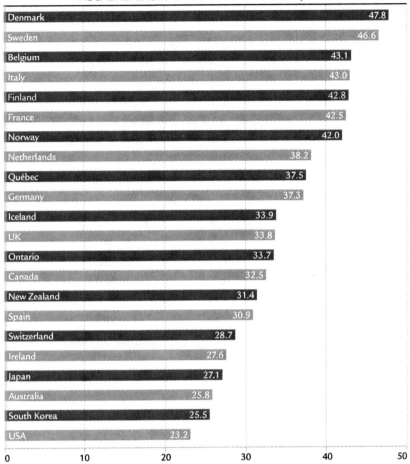

Denmark	47.8
Sweden	46.6
Belgium	43.1
Italy	43.0
Finland	42.8
France	42.5
Norway	42.0
Netherlands	38.2
Québec	37.5
Germany	37.3
Iceland	33.9
UK	33.8
Ontario	33.7
Canada	32.5
New Zealand	31.4
Spain	30.9
Switzerland	28.7
Ireland	27.6
Japan	27.1
Australia	25.8
South Korea	25.5
USA	23.2

Source: Centre for Productivity and Prosperity, HEC Montreal.

but Ontario and the State of New York. This limits our wiggle-room, because governments must take into account the ways of doing business and citizen reactions to tax hikes. Citizens can shop, invest and move elsewhere. Businesses especially can often choose where they will set up and invest. The more taxes rise, the more taxpayers are likely to react. They and businesses can also modify their habits and behaviour toward tax evasion: not selling a building so as not to pay capital gains tax, or refusing to work overtime and turn the extra money over to the taxman, with the consequences often being that tax receipts are lower than expected.

This may shock many, but one can see the reticence of taxpayers. Québécois, rich or poor, are not Scandinavians solely because of their geography, but also because the social contract is more fragile. We are at peace with paying taxes willingly if, and only if, we are convinced they are legitimate. The perception of waste and lack of care in spending is strong enough to incur resistance to any large increase.

Finally, it must be considered that tax increases have a negative impact on the economy, because of their influence on choices and behaviour. Such an impact will vary according to the type of tax, some taxes being more neutral than others. According to the CPP, an increase of $1 billion in the income tax will have a long term negative cost in GDP of $890 million. The cost of that billion in income tax will be $760 million, and for $280 million in sales tax, it will be $410 million.

There are certainly other tax trails to follow, ones which will be less damaging to the economy. The door to further property taxes is also firmly shut.

BACK INTO DEBT

There is another way out of this: pay later, agree to spend more than we have and be back in deficit, in the full knowledge that this will inflate the debt we will eventually have to reimburse. Saying this here and now may seem like heresy, unless one is a militant in Québec solidaire, but for decades, that has been the normal way of doing things.

In a 2013 interview on RDI (Réseau de l'information, the French-language counterpart to CBC Newsworld), Jacques Parizeau asserted that we had to stop spooking ourselves with the financial situation in Québec. "We are desperately normal with regard to the deficit and debt," he said, adding, "We worry too much about it." He was reflecting the view of his generation. The swing happened after his time, in the mid-1990s, when the Chrétien government in Ottawa and the Bouchard government in Québec City succeeded in passing the rule of deficit zero—a long-consecrated dogma enshrined in law, such that it was normal for a government not to spend more than it took in. Thus it is forbidden to pay current expenses with increased debt—i.e. to borrow for groceries. This was fortunate, for it is unacceptable ethically to fill the present needs of the population by asking their descendants to pay for it, a simple matter of intergenerational equity that has begun to take root.

Debt has still continued to climb, because governments have continued to finance building projects with further borrowing, such as the building of roads or schools. This idea is defensible on financial and ethical levels, since it is long-term collective infrastructure that will be amortized over a lengthy period. It is logical to pay the price for a long time and have future cohorts pay as well, for they will benefit from them.

The gross debt in Québec from the year 2000 to the crisis in 2008–2009 increased by $31.9 billion in eight years, going from $120.6 billion to $152.5 billion, a rise of 26.4% for an average of $3.9 billion a year. That is a lot, but the debt increase was less rapid than the growth in the economy, to the extent that the gross debt dropped from 52.3% to 48.6% of GDP during this period.

Starting with 2009, the process was inverted. That year, two things happened: a vast infrastructure plan to repair equipment that was falling to pieces, and the economic crisis. Building works added $5 billion a year to the debt, while budget deficits brought on by the crisis piled on, for an average annual debt of $8.5 billion for 2009 to 2012.

It is pure chance that the infrastructure work and the crisis coincided. It was providential though: it allowed Québec to better resist the recession and leave it behind more rapidly than our neighbours. These investments filled a gaping and long overdue need, but, more than that, they also served, here as everywhere in the world, to restart the economy.

Nevertheless, the cumulative effect of these two forms of debt is still very disquieting. Since the crisis, debt has gone from $152.5 billion in 2008–2009 to $206.8 billion in 2014–2015, a rise of 35.6% in six years, and took gross debt to an all-time high, 54.9% of GDP. On the other hand, combatting the deficit is working: debt should decline to 50% of GDP in 2019–20.

For gross debt (overall debt contracted on financial markets plus retirement liabilities, a measure preferred by the government of Québec) we were the champions of North America in 2013 in all categories at 53.6% of GDP—by far the highest in Canada, and clearly beyond Ontario (44%), Nova Scotia (38.7%), Manitoba (36.8%), and New Brunswick (32.9%) and the other indebted provinces, as shown by the graph below.

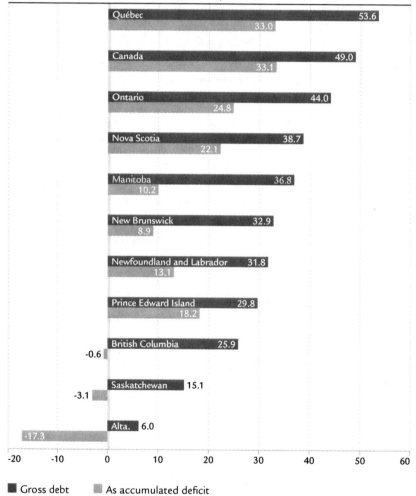

PUBLIC DEBT IN CANADA
% OF GDP, 2013

■ Gross debt   As accumulated deficit

Source: Québec Ministry of Finance.

Furthermore, if we use another measure, that of net debt, and thus take account of financial assets held by the government, so as to better reflect our capacity to reimburse public debt, the figures are not any prettier. This represents a net debt which is 49% of GDP, placing us far ahead of other provinces once again: 37.4% in Ontario, 17.3% in British Columbia and 0% in Alberta. A comparison with the US by the Fraser Institute shows, moreover, that the bond debt, close to 45% of Québec GDP, does not rise beyond 15% in American states.

Comparisons on an international scale are more difficult, notably because Québec is not enumerated as an independent country. The government of Québec performed the exercise in 2010 (for the year 2008, before the crisis) using the OECD method and in attributing to the province a portion of the federal debt. According to these data, Québec was 5th in the world at 94.0% of GDP (behind Japan, with a debt equivalent to 172.1% of GDP; Italy, at 114.2%; Greece, at 102.6%; and Iceland, at 96.3%). Our debt was certainly higher than the OECD average (78.4%) or Canada (69.7%). We should not be too quick in jumping to conclusions based on these figures, but must bear in mind that Québec is heavily in debt.

One might add that Québec is in debt in a bad way. Budgetary data allow us to distinguish that portion of the debt used to finance construction from debt contracted to pay for current expenses. This debt, due to annual deficits serving to finance these expenditures, was equivalent to 33% of GDP in 2013. This corresponds to $118 billion or 67% of net debt, far, far more than that of the other provinces: 24.8% in Ontario, 22.1% in Nova Scotia and below 20% everywhere else except the three western provinces with 0%. Québec alone has massively financed programs by going into debt, especially in the name of future generations.

This too has consequences. First, interest must be paid, which considerably reduces the government's margin for manoeuvre. In 2014–15, on overall expenditures of $72.3 billion, $8.6 billion (11.6%) were for service on the debt—$8.6 billion, which would have been far more useful were we not so indebted, especially when we consider that two-thirds of this amount is to reimburse expenditures from some 10, 15 or 20 years past.

Heavy debt also means financial vulnerability to creditors and the risk of a credit-rating change if the situation becomes too precarious. What credit agencies most look to is debt much more than deficit. It was a serious enough problem for Finance Minister Carlos Leitão to be forced, in his first budget, to abandon an election promise to speed up public investment.

Shamefully, Québec has gone further into debt to solve its financial needs year after year, posing in a very acute way the question of intergenerational equity. It explains, in part, how Québec has succeeded in paying for the continent's Cadillac of public services, without actually being rich. The level of debt in the province is such that the government is now very vulnerable. It must quickly reduce its deficit to avoid aggravating the situation. There is, to be sure, no room to manoeuvre in this matter. Again a door slams shut.

FEDERAL LARGESSE

There remains one other door, the federal government, on whose door successive Québec governments have reflexively knocked when they were out of money. The style varies according to the constitutional orientation of each government (sovereignist or federalist), but there is remarkable continuity among them in denouncing the fiscal imbalance, one way or another. Each budget, whether Liberal or Péquiste, has its chapter on the inadequacy of federal funding.

I have no intention of launching into this complicated and interminable discussion. I simply wish to refresh our faulty memory of how important federal transfers are to Québec and that they play a central role in our financial equation. In 2012, Ottawa drew $44.5 billion in income tax from Québec, both from citizens and from companies, GST, fees, etc., but spent $60.8 billion on the province in salaries for its employees, in goods and services, in payments and pensions, in interest on the debt and in transfers to the government of Québec.

In other words, overall spending by the federal government surpassed its revenues from the province by $16.3 billion. These figures from the *Comptes économiques des revenus et dépenses du Québec* (*Economic Accounts of Income and Spending*) and from the Institut de la statistique du Québec (Québec Institute of Statistics), show clearly what many still do not know, or choose not to acknowledge: Québec does not subsidize Confederation, but rather the reverse.

Even if the discussion on sovereignty is currently on the back burner, these data throw into question, once again, one of the recurrent themes in the sovereignist discourse as to whether independence would be financially feasible and allow Québec to get its money back. This gap is so great that no amount of statistical acrobatics can make it go away.

The gap between federal spending and revenue in Québec has exploded since 2007, when it was $7.3 billion. This gulf has now climbed to $19.3 billion in 2010, back down to $16.3 billion two years later, essentially because Ottawa's record deficits, since the crisis, have themselves passed their peak at $50 billion.

Within federal spending, transfers to the provincial government reached $16.7 billion in 2014–2015 and then increased by 3% to 3.5% per year. The Ministry of Finance estimates that these increases are not enough. It is noteworthy that this progression resembles that of Québec's own revenues.

Transfer payments from Ottawa totalled $9.3 billion in 2014–2015. These payments compensate for the insufficient fiscal balance of certain provinces and clearly constitute a transfer from rich provinces to the poor ones, such as Québec. We receive the largest transfer payments—more than half—although per capita, we are far from being the principal beneficiary.

Why have we been a poor province ever since the transfer payment program began? Why does this fact not seem to bother us much? Québec has rooted itself in a culture of dependency on Confederation. This has created a malaise within the rich provinces who have the impression that Québec is not doing all it can to improve the situation, notably in resource development. We say no to gas and oil, we look down on provinces that produce them, but we accept their money.

This imbalance illustrates in another way how fragile the foundation of the Québec model really is. How, with a lower standard of living, does Québec manage to maintain a more complete social safety net than anywhere else in Canada? This miracle can be explained by our higher taxes and debt, but also by this federal boost. In fact, our quality of life also has a Canadian component via federal social programs, as well as the mechanisms of interprovincial redistribution, including federal transfer payments.

Québec is accused of paying for better public services out of other provinces' pockets, who cannot afford the same for themselves. The accusation is false, because it is possible to show that, with its much heavier tax burden, Québec finances programs that do not exist elsewhere. Still, these reactions do indicate that the rationale for transfer payments is contested, and that probably Québec cannot count as much on federal pennies from heaven in future.

AN UNVIABLE MODEL

In brief, then: finances in Québec are structurally unbalanced, and this becomes worse as the population ages; the economy is not robust enough to support present levels of public spending (there is no more fiscal wiggle-room); taxes cannot really be increased further, and we cannot forever count on the shower of money from the federal government. Nor can we indebt ourselves any more.

In the final analysis, our model is simply not viable. On average, we will have less and less with which to maintain the system. Since the sole way left for us to rebalance our finances is to control spending, the necessary reductions risk wiping out our past achievements, hollowing out our purposes and compromising the quantity and quality of service and support to the population.

This brings us back to the same problem we have been harping on. If Québec wants to remain a generous society, it must give itself the means to do so and be sure to maintain the standard of living and the resources it requires. This will remind us why economic growth and wealth-creation should be first in our minds, and, yes, even obsess us. It is a collective necessity and a moral obligation.

If a social contract exists in Québec, and we wish to preserve it, there is a choice to be made. What is really at stake is this: are we ready to abandon our model, or better yet, do we wish to do what is needed to protect it? Recurring cuts by government are emergency measures and expedients more often temporary than not. If we wish sustainable solutions, we need to reflect on this social contract, define what is essential to be preserved, then accept the sacrifice that comes with it. It is not the consensus which needs to be challenged, not its grand principles, but the culture of the status quo it fosters.

This much is clear: if we do not change our way of doing things, if our social objectives are not linked to an obligation to develop the economy, if we do not rethink how we manage the state and ensure public services, what we call the Québécois model will slowly but surely die away to become increasingly a shadow of its former self.

CONCLUSION

TIME TO CHOOSE

This book has been, at times, depressing. I know
this perfectly well. Why is it? Our main objective
has been to deflate at all costs the balloons we
collectively have been blowing up for far too
long, and instead paint a more realistic portrait
of Québec society. It was predictable that this
exercise in lucidity, in which I have attempted to
counteract our self-congratulation, would reveal a
Québec which is less remarkable and less unique
than we are used to thinking. All of this must,
however, never make us forget that the Québec
adventure is a success overall. Yet it is one that
may turn out badly if we do not get to work.

We must remember that if we do not always come out best in certain comparisons, we are still ranked with the best. Québec is one of very few societies in which it is good to live. Like Canada as a whole, we have succeeded in balancing social progress and economic logic, in reconciling growth and quality of life with social and collective concerns. The single greatest criticism we can make is that we have stalled along the way, underused our potential, and not fully exploited many of our advantages and talents. This lack of energy and willpower to do even better is largely due to our attachment to the status quo and to our self-satisfaction, to our mistaken impression that we have already peaked.

I would like Québec to do even better, yes, but not because I am a fan of performance. In fact, it is sad for a society to underuse its potential: first, because of the enormous waste in talent; next, because Québec and its people, would be much better off if the economy were more dynamic and if our social organization were less slipshod.

Add to this a present feeling of urgency. Equilibrium in our society is threatened by an ageing population, the sluggish economy and the crisis in state finances. We are truly at a crossroads, to recycle the old cliché. Without a change of course, the type of society we prize—the Québécois —is threatened.

This does not mean that we are on the edge of a precipice. Our economy is not dynamic, but it is healthy. There exists no dramatic social fracture. While our governments are in bankruptcy, our situation in a way resembles those of Italy, Greece, Spain or Japan. The threat we face is rather one of slow decline, of a society lacking the means for its ambitions and which must gradually start to aim lower. We are not powerless against our destiny, like France, whose sclerosis is such that we all wonder how it will resolve its crisis. We have all we need to make it through and forward. What slows us down is our attachment to acquired rights and the status quo. What we lack is a sense of urgency and desire to change direction.

We are on the verge of a great questioning of our public programs and of our relation to the economy, as well as our individual and collective responsibilities. Our governments cannot do it all. Choices must be made for this to happen, and we will need to establish our fundamental values clearly, define the programs and services we deem essential to preserve the essence of our model, to distinguish between what is important and what we cling to out of habit or conditioned reflex. We must also better identify the more fragile elements of our model to better reinforce them, and take stock of the forces we can rely upon.

If this book is to be useful, it will be to help us see all this more clearly.

NOTES

CHAPTER 3

1 "Enquête québécoise sur le développement des enfants à la maternelle," Institut de la statistique du Québec, 2012.

2 Pierre Fortin, "Les sans-diplôme au Québec," 2008.

3 "Savoir pour pouvoir: Entreprendre un chantier national pour la persévérance scolaire," rapport du Groupe d'action sur la persévérance et la réussite scolaires au Québec, 2009.

4 "Indicateurs de l'éducation au Canada: une perspective internationale," Statistique Canada, 2012.

CHAPTER 4

5 "Regards sur l'éducation," OECD, 2013.

6 "Indicateurs de l'éducation au Canada: une perspective internationale," Statistique Canada, 2012.

7 Quacquarelli Symonds, www.topuniversities.com/university-rankings.

CHAPTER 5

8 "Mesurer et comprendre l'économie créative du Canada," Conference Board du Canada, 2008.

9 Richard Florida, *The Rise of the Creative Class: And How It's Transforming Work, Leisure, Community, and Everyday Life*, Basic Books, 2002.

10 "Artists in Canada's Provinces and Territories Based on the 2006 Census," Hill Strategies Research Inc.

11 "L'évolution des dépenses culturelles des ménages québécois, de 1997 à 2009," *Optique*, Number 19, May 2012, OCCQ.

12 "Dépenses de consommation au chapter de la culture en 2008," Hill Strategies, 2010.

13 "Profil des acheteurs de livres et de revues au Canada en 2008," Hill Strategies.

CHAPTER 6

14 "Caractéristiques linguistiques des Canadiens," Statistique Canada, 98-314-X2011051.

15 "Redynamiser la politique linguistique du Québec," OQLF, 2011.

16 Francotropes are allophones (non-speakers of English or French originally) more likely to adopt French than English.

17 "Lecture et achat de livres pour la détente," Sondage national 2005, Rapport présenté à Patrimoine canadien, 2005.

18 "Un engagement collectif pour maintenir et rehausser les compétences en littératie des adultes," Conseil supérieur de l'éducation, September 2013.

CHAPTER 7

19 *Portrait des Québécoises en huit temps*, 2014 Edition, Conseil du statut de la femme.

20 "Annuaire québécois des statistiques du travail. Portrait des principaux indicateurs du marché et des conditions de travail, 2003–2013," Volume 10, Institut de la statistique du Québec.

21 "Enquête Catalyst 2013: les femmes membres de conseils d'administration selon le classement Financial Post 500," www.catalyst.org.

CHAPTER 8

22 *All on Board: Making Inclusive Growth Happen*, OECD, 2014.

23 "Productivité et prospérité au Québec: Bilan 2013," Centre sur la productivité et la prospérité, 2014.

24 Luc Godbout, Michaël Robert-Angers, and Suzie St-Cerny, "La charge fiscale nette: concept, résultats pancanadiens et positionnement du Québec," Université de Sherbrooke, 2013.

25 Mireille Vézina and Susan Crompton, "Le bénévolat au Canada," Statistique Canada, 2012.

26 "Revenus de bien-être social 2009," Conseil national du bien-être social, Canada, 2010.

CHAPTER 9

27 "Meilleure santé, meilleurs soins, meilleure valeur pour tous: recentrer la réforme des soins de santé au Canada," Conseil canadien de la santé, September 2013.

28 "Analyse comparative du système de santé du Canada: comparaisons internationales," Institut canadien d'information sur la santé, November 2013.

29 "Mirror, Mirror on the Wall, 2014 Update: How the U.S. Health Care System Compares Internationally," Commonwealth Fund.

30 Claude E. Forget, "Le mystère des médecins québécois 'évanouis': comment

améliorer l'accès aux soins," *Commentaire*, Number 410, Institut C.D. Howe, 2014.

31 "Paving the Road to Higher Performance: Benchmarking Provincial Health Systems," Conference Board of Canada, 2013.

CHAPTER 10

32 Éditions Voix Parallèles, 2007.

33 "Rapport d'inventaire national 1990–2012: sources et puits de gaz à effet de serre au Canada – Sommaire," Environnement Canada, 2012.

34 "De la réduction des gaz à effet de serre à l'indépendance énergétique du Québec," document de consultation, Commission sur les enjeux énergétiques du Québec, 2013.

35 "Rapport de 2011 sur l'utilisation de l'eau par les municipalités, statistiques de 2009," Environnement Canada, 2011.

36 One øre is worth about 0.15 cents CAD. There are 100 øre in a Norwegian krone.

CHAPTER 12

37 "Course Correction: Charting a New Road Map for Ontario," Institute for Competitiveness and Prosperity, 2013.

38 "Budget 2013–2014: investir pour assurer notre prospérité—la vision économique du gouvernement," Gouvernement du Québec, 2012.

39 "Productivité et prospérité au Québec: Bilan 2013," Centre sur la productivité et la prospérité, 2014.

40 "L'investissement au Québec: on est pour," Rapport du Groupe de travail sur l'investissement des entreprises, Ministère des Finances du Québec, 2008.

41 "Budget 2013–2014: investir pour assurer notre prospérité—la vision économique du gouvernement," Gouvernement du Québec, 2012.

CHAPTER 14

42 Andrew Sharpe and Evan Capeluck, "Canadians Are Happy and Getting Happier: An Overview of Life Satisfaction in Canada, 2003–2011," Centre for the Study of Living Standards, Ottawa, September 2012.

CHAPTER 15

43 Claude Montmarquette, Pierre Fortin, Luc Godbout, and Robert Gagné, "Le Québec face à ses défis. Fascicule 3: Une voie durable pour rester maîtres de nos choix," Gouvernement du Québec, 2010.

44 Luc Godbout, Suzie St-Cerny, Matthieu Arseneau, Ngoc Ha Dao, and Pierre Fortin, "La soutenabilité budgétaire des finances publiques du gouvernement du Québec," Université de Sherbrooke, 2014.

45 "Choc démographique et finances publiques: pour un contrat social durable," Institut du Québec, 2014.

46 "Le bilan démographique du Québec, édition 2013," Institut de la statistique du Québec.

ABOUT THE AUTHOR AND TRANSLATOR

ALAIN DUBUC, a federalist in politics, obtained a master of science in economics at the Université de Montréal, where he was also a researcher in economics from 1973 to 1976. In 1976, he became a *La Presse* columnist specializing in economics. From 1985 to 1988, he hosted the weekly television show *Questions d'argent* on Radio-Québec (now Télé-Québec) on economics and personal finances. In 1988, Dubuc was appointed chief editorialist of *La Presse*, a position he held until 2001. He was president and editor of the daily *Le Soleil* in Québec from 2001 to 2004. A renowned speaker, Dubuc has accumulated many journalism awards throughout his career. He was inducted as an Officer of the Order of Canada in 2011. He is also Visiting Fellow at CIRANO, the Center for Interuniversity Research and Analysis of Organizations.

NIGEL SPENCER is one of Canada's outstanding translators. He has won three Governor General's Awards for translations of Marie-Claire Blais' novels: *Thunder and Light*, *Augustino and the Choir of Destruction*, and *Mai at the Predators' Ball*. For Ronsdale Press he has translated Jean-Pierre Rogel's *Evolution: the View from the Cottage* as well as Marie-Claire Blais' collection of short stories *The Exile & the Sacred Travellers* and her collection of plays *Wintersleep*. He makes his home in Montreal.

MARQUIS

Québec, Canada

RECYCLED
Paper made from
recycled material
FSC® C103567

Printed on Rolland Enviro, which contains 100% post-
consumer fiber, is ECOLOGO, Processed Chlorine Free,
Ancient Forest Friendly and FSC® certified
and is manufactured using renewable biogas energy.

PERMANENT

100%

Ancient
Forest
Friendly™